SuSE Linux and Netfinity® Server Integration Guide

*Jakob Carstensen, Lenz Grimmer, Ivo Gomilsek,
Jay Haskins, and Joe Kaple*

International Technical Support Organization

www.redbooks.ibm.com

SuSE Linux and Netfinity® Server Integration Guide

ISBN 0-13-028675-3

90000

9 780130 286758

The ITSO Networking Series

SuSE Linux and Netfinity® Server Integration Guide

JAKOB CARSTENSEN ▪ LENZ GRIMMER ▪
IVO GOMILSEK ▪ JAY HASKINS ▪
JOE KAPLENK

PRENTICE HALL PTR, UPPER SADDLE RIVER, NEW JERSEY 07458
www.phptr.com

First Edition (December 1999)

This edition applies to preparing for or installing SuSE Linux on IBM Netfinity systems.

Comments may be addressed to:
IBM Corporation, International Technical Support Organization
Dept. HZ8 Building 678
P.O. Box 12195
Research Triangle Park, NC 27709-2195

When you send information to IBM, you grant IBM a non-exclusive right to use or distribute the information in any way it believes appropriate without incurring any obligation to you.

Published by Prentice Hall PTR
Prentice-Hall, Inc.
Upper Saddle River, NJ 07458

Prentice Hall books are widely used by corporations and government agencies for training, marketing, and resale.
The publisher offers discounts on this book when ordered in bulk quantities. For more information, contact Corporate Sales Department, Phone 800-382-3419; FAX: 201-236-7141, E-mail: corpsales@prenhall.com; or Write:

Prentice Hall PTR
Corporate Sales Department
One Lake Street
Upper Saddle River, NJ 07458

> **Take Note!** Before using this information and the product it supports, be sure to read the general information under Appendix B, "Special Notices" on page 251.

Printed in the United States of America

10 9 8 7 6 5 4 3 2 1

ISBN   0-13-028675-3

Prentice-Hall International (UK) Limited, *London*
Prentice-Hall of Australia Pty. Limited, *Sydney*
Prentice-Hall Canada Inc., *Toronto*
Prentice-Hall Hispanoamericana, S.A., *Mexico*
Prentice-Hall of India Private Limited, *New Delhi*
Prentice-Hall of Japan, Inc., *Tokyo*
Pearson Education Asia Pte Ltd.
Editora Prentice-Hall do Brasil, Ltda., *Rio de Janeiro*

Contents

Preface

This redbook will help you install, tailor and configure the SuSE Linux 6.2 distribution on different servers of the Netfinity class. You will be instructed on how to do the basic installation, installing and configuring different services like Apache (http-Server), Samba (Fileserver for Windows-based networks) and several other servers. Even though SuSE Linux 6.3 will already be out at the time this book will be published, most of the content still applies to SuSE Linux 6.3 as well. In fact, some things might be much easier and workarounds that were needed for 6.2 will not be necessary anymore.

Linux is a very mature and stable operation system but the Linux Kernel is constantly being updated in order to make the operating system better. This can make it difficult for Linux beginners, so be prepared for a bumpy ride and a steep learning curve. But it is worth the effort and, as they say at SuSE, don't forget to have a lot of fun...

The team that wrote this redbook

This redbook was produced by a team of specialists from around the world working at the International Technical Support Organization Raleigh Center.

Jakob Carstensen is an Advisory Specialist for Netfinity Servers at the International Technical Support Organization, Raleigh Center. He manages residencies and produces redbooks. His most recent publication was *Linux for WebSphere and DB2 Servers*. Before joining the ITSO, he worked in Denmark both for the IBM PC Institute teaching TechConnect and Service Training courses, and for IBM PSS performing level-2 support of Netfinity products. He has a Bachelor of Electronic Engineering degree and has worked for IBM for the past nine years.

Lenz Grimmer is a Software Engineer at SuSE GmbH in Nuremberg, Germany. He belongs to the distribution development team and is responsible for a number of packages on the distribution. He has five years of experience with Linux (since Kernel 0.99.xx) and holds a degree in Computer Science from the Berufsakademie in Mannheim, Germany. Before he started working for SuSE in April 1998, he worked as a system administrator for a local Internet service provider that used Linux exclusively for its servers. His areas of expertise include setting up different Linux services such as Apache, Samba and Squid. In addition to trying to be helpful on several SuSE mailing lists, he has written the SuSE FAQ, which is available online at
http://www.suse.com/Support/Doku/FAQ/

Ivo Gomilsek is a Product Specialist for PC Hardware in IBM Slovenia. He is IBM Certified Professional Server Specialist, Red Hat Certified Engineer, OS/2 Warp Certified Engineer and Certified Vinca Co-StandbyServer for Windows NT Engineer. Ivo was a member of the team that wrote the redbook *Implementing Vinca Solutions on IBM Netfinity Servers.* His areas of expertise include IBM Netfinity servers, network operating systems (OS/2, Linux, Windows NT) and Lotus Domino Servers. During his career he has worked as a Systems Engineer in PSG and is now working in Product Support Services (PSS) as level-2 support for IBM Netfinity servers, and high availability solutions for IBM Netfinity servers and Linux. Ivo has been employed at IBM for three years.

Jay Haskins is a Systems Architect for IBM Global Services Enterprise Architecture and Design in Seattle, Washington. He has been a Linux and Open Source advocate for more than five years and currently spends most of his time developing dynamic monitoring tools using Perl and the Apache Web server. Before joining IBM, Jay worked in several different areas of the information technology field including UNIX system administration, database design and development, Windows application development, and network administration.

Joe Kaplenk is a Senior Systems Management Integration Professional for IBM Global Services/DAAS in Lisle, Illinois. He has 20 years of experience in the computer field. He holds a degree in Physics from the University of Utah. His areas of expertise include UNIX system administration and computer science education. He has written several books on UNIX and Linux system administration, including the *UNIX System Adminstrator's Interactive Workbook* and the *Linux Network Administrator's Interactive Workbook,* both published by Prentice-Hall, as well as contributing articles to Linux journals. He has worked with IBM for three years. He has also been teaching Computer Science part-time at the College of DuPage in Glen Ellyn, Illinois for 16 years and UNIX administration for seven years.

Thanks to the SuSE development team for their support and a great distribution.

Thanks to the following people from the International Technical Support Organization, Raleigh Center:

Diane O'Shea
Gail Christensen
Shawn Walsh
Linda Robinson
David Watts
Rufus Credle

Margaret Ticknor
Mike Haley
Linda Robinson

Thanks to the following IBM employees:

Egan Ford, Advanced Technical Support
Karl Schultz, Netfinity ServerProven
Julie Briddon, Marketing Communications
Bo Brun, PC Institute

Comments welcome

Your comments are important to us!

We want our redbooks to be as helpful as possible. Please send us your comments about this or other redbooks in one of the following ways:

- Fax the evaluation form found in "IBM Redbooks evaluation" on page 267 to the fax number shown on the form.

- Use the online evaluation form found at `http://www.redbooks.ibm.com/`

- Send your comments in an Internet note to `redbook@us.ibm.com`

Chapter 1. Introduction

Linux, the free UNIX-like operating system that was originally invented by Linus Torvalds, is gaining more and more popularity these days. Its unmatched stability along with the availability of the full source code and its broad range of supported hardware make it a viable alternative as a server operating system in all areas of today's IT environments.

Actually, the term "Linux" comprises the core of the operating system, the kernel, and its device drivers. However, the kernel itself is not very useful without some helper programs. The collection of the Linux kernel with tools and applications is called a distribution. There are quite a number of Linux distributions available, each of them with its unique features and properties.

This redbook describes the installation of the SuSE Linux 6.2 distribution on IBM Netfinity servers in different configurations. Moreover, it discusses how to install and configure some of the most popular services and gives various tuning and configuration tips.

SuSE Linux 6.2 is the latest Linux distribution produced by SuSE GmbH, a Germany-based Linux distributor. The cardboard box consists of six CD-ROMs containing more than 1300 applications and utilities, a 400+ page manual, and 60 days of free installation support by e-mail or telephone.

With about 180 employees and over 50,000 business customers around the world, SuSE (`http://www.suse.de/en/`) is one of the leading Linux distributors worldwide. SuSE was founded in 1992 and started distributing Linux in early 1993. Apart from its flagship product, SuSE Linux, SuSE also offers a broad range of products and services in the Linux domain. In addition to providing professional support for business customers, SuSE also offers personal training courses and workshops.

SuSE recently founded the SuSE Labs - a global collaboration of developers that promote the development of free software projects, such as ALSA (Advanced Linux Sound Architecture), KDE (KDE Desktop Environment), XFree86 and USB-support for the Linux kernel. The SuSE developers also contribute to the development of the Linux kernel itself, to the GNU C-Library glibc and numerous other free software projects.

In addition to providing code and enhancements to the Linux community, SuSE also supports several Linux standardization efforts, such as the Linux Standard Base (LSB, found at `http://www.linuxbase.org`), The Linux Professional Institute (LPI, found at `http://www.lpi.org`) and The Linux Internationalization Initiative (Li18nux, found at `http://www.li18nux.org/`).

Besides its German branch offices in Frankfurt, Hamburg, Munich and Stuttgart, SuSE also has international subsidiaries in Oakland, California (http://www.suse.com), Prague in the Czech Republic and Borehamwood/London in the UK, which provide marketing, distribution and technical support for these countries.

Chapter 2. Linux installation

This chapter discusses the basic installation of SuSE Linux 6.2 on different models of IBM Netfinity servers and how to work around common problems. Since it is almost impossible to cover all hardware combinations, we have concentrated on typical configurations, which are representative examples:

- IBM Netfinity 3000
- IBM Netfinity 3500 M10
- IBM Netfinity 5000 with ServeRAID controller
- IBM Netfinity 5500 with ServeRAID controller
- IBM Netfinity 5600 with ServeRAID controller
- IBM Netfinity 7000 with ServeRAID controller
- IBM Netfinity 8500 with ServeRAID controller

We strongly recommend that you also have a look at the extensive SuSE manual, which covers the installation process in more detail and more variations than we will describe it here. It also gives you a lot of background information to begin with. Before you start the installation, make sure that you check the SuSE web site for updates and bug fixes. Linux is a fast-moving target, and the development is a continously ongoing process. There might be new boot floppy images or kernel patches that contain newer drivers. Also make sure that you add all security fixes if you plan to connect your machine to the Internet. Updates and bug fixes for SuSE Linux 6.2 can be found at:

    http://www.suse.de/en/support/download/updates/62_update.html

The updates are located on the SuSE FTP server at the following address:

    ftp://ftp.suse.com/pub/suse/i386/updates/6.2/

> **Note**
>
> Although this chapter covers the installation of SuSE Linux 6.2, most of this still applies to SuSE Linux 6.3 as well. At the time of this writing, SuSE Linux 6.3 was still in beta phase and it was too early to base this book on this version. SuSE Linux 6.3 now offers a graphical installation program to ease the basic installation for the unexperienced user. However, you can still use the text-based installation program described in this chapter by booting from the second CD-ROM instead of the first one. In fact, using the traditional installation routine is recommended, if you want to set up a server system and want to have some more control and flexibility over your installation process. A SuSE Linux 6.3 installation might be slightly different in some options. For example, it will offer an additional installation target by using a logical volume manager (LVM).
>
> However, this chapter should still be a helpful aid for this task. Please refer the the SuSE Linux 6.3 Installation Manual, if you run into any problems resulting of differences to this chapter.

2.1 Hardware considerations

Before installing SuSE Linux, it is helpful to know the hardware components in the computer that will be used for the installation. SuSE Linux is capable of detecting most of these components correctly. However, you should still try to gather information about the following components of your machine:

- **SCSI adapter** - manufacturer and model number
- **Hard drives** - interface type (SCSI or IDE) and size
- **CD-ROM** - interface type (SCSI or IDE)
- **Display Adapter** - manufacturer, model and video memory size
- **Mouse** - mouse type and connector type
- **Network card** - manufacturer and model
- **RAM** - the amount of RAM in your system
- **CPU** - the type and number of processors
- **Monitor** - manufacturer and model, horizontal and vertical frequency range

A very helpful resource for information about IBM Netfinity servers and other IBM products including monitors and SCSI adapters can be found on the following site:

```
ftp://ftp.pc.ibm.com/pcicrse/psref
```

This archive contains Personal Systems Reference sheets (PSREF) for all IBM PC products, current and withdrawn. You can also get a lot of useful information about IBM hardware at the following Web sites:

```
http://www.pc.ibm.com/support/
http://www.pc.ibm.com/us/netfinity/tech_library.html
```

SuSE also maintains an online database of supported hardware for Linux, which is available at:

```
http://cdb.suse.de/cdb_english.html
```

In addition to that, SuSE certifies IBM Netfinity systems for compatibility with SuSE Linux and is in close contact with the developers at IBM.

Keylabs is also running a Linux hardware certification program, which lists IBM products as well:

```
http://www.keylabs.com/linux/linux_results.html
```

2.2 Making the CD-ROM bootable

If you plan on booting the system directly from the CD-ROM, make sure the CD-ROM drive is the initial boot device prior to the installation. This can be accomplished by following the ensuing steps:

1. Power on the server.

2. When you see the IBM logo press F1 to enter the setup utility.

3. From the setup utility select **Start Options**.

4. From the Start Options select **Startup Sequence**.

5. Make sure that your CD-ROM is the initial boot device.

6. Press Esc until you see the setup utility main screen and select **Save Settings**.

7. Press Enter to confirm saving the current settings.

8. Exit the setup utility.

> **Note**
>
> Making the CD-ROM bootable can also be done by loading the default settings from the setup utility, but be aware that all other settings will be set to default as well.

2.3 Basic Linux installation

We will begin with the installation procedure on an IBM Netfinity without ServeRAID controller. Most of the following steps are identical to the procedure for installing on a system equipped with the ServeRAID interface. 2.4, "Installation with ServeRAID" on page 40 explains the differences.

SuSE Linux already contains all the necessary drivers, so you can start the installation by booting directly from the first CD-ROM. The installation will not be different from on any other regular PC. The only obstacle is the onboard S3 video chipset on some models, which is not very well supported by the version of XFree86 that is included on the CD-ROM (the driver first appeared with XFree86 3.3.4). The X Server tends to crash the machine with certain modelines (resolutions). See 2.5, "XFree86 configuration" on page 44 for more information.

The installation workflow of SuSE Linux is illustrated in Figure 1.

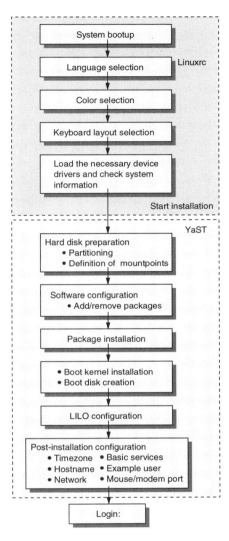

Figure 1. SuSE Linux installation workflow

The installation process is performed by two programs. Stage 1, the initial bootup process and the loading of driver modules, is fulfilled by Linuxrc, which can be loaded from either floppy disk or the CD-ROM. Linuxrc will then start YaST (Yet another Setup Tool) to perform tasks like partitioning, definition of mount points and installing the software packages. YaST can either be loaded from a local installation medium like the CD-ROM or the hard disk, or it can be loaded over the network to do a network installation. After

YaST has finished its job, it will boot directly into the freshly installed system. However, YaST will not only be used for the initial installation. You can use it for system administration and package management later on. Start it by typing "yast" as the root user. See Chapter 3, "Basic system administration" on page 51 for details.

2.3.1 Booting the installation system

Insert the first SuSE Linux 6.2 CD-ROM in your CD-ROM drive (and the boot floppy disk, if booting from CD-ROM is not supported) and reboot or power up the system. After a short moment you should see the bootup splash screen shown in Figure 2. If this fails, make sure that the PC is really configured for booting from CD-ROM or Floppy!

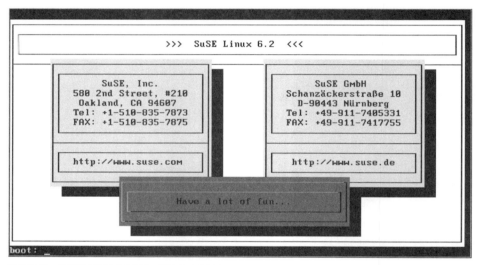

Figure 2. SuSE Linux bootup splash screen

The boot prompt enables you to enter special boot parameters. This may be necessary, if the system does not recognize certain hardware components. Section 2.7.6, "Kernel parameters" in the SuSE manual gives you more information about this feature. We did not experience any problems with IBM Netfinity hardware; therefore, you should not need this.

The installation system will automatically continue the boot process after a few seconds. If you press Enter, it will boot up immediately.

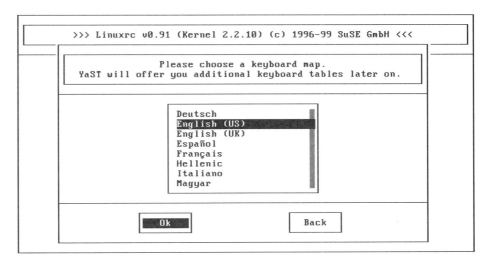

Figure 3. Language selection screen

First you have to select your desired language. This is the language that will be used during the installation process. Use the Up/Down cursor keys to highlight your selection and click **Ok** to continue.

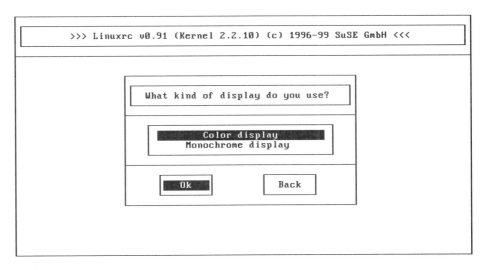

Figure 4. Color selection screen

Select what kind of display you will use. We recommend you select **Color display**, since this is what most modern PCs presently use.

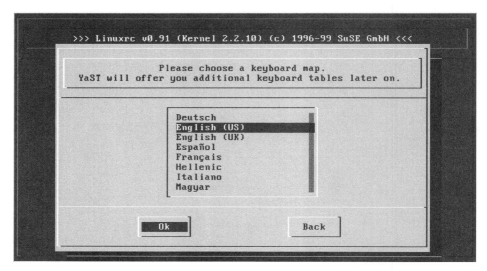

Figure 5. Keyboard selection window

Now you have to select the required layout for your keyboard. Click **Ok** to advance to the Linuxrc main menu.

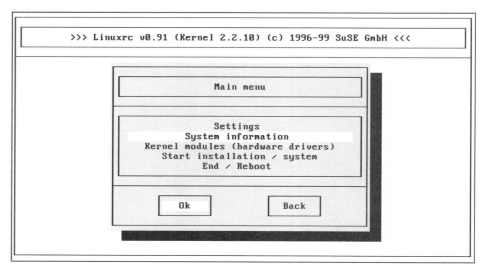

Figure 6. Linuxrc - main menu

Figure 6 shows the Linuxrc main menu. It offers the following options:

Settings - This option enables you to modify the language, screen or keyboard settings, if you need to revise the selection you made during the bootup process.

System information - This menu option gives you detailed information about the hardware that has already been recognized.

Kernel modules (Hardware drivers) - Use this menu to load device drivers for special SCSI devices, network cards and other devices.

Start installation / System - After you have loaded the necessary device drivers, select this option to continue the installation.

End / Reboot - This aborts the installation and reboots the system.

Before you can start the installation, you should make sure that the system detected your hard disk(s) and CD-ROM drive. If you intend to make a network installation or if you want to use a network connection later on, you should also load the respective network driver. Select **System Information > Harddisks / CD-ROMs** to determine which devices have been detected. Devices that are connected to the Adaptec SCSI Hostadapter, which is used in most IBM Netfinity servers, should already show up in this list. Return to the main menu and select **Kernel modules (hardware drivers)** to load the network and additional SCSI drivers.

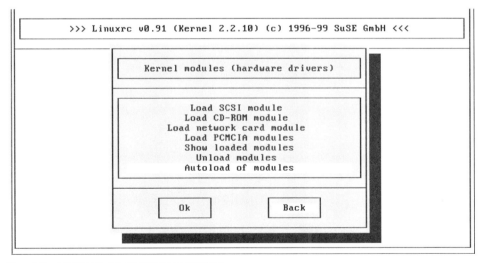

Figure 7. Hardware driver selection window

Select **Load network card module** to load the network card driver. You can also select **Autoload of modules** to let the system try to automatically probe for additional devices. However, this may freeze the machine or will not detect all components. This is especially true for the IBM ServeRAID driver - autoprobing this module will freeze the machine. Do this only if you absolutely do not know what kind of hardware you have.

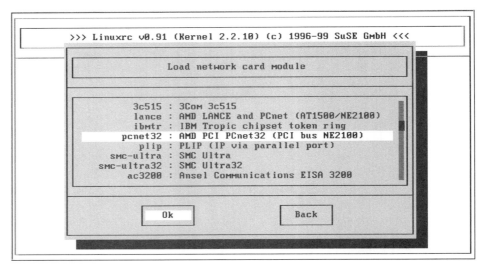

Figure 8. Network module selection window

Load the network card module that fits your network card. Select **eepro100** if you have an Intel network card, or select the **pcnet32** driver from the separate modules disk if your PC uses a card with the AMD chipset. Before loading the driver, you can again pass parameters to it (for example, interrupt and I/O address). This is not necessary for most modern PCI cards; you can just click **Ok** here. Linuxrc will now attempt to load the kernel module and informs you of the success or failure including the output of the device driver startup. This procedure may take a while with some drivers, so please be patient if the system does not react immediately.

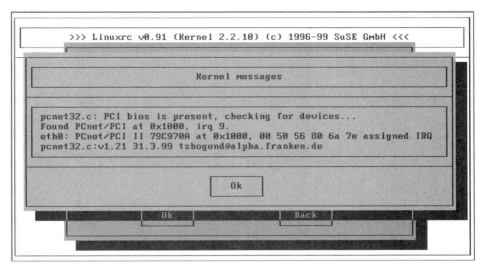

Figure 9. Network driver debug messages

After loading all necessary drivers, select **Back** to return to the Linuxrc main menu shown in Figure 6 on page 10. Select **Start installation / system** to begin the installation.

2.3.2 Starting the installation

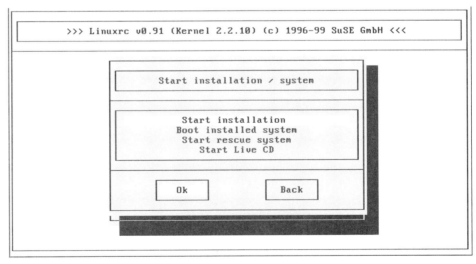

Figure 10. Linuxrc: start installation

This is an explanation of Figure 10:

Start installation to begin a regular installation.

Boot installed system comes in handy, if an already installed system fails to boot from the hard disk and you do not have a special boot disk.

Start rescue system enables you to start a minmal Linux system in a RAM disk, which you can use to do system maintenance or repair a corrupted installation.

Start Live CD enables you to run a full-fledged Linux system (including XFree86, KDE and compilers) directly from CD-ROM without installing Linux on your hard drive. You need to have the special Live-CD-ROM to do this, which is a separate product and is no longer included in the SuSE Linux box.

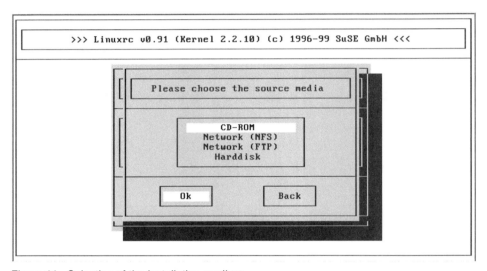

Figure 11. Selection of the installation medium

Please choose your source medium here. In our case, select **CD-ROM**. YaST will now be loaded and started to continue the installation. You can also set up a file server that serves the installation CD-ROMs over the network using NFS or FTP. However, this is beyond the scope of this manual and will not be discussed. Please see the SuSE manual for further details about this.

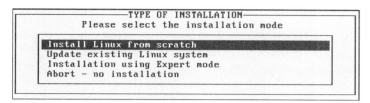

```
┌──────────────TYPE OF INSTALLATION──────────────┐
│            Please select the installation mode  │
│  ┌──────────────────────────────────────────┐  │
│  │ Install Linux from scratch               │  │
│  │ Update existing Linux system             │  │
│  │ Installation using Expert mode           │  │
│  │ Abort - no installation                  │  │
│  └──────────────────────────────────────────┘  │
└─────────────────────────────────────────────────┘
```

Figure 12. Type of selection

Select **Install Linux from scratch** to advance to the next section. If you intend to update an existing SuSE Linux, use **Update existing Linux system** here. Do not try to update distibutions other than SuSE Linux with this feature! This can cause severe chaos in your installation. Choosing **Installation using Expert mode** gives you some more control over the installation process, but will not be discussed here.

2.3.3 Partitioning and creation of filesystems

In order to be able to install Linux on your hard drive, you need to have some free space on your hard disk. This free space has to be divided among several partitions. Similar to fdisk in MS-DOS/Windows, SuSE Linux provides a tool to create the partitions and define their size and the partition type. After you have created the partitions, filesystems have to be created on them (they need to be formatted) so that Linux can access them. Linux does not know about drive letters like A:, C: or D:. Everything lives below a single directory tree (the root directory). Filesystems on other partitions will be mounted to a subdirectory of the root directory. You will also have to define these mountpoints when creating the file systems on your partitions.

Devices also use a different naming scheme from the Microsoft operating systems. Instead of using the above-mentioned drive letters, all drives in Linux are named alphabetically. Each partition on this drive has another number (CD-ROMs do not have partitions). For example:

- /dev/hda is the first IDE drive (master on the first IDE channel).
- /dev/hdc would be the first IDE drive on the second IDE channel.
- /dev/hdb1 is the first primary partition on the slave drive of the first IDE channel.
- /dev/sda names the first SCSI hard disk.
- /dev/sdb5 names the first logical partition on the second SCSI disk.

For more information about devices, see Appendix D1, "Device files in the /dev directory" in the SuSE manual.

---- Note --

Even though the partitioning tool is capable of creating partitions for
MS-DOS or Windows, you should not use it for creating partitions for
operating systems other than Linux. Please use the fdisk that ships with
MS-DOS/Windows to create such partitions.

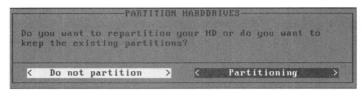

Figure 13. Selection: Hard drive partitioning

At first you will be prompted if you want to create partitions on your hard
disk(s). Select **Partitioning**, if you have not defined any partitions for Linux
yet. If you want to keep previously defined partitions, choose **Do not
partition** here.

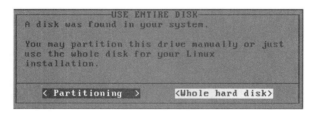

Figure 14. Selection: partitioning method

If you have multiple hard disks, you will be prompted to select the drive you
want to use for the partitioning. You will then return to this screen, after you
have created partitions on one of these to be able to partition the other disks
as well. Linux can be spread over multiple disk drives without problems.

If you choose **Whole hard disk** here, YaST will automatically partition the
selected disk for you by creating one swap partition, a small partition for the
/boot directory and one large partition for the root directory and all its
subdirectories. It will also automatically define these mount points and
advance to the package installation menu shown in Figure 26 on page 24.

While automatic partitioning is fine for home or workstation use, you should
consider partitioning your disks manually to better fit your needs.

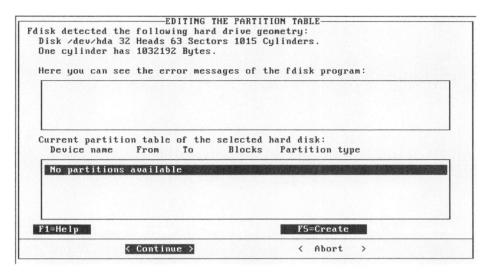

```
                       EDITING THE PARTITION TABLE
Fdisk detected the following hard drive geometry:
  Disk /dev/hda 32 Heads 63 Sectors 1015 Cylinders.
  One cylinder has 1032192 Bytes.

  Here you can see the error messages of the fdisk program:




  Current partition table of the selected hard disk:
    Device name    From    To       Blocks    Partition type

    No partitions available




    F1=Help                                  F5=Create

          < Continue >                  <  Abort   >
```

Figure 15. Fdisk main screen (no partitions defined)

If the current hard disk has not been used before, you will start with an empty partition table as shown in Figure 15. You can now start adding partitions with the F5 key. Use F4 to delete previously defined partitions.

Note

Partitioning your hard disks is highly dependent on the purpose of your system. Depending on the intended services, you may need to create one especially large partition (for example for a file server). There is no general rule for this and it's almost impossible to give recommendations. See section 2.10, "Partitioning for experts" in the SuSE manual for more information about this issue.

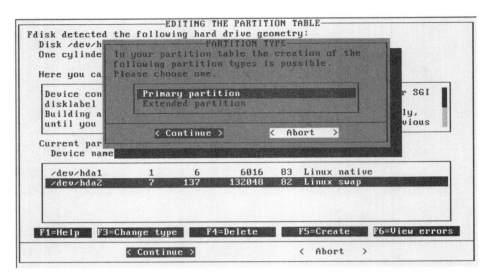

Figure 16. Selection: partition type

Depending on the already existing partitions, you can now define the partition type. A hard disk can consist of a maximum of four primary partitions, or up to three primary and one extended partition. An extended partition can contain multiple logical partitions. See section 2.9, "Partition types on a PC" in the SuSE 6.2 manual for a detailed description of the different partition types on a PC. Linux can be installed in either partition type.

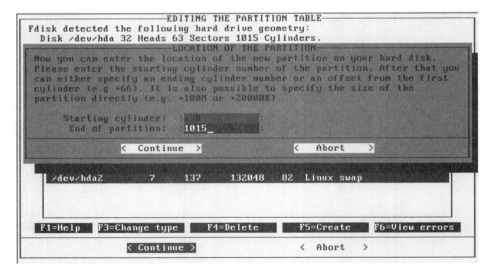

Figure 17. Selection: partition size

After defining the partition type, you now have to enter the size and location of that partition by supplying the starting and ending cylinder. By default, YaST uses the next available starting cylinder for the beginning of the new partition and the last available cylinder as the end (grow to fill). To define the size and location, you can either enter absolute cylinder numbers here, or you can use the default start cylinder and enter the size of this partition in kilobytes or megabytes (for example entering +10M would create a 10 MB partition).

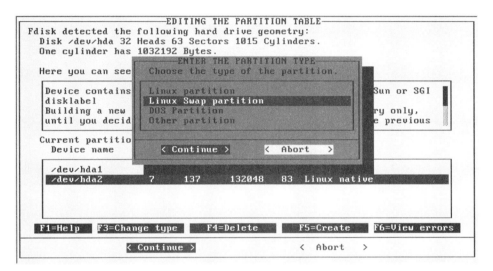

Figure 18. Selection: Linux Swap partition

By default, YaST creates Linux native partitions. To create partitions of another type (for example Swap), press F3 after you have selected the desired partition you want to change. Note that this procedure only sets the partition ID of this partition. It does not modify the partition's content or size. Partition the drive(s) to suit your needs.

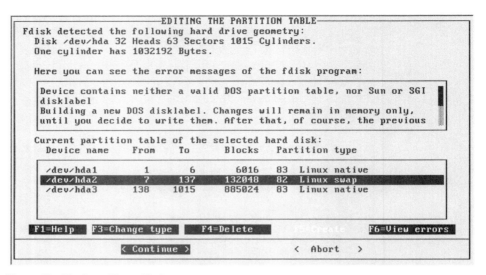

```
                      ┌─────────────EDITING THE PARTITION TABLE──────────────┐
                      Fdisk detected the following hard drive geometry:
                        Disk /dev/hda 32 Heads 63 Sectors 1015 Cylinders.
                        One cylinder has 1032192 Bytes.

                        Here you can see the error messages of the fdisk program:
                      ┌──────────────────────────────────────────────────────────────┐
                      │Device contains neither a valid DOS partition table, nor Sun or SGI │
                      │disklabel                                                       │
                      │Building a new DOS disklabel. Changes will remain in memory only, │
                      │until you decide to write them. After that, of course, the previous │
                      └──────────────────────────────────────────────────────────────┘
                      Current partition table of the selected hard disk:
                        Device name      From      To       Blocks    Partition type
                      ┌──────────────────────────────────────────────────────────────┐
                      │ /dev/hda1         1         6        6016      83   Linux native │
                      │ /dev/hda2         7        137      132048     82   Linux swap   │
                      │ /dev/hda3        138       1015     885024     83   Linux native │
                      │                                                              │
                      └──────────────────────────────────────────────────────────────┘

                      F1=Help    F3=Change type     F4=Delete       F5=Create     F6=View errors

                              < Continue >                    <  Abort   >
```

Figure 19. Final partition table layout

After the partition table is finished, click **Continue** to write the partition table
to disk and proceed to the filesystem creation dialog.

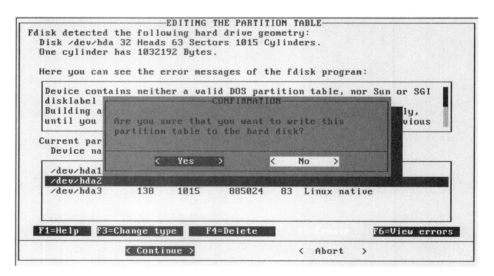

```
                      ┌─────────────EDITING THE PARTITION TABLE──────────────┐
                      Fdisk detected the following hard drive geometry:
                        Disk /dev/hda 32 Heads 63 Sectors 1015 Cylinders.
                        One cylinder has 1032192 Bytes.

                        Here you can see the error messages of the fdisk program:
                      ┌──────────────────────────────────────────────────────────────┐
                      │Device contains neither a valid DOS partition table, nor Sun or SGI │
                      │disklabel        ┌──────────CONFIRMATION──────────┐            │
                      │Building a       │                                │     ly,    │
                      │until you        │ Are you sure that you want to write this │ vious │
                      │                 │ partition table to the hard disk? │            │
                      Current par       │                                │
                        Device na       │     <   Yes    >      <   No   >  │
                      ┌─────────────────│                                │──────────────┐
                      │ /dev/hda1       └────────────────────────────────┘            │
                      │ /dev/hda2                                                      │
                      │ /dev/hda3        138       1015     885024     83   Linux native │
                      │                                                              │
                      └──────────────────────────────────────────────────────────────┘

                      F1=Help    F3=Change type     F4=Delete       F5=Create     F6=View errors

                              < Continue >                    <  Abort   >
```

Figure 20. Writing the partition table

Click **Yes** if you want to write the new partition table to this disk. Selecting **No**
will abort the partitioning.

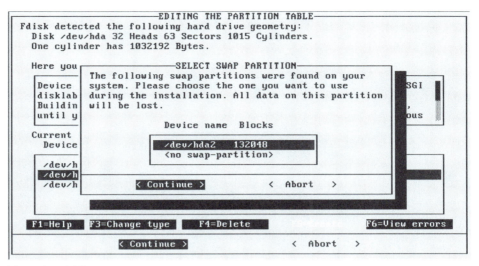

Figure 21. Adding swap space

If you have created a swap partition, YaST will immediately attempt to use it to have more virtual memory for the further installation procedure. Select **Continue** to make use of this. The content of this partition will be deleted!

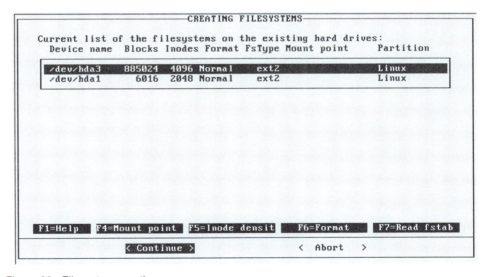

Figure 22. Filesystem creation

After the partition table has been written, you need to create filesystems on all partitions that you want to use for Linux (this is similar to formatting them).

Additionally you have to define mount points, which partition will act as your root filesystem, and where other partitions should be mounted to. Press F4 to open the mount point dialog.

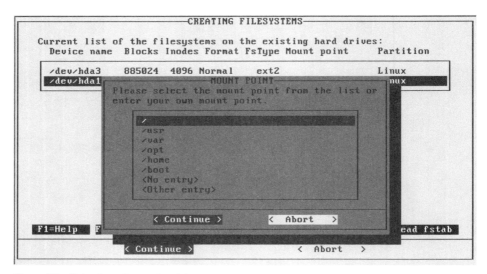

Figure 23. Selection of mount points

YaST offers a list of commonly used mount points. You can either select one of the list or select **Other entry** to freely define another mount point.

Note

One of your partitions must to be mounted to "/". This will be your root partition. YaST will check for the existence of this mount point before you can proceed.

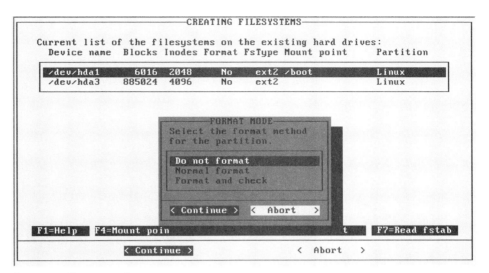

Figure 24. Format mode

After the definition of mount points and the type of formatting, select **Continue** to proceed to the actual creation of these filesystems. *This is the same as formatting your hard disk! You will not be able to recover any data that has not been backed up yet!* If you are sure, that you want to proceed, select **Yes**.

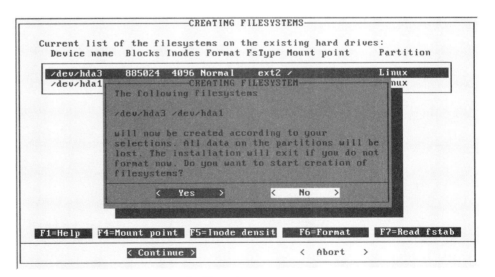

Figure 25. Confirmation to create the filesystems

The creation of file systems may take some time, depending on the size of your partitions. You should note some hard disk activity during this process.

After the filesystems have been successfully created, you will reach YaST's package selection screen.

2.3.4 Software package selection and installation

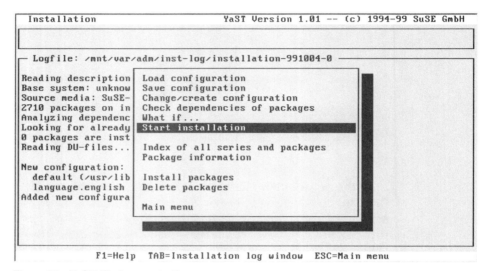

Figure 26. YaST: Package selection

After you have finished the creation of partitions and filesystems, the installation program needs to know which software you want to install. Since SuSE Linux offers a broad variety of software packages, it would be a very time consuming task to check each single package for installation.

The window shown in Figure 26 enables you to define the software packages that will be installed on your system. You will be able to add or remove packages later on; therefore ,we will stick with the default configuration here. SuSE also created a number of predefined package selections (configurations), which you can choose with the menu option **Load configuration**.

More information about package management can be found in 3.1, "Adding and removing software packages using YaST" on page 51.

The only package that we will be adding here is the correct driver for the video card, also referred to as the X server.

Select Change/create configuration

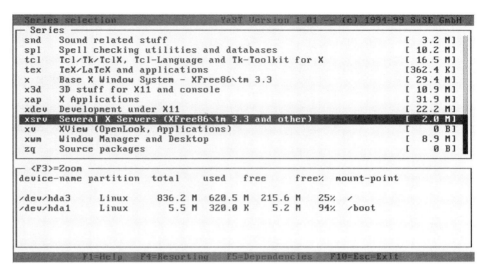

Figure 27. YaST: Series selection

Figure 26 show the series selection of YaST. All software packages have been categorized into different series, to make it easier to find the correct program for your needs.

Select xsrv to open the list of available X servers.

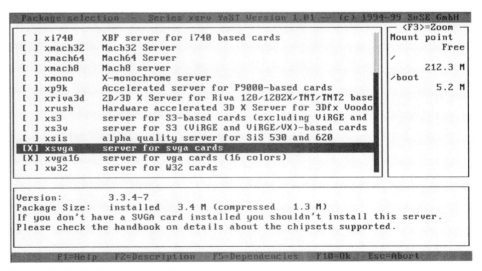

Figure 28. YaST: Package selection

After you have selected a series, you will see a list of all packages available in this series. Select **xsvga**. F2 will give you a more detailed description of the current package. To confirm you selection, press F10 to return to the package series selection menu. You can now select or deselect packages from other series or press F10 to continue.

Now the selection is finished and you can start the actual installation of the selected packages by choosing **Start installation**.

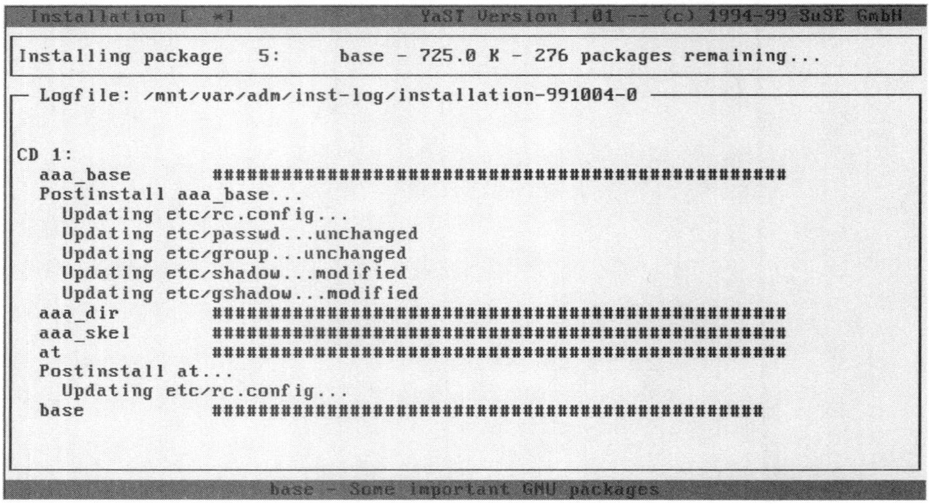

```
Installation [ *]                    YaST Version 1.01 -- (c) 1994-99 SuSE GmbH

Installing package    5:      base - 725.0 K - 276 packages remaining...

  Logfile: /mnt/var/adm/inst-log/installation-991004-0

CD 1:
  aaa_base        ###############################################################
  Postinstall aaa_base...
    Updating etc/rc.config...
    Updating etc/passwd...unchanged
    Updating etc/group...unchanged
    Updating etc/shadow...modified
    Updating etc/gshadow...modified
  aaa_dir         ###############################################################
  aaa_skel        ###############################################################
  at              ###############################################################
  Postinstall at...
    Updating etc/rc.config...
  base            ###############################################################

                     base - Some important GNU packages
```

Figure 29. YaST: Package installation in progress

Now the installation of software packages from the CD-ROM to your hard disk is being performed. Depending on the speed of your CD-ROM and the number of packages, this may take a while. You will be prompted to change the CD-ROM from time to time, to install the remaining packages.

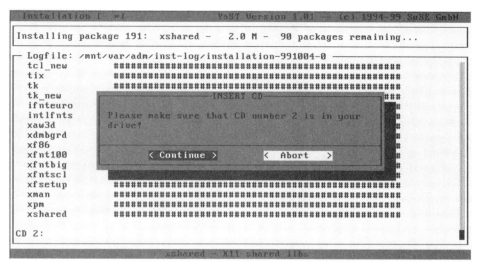

Figure 30. YaST: CD changing prompt

After the installation of packages has been finished, YaST will return to the package installation menu shown in Figure 26 on page 24. You are free to add or remove further software packages and reiterate through this process. To continue the installation of SuSE Linux, select **Main menu**.

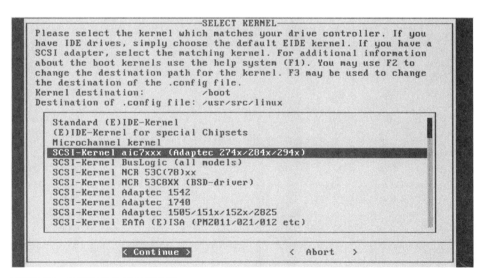

Figure 31. YaST: Kernel selection

In order to be able to boot the installed system from hard disk, you need to install a Linux kernel that includes support for your SCSI adapter. If your system uses the Adaptec SCSI controller, select **SCSI Kernel aic7xxx** here.

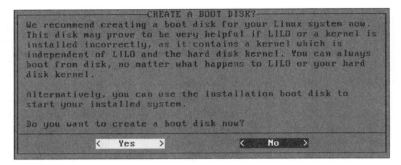

Figure 32. YaST: Bootdisk creation

You now have the possibility to create a boot disk with the previously selected kernel image. We recommend you select **No** here, because you can also use the installation floppy or the first CD-ROM to boot the system in case of an accident.

You will now be prompted if you want to configure LILO, the Linux Loader. Select **Yes**.

2.3.5 LILO - the Linux Loader

```
┌─────────────────────────────LILO INSTALLATION─────────────────────────────┐
│ LILO (the Linux Loader) allows you to boot Linux from a hard disk.  To     │
│ configure LILO, fill in the following fields. Then, create and/or edit your│
│ boot configurations.  The first boot configuration will be booted          │
│ automatically after the boot delay. You must create at least one boot      │
│ configuration (using F4).  After that, you can commit your configuration by │
│ pressing <CONTINUE> and LILO will be installed.                            │
│                                                                            │
│                                                                            │
│ Append-line for hardware parameter    :███████████████████████████████:    │
│                                                                            │
│ Where do you want to install LILO      [Master boot record              ]   │
│                                                                            │
│ Boot delay             :███████:       [ ] 'linear' option                  │
│                                                                            │
│                                        ┌────────────────────────────────┐  │
│ The following boot configurations      │ Linux                          │  │
│ are currently available                │                                │  │
│                                        │                                │  │
│                                        └────────────────────────────────┘  │
│                                                                            │
│   ████ F1=Help ████      ███ F4=New Config ███                             │
│          < Continue >                        <   Abort   >                 │
└────────────────────────────────────────────────────────────────────────────┘
```

Figure 33. YaST: LILO configuration

LILO, the Linux Loader, is a boot manager that allows you to boot multiple operating systems that can reside on different hard disk partitions or even on different hard disks. Even if you do only have Linux installed, you still need to create a boot configuration for Linux. Linux cannot be booted without LILO.

For an exhaustive explanation of LILO and boot concepts, see Chapter 4, "Booting and boot managers: LILO, loadlin, etc." in the SuSE manual.

Figure 33 shows YaST's LILO main configuration window. You can stick with these default values. However, you might want to decrease the Boot delay from 10 seconds (default) to a lower value to save some time during the system startup. By default, LILO will be written to the master boot record of your primary hard disk. Alternatively you can write it to a floppy disk, which has to be inserted during the system bootup.

Press F4 to create a new boot configuration.

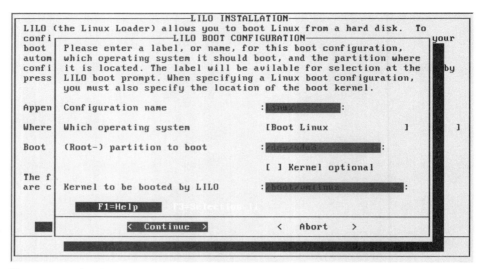

```
┌──────────────────────LILO INSTALLATION──────────────────────┐
│ LILO (the Linux Loader) allows you to boot Linux from a hard disk.  To │
│ confi ┌──────────────────LILO BOOT CONFIGURATION──────────────────┐ your │
│ boot  │ Please enter a label, or name, for this boot configuration, │      │
│ autom │ which operating system it should boot, and the partition where │   │
│ confi │ it is located. The label will be avilable for selection at the │ by │
│ press │ LILO boot prompt. When specifying a Linux boot configuration, │    │
│       │ you must also specify the location of the boot kernel.        │     │
│       │                                                               │     │
│ Appen │ Configuration name              :▓Linux▓▓▓▓▓▓▓:              │     │
│       │                                                               │     │
│ Where │ Which operating system          [Boot Linux            ]    │ ]   │
│       │                                                               │     │
│ Boot  │ (Root-) partition to boot       :▓/dev/sda3▓▓▓▓▓▓:         │     │
│       │                                                               │     │
│       │                                 [ ] Kernel optional          │     │
│ The f │                                                               │     │
│ are c │ Kernel to be booted by LILO     :▓/boot/vmlinuz▓▓▓:        │     │
│       │    ▓▓▓F1=Help▓▓▓          ▓F3=Selection 1▓                  │     │
│  ▓▓  │ ┌──────────────────────────────────────────────────────────┐ │
│       │ │      <  Continue  >            <   Abort   >            │ │
└───────┴────────────────────────────────────────────────────────────┘
```

Figure 34. YaST: Create LILO boot configuration

Figure 34 shows the boot configuration dialog. You need to create such a configuration for each operating system you want to boot.

Enter Linux as the configuration name. This name identifies your boot configuration and it must be unique for each configuration you create. If you want to boot an operating system later on, you have to enter this name at the LILO: prompt.

In the Which operating system field, enter Boot Linux. Choose the correct value if you want to boot another operating system.

In the (Root-) partition to boot field, enter /dev/sda3, where 3 is the partition number. You have to select your root-partition here (the partition that is mounted to /) - not the Boot-Partition! Usually this is already correctly preselected.

In the Kernel to be booted by LILO field, enter /boot/vmlinuz. LILO needs to know where the kernel image to be booted is located.

Highlight **Continue** using the Tab key to create this new boot configuration. When you have added all necessary boot configurations, select **Continue** in the LILO main menu to write the new boot record.

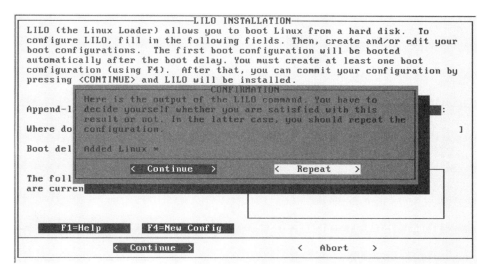

```
                    ┌────────────LILO INSTALLATION────────────────────────────┐
                    │ LILO (the Linux Loader) allows you to boot Linux from a hard disk.  To │
                    │ configure LILO, fill in the following fields.  Then, create and/or edit your │
                    │ boot configurations.  The first boot configuration will be booted │
                    │ automatically after the boot delay. You must create at least one boot │
                    │ configuration (using F4).  After that, you can commit your configuration by │
                    │ pressing <CONTINUE> and LILO will be installed. │
                    │          ┌──────────────CONFIRMATION──────────────┐      │
                    │          │ Here is the output of the LILO command. You have to │  │
                    │ Append-l │ decide yourself whether you are satisfied with this │ : │
                    │          │ result or not. In the latter case, you should repeat the │  │
                    │ Where do │ configuration. │                                     ] │
                    │          │                                         │        │
                    │ Boot del │ Added Linux * │                                    │
                    │          │                                         │        │
                    │          │  <   Continue   >        <   Repeat   > │        │
                    │ The foll │                                         │        │
                    │ are curren                                        │        │
                    │                                                            │
                    │                                                            │
                    │  ██ F1=Help ██        ██ F4=New Config ██                   │
                    ├────────────────────────────────────────────────────────────┤
                    │       <  Continue  >              <   Abort   >             │
                    └────────────────────────────────────────────────────────────┘
```

Figure 35. YaST: LILO output

After LILO has performed the creation of the new boot block, you have the possibility to review LILO's output. Click **Continue** to proceed to the time zone and clock settings.

2.3.6 Time zone and clock settings

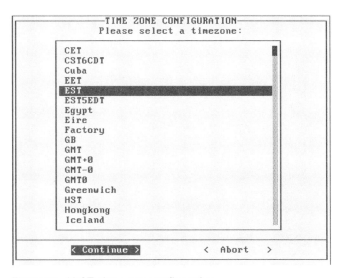

```
              ┌──────────────TIME ZONE CONFIGURATION───────────┐
              │              Please select a timezone:          │
              │  ┌──────────────────────────────────────────┐  │
              │  │ CET                                      █ │  │
              │  │ CST6CDT                                  █ │  │
              │  │ Cuba                                     █ │  │
              │  │ EET                                      █ │  │
              │  │ EST                                      █ │  │
              │  │ EST5EDT                                  █ │  │
              │  │ Egypt                                    █ │  │
              │  │ Eire                                     █ │  │
              │  │ Factory                                  █ │  │
              │  │ GB                                       █ │  │
              │  │ GMT                                      █ │  │
              │  │ GMT+0                                    █ │  │
              │  │ GMT-0                                    █ │  │
              │  │ GMT0                                     █ │  │
              │  │ Greenwich                                █ │  │
              │  │ HST                                      █ │  │
              │  │ Hongkong                                 █ │  │
              │  │ Iceland                                  █ │  │
              │  └──────────────────────────────────────────┘  │
              ├────────────────────────────────────────────────┤
              │   < Continue >          <   Abort   >           │
              └────────────────────────────────────────────────┘
```

Figure 36. YaST: time zone configuration

Select your desired time zone here. This is important for automatic switching between summer or winter time. You can also change this value later on, which is helpful if you use your Linux system in different locations (for example on a laptop computer).

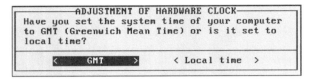

Figure 37. YaST: system clock selection

Now the setting of your BIOS clock has to be selected. Click **Local time** if you are booting other operating systems on this box, or **GMT** otherwise.

2.3.7 Network configuration

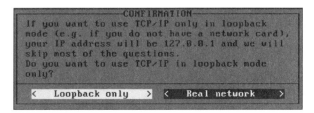

Figure 38. YaST: host name configuration

Enter your host and domain name here. Each host in a TCP/IP network must have a unique host name. If you do not know this, please ask the network administrator of your local network for assistance. If you do not intend to use this system in a networked environment, you can freely choose your host and domain name.

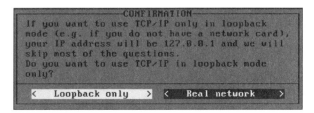

Figure 39. YaST: network type selection

If your system will be connected to a LAN, select **Real network**.

Otherwise, select **Loopback only**. This will skip the following questions and continues with the Sendmail configuration shown in Figure 42 on page 35.

For DHCP client selection, select **No**, if you will use a static IP address for the network card (which is recommended for a server). If you select **Yes** here, the system will act as a DHCP client in your network and will obtain its IP address from a DHCP server in your local network. In this case, the dialog shown in Figure 40 will not appear.

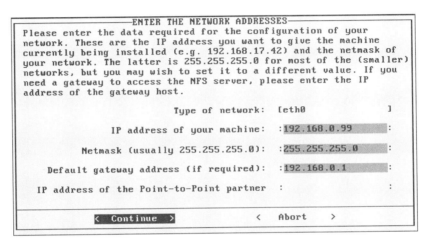

Figure 40. YaST: network configuration

The window shown in Figure 40 enables you to configure your TCP/IP configuration. You need an IP address to be able to communicate with other hosts in your network. Please ask your network administrator for the correct values for your network.

Type of network - select the desired network card here. Select **eth0** to use the first Ethernet card, **tr0** if you use a token-ring adapter.

Enter the correspondent values for your local network and click **Continue**.

You will now be prompted if you want to start the inetd service. Inetd is needed for invoking certain services on demand, such as telnet, finger, ftp and others. Inetd should always be started; otherwise, the above-mentioned services will not be available. If your system will be connected to the Internet, you may want to restrict access to certain services. Please see section

18.2.2, "inetd" in the SuSE manual for more info about inetd. In most cases it is safe to select **Yes** here.

If you want to use this system as an NFS or NIS server, you will need to start the portmapper service at boot-up. Therefore, the question "START THE PORTMAPPER?" should be answered with **Yes**.

If you have decided to start the portmapper, you will now be prompted, if you want to start the NFS server as well. Select **Yes** if you plan to share files using NFS.

The ADJUST NEWS FROM-ADDRESS dialog enables you to modify the sender address, if you intend to use Usenet News. The default is fine here for most cases; select **Continue** to proceed.

If your system is connected to a network and you would like to access a Domain Name System (DNS) server, select **Yes** at the CONFIRMATION (nameserver) dialog. If your system will act as the DNS, select **Yes**, too.

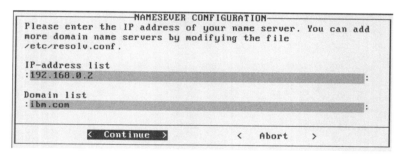

Figure 41. YaST: nameserver configuration

Figure 41 shows the name server configuration dialog. You can enter your name server's IP address on the first line. If you want to access multiple name servers, separate the entries with blanks. Adjust the domain list to your local domain.

If you want to run a DNS server on this system, you still have to configure the system to query the local running name server. Select the loopback interface (127.0.0.1) as the name server's IP address.

Choose **Continue** to advance to the next window.

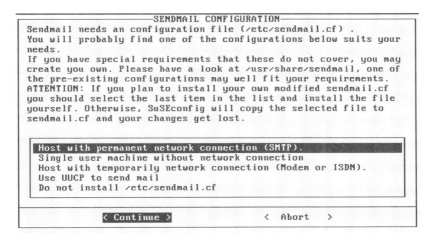

```
───────────SENDMAIL CONFIGURATION───────────
Sendmail needs an configuration file (/etc/sendmail.cf) .
You will probably find one of the configurations below suits your
needs.
If you have special requirements that these do not cover, you may
create you own. Please have a look at /usr/share/sendmail, one of
the pre-existing configurations may well fit your requirements.
ATTENTION: If you plan to install your own modified sendmail.cf
you should select the last item in the list and install the file
yourself. Otherwise, SuSEconfig will copy the selected file to
sendmail.cf and your changes get lost.

  ┌──────────────────────────────────────────────────────┐
  │ Host with permanent network connection (SMTP).        │
  │ Single user machine without network connection        │
  │ Host with temporarily network connection (Modem or ISDN). │
  │ Use UUCP to send mail                                 │
  │ Do not install /etc/sendmail.cf                       │
  └──────────────────────────────────────────────────────┘

      < Continue >              <  Abort  >
```

Figure 42. YaST: Sendmail configuration selection

You will now be asked how you want to install the Sendmail service. The default selection is good for most configurations. Press **Continue** after you have made your choice.

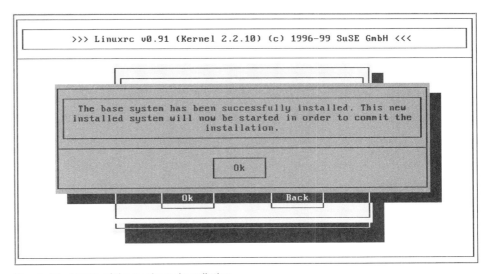

```
>>> Linuxrc v0.91 (Kernel 2.2.10) (c) 1996-99 SuSE GmbH <<<

     The base system has been successfully installed. This new
     installed system will now be started in order to commit the
                          installation.

                             Ok

          Ok                      Back
```

Figure 43. Finish of the package installation

After you have entered all the necessary values, the system will now be booted up.

```
Mounting local file systems...
proc on /proc type proc (rw)
/dev/hdb1 on /usr type ext2 (rw)
/dev/hda1 on /boot type ext2 (rw)                                    done
Setting up /etc/ld.so.cache                                          done
Setting up timezone data                                             done
Setting up loopback device                                           done
Setting up hostname                                                  done
Setting up the CMOS clock                                            done
Running /sbin/init.d/boot.local                                      done
Creating /var/log/boot.msg                                           done
Disabling IP forwarding                                              done
Starting syslog services                                             done


--------------------------------------------------------------------------------

                         Welcome to SuSE Linux

--------------------------------------------------------------------------------

    You should set a password for root first. If you don't want a
    password for root, simply hit enter.

New password: _
```

Figure 44. Definition of the root password

The installation program will now start to boot up from the freshly installed
system. Since Linux is a multi-user operating system, you have to define user
accounts first. The most important user account is the root account, which
identifies the system administrator (username "root") of this system. Each
user account is protected by a password. Therefore you will now be prompted
to enter a password for the root user twice. Please note that passwords in
Linux are case-sensitive!

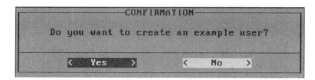

Figure 45. Confirmation: example user

After defining the root password, you will be asked if you would like to create
a sample user account. We strongly recommend you do so, since you should
not use the root account for your regular work! The root login should only be
used for system maintenance. The root user has full access to the system
configuration files and it is very easy to render the system unusable by
accident. Therefore, click **Yes** here. If you choose not to create a sample user
account, click **No**. This will skip the following screen.

```
                    ──ENTER USERNAME──
 Please enter username, description and password of
 the sample user.

 Login name                    :lxuser          :

 Password                      :******          :

 Re-enter password             :******          :

 Description of user
 :Example user SuSE Linux 6.2                    :


        <  Continue  >          <   Abort    >
```

Figure 46. YaSY: adding a user account

Figure 46 shows the sample user creation form. Select a login name (do not use capital letters) and a password. The login name should be short, for example the first name of this user or an abbreviation of first and last name. The description of the user should be the full name or a short statement about this user account. Click **Continue** to create the user account.

The next window will ask you to set up your modem. If you have one, click **Yes**. Clicking **No** will skip the following window.

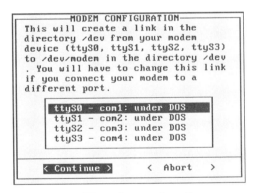

Figure 47. YaST: modem configuration

Figure 47 displays the modem configuration screen. Select the serial port where your modem is connected to. YaST will create a symbolic link /dev/modem that will point to the respective serial device. Please note that this is only the first step in configuring your modem for Linux. The symbolic link just makes it easier for other applications to find the modem. However, these applications still have to be configured manually to be able to "talk" with the modem later on. Click **Continue** to create the link.

2.3.8 Mouse configuration

After configuring your modem, you can now configure the mouse. If you intend to use the X-Windows system later on or want to use the mouse on the text console, click **Yes**. If you do not need a mouse, click **No** to skip the following mouse configuration dialogs.

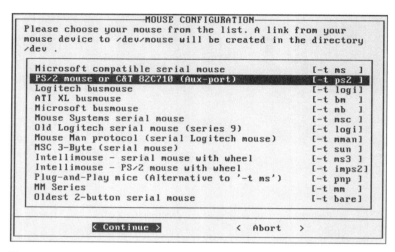

```
┌──────────────────MOUSE CONFIGURATION──────────────────┐
│ Please choose your mouse from the list. A link from your │
│ mouse device to /dev/mouse will be created in the directory │
│ /dev .                                                   │
│  ┌────────────────────────────────────────────────────┐ │
│  │ Microsoft compatible serial mouse        [-t ms  ]  │ │
│  │ PS/2 mouse or C&T 82C710 (Aux-port)      [-t ps2 ]  │ │
│  │ Logitech busmouse                        [-t logi]  │ │
│  │ ATI XL busmouse                          [-t bm  ]  │ │
│  │ Microsoft busmouse                       [-t mb  ]  │ │
│  │ Mouse Systems serial mouse               [-t msc ]  │ │
│  │ Old Logitech serial mouse (series 9)     [-t logi]  │ │
│  │ Mouse Man protocol (serial Logitech mouse) [-t mman] │ │
│  │ MSC 3-Byte (serial mouse)                [-t sun ]  │ │
│  │ Intellimouse - serial mouse with wheel   [-t ms3 ]  │ │
│  │ Intellimouse - PS/2 mouse with wheel     [-t imps2] │ │
│  │ Plug-and-Play mice (Alternative to '-t ms') [-t pnp] │ │
│  │ MM Series                                [-t mm  ]  │ │
│  │ Oldest 2-button serial mouse             [-t bare]  │ │
│  └────────────────────────────────────────────────────┘ │
│                                                          │
│      < Continue >              <   Abort   >             │
└──────────────────────────────────────────────────────────┘
```

Figure 48. YaST: mouse configuration

First, you have to choose the type of mouse you have. The two most common types are Microsoft compatible or PS/2 mouse. IBM Netfinity servers use PS/2, therefore select **PS/2 mouse**. If your mouse is connected to a serial port, it is most likely a Microsoft compatible mouse. If you choose a serial mouse, you will also have to select the correct serial port as shown on Figure 49.

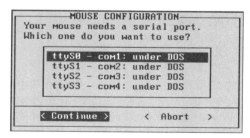

```
┌──────────MOUSE CONFIGURATION──────────┐
│ Your mouse needs a serial port.        │
│ Which one do you want to use?          │
│  ┌──────────────────────────────────┐ │
│  │ ttyS0 - com1: under DOS           │ │
│  │ ttyS1 - com2: under DOS           │ │
│  │ ttyS2 - com3: under DOS           │ │
│  │ ttyS3 - com4: under DOS           │ │
│  └──────────────────────────────────┘ │
│                                        │
│  < Continue >        <  Abort  >       │
└────────────────────────────────────────┘
```

Figure 49. YaST: serial mouse port selection

YaST will create a symbolic link /dev/mouse, that will point to the correct mouse device (for example /dev/psaux for PS/2 mice or /dev/ttyS0 for a serial mouse on the first serial port).

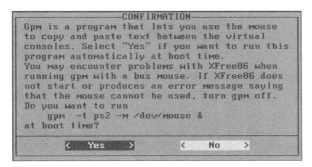

Figure 50. YaST: GPM configuration

GPM is a helpful program, if you do a lot of work on the command line in text mode. It enables you to copy and paste text between virtual consoles by highlighting the text with the mouse. Some applications, like the Midnight Commander (MC) can also be operated with the mouse. Select **Yes** if you want GPM to be started on system startup. Selecting **No** will skip the following window.

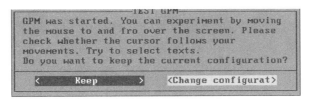

Figure 51. YaST: GPM test window

YaST will now start GPM to let you test your configuration. Try to move the mouse around, the cursor should follow your mouse movement. Also try to select some text by highlighting it with the left mouse button. If the cursor does not move at all, or jumps randomly across the screen, you have most likely chosen the wrong mouse protocol. Click **Change configuration** to return to the previous screen and try another mouse protocol. If everything is working fine, click **Keep** to continue. And no, unfortunately you cannot use the mouse for this :-)

YaST will now terminate and finish to boot the system.

```
Configuring serial ports
ttyS0 at 0x03f8 (irq = 4) is a 16550A
ttyS1 at 0x02f8 (irq = 3) is a 16550A
ttyS2 at 0x03e8 (irq = 4) is a 16550A
ttyS3 at 0x02e8 (irq = 3) is a 16550A                             done
Setting up network device eth0                                    done
Setting up routing (using /etc/route.conf)                        done
Re-Starting RPC portmap daemon                                    done
Re-Starting syslog services                                       done
Initializing random number generator                              done
Starting NFS server                                               done
Starting INET services (inetd)                                    done
Loading keymap qwerty/us.map.gz                                   done
Initializing SMTP port. (sendmail)                                done
Starting CRON daemon                                              done
Starting Name Service Cache Daemon                                done
Master Resource Control: runlevel 2 has been

      Please enter "root" to login as user root...


Welcome to SuSE Linux 6.2 (i386) - Kernel 2.2.10 (tty1).

SuSE login: _
```

Figure 52. SuSE Linux login

Log in as user root with the password you provided during the installation to finalize the installation. Of course you can also log in and start working with the regular user account you have created.

Congratulations! The basic installation of SuSE Linux is now finished. Now you can start configuring the X-Windows system (2.5, "XFree86 configuration" on page 44) and the additional services.

2.4 Installation with ServeRAID

The Installation of SuSE Linux 6.2 on servers with IBM ServeRAID controllers is a bit different from the installation procedure described in the previous section, because the ServeRAID driver is very new and has been updated and improved after the distribution was finished. Future releases of SuSE Linux will not have this limitation and you will be able to install it on a ServeRAID system without these additional steps.

Nevertheless, SuSE Linux 6.2 contains an early version of the driver, you can boot and install the system with it. However, we recommend you download the latest boot image for the installation and you should definetely use the latest driver, if you intend to use this Linux system in a production environment.

Before starting the actual installation, we advise you to update the server's BIOS and the ServeRAID firmware (use Version 3.50B or later) as well. The required files can be found at:

```
http://www.pc.ibm.com/support
```

After upgrading the firmware, create the desired RAID partitions first by booting off the ServeRAID DOS diskette or the ServeRAID CD. Please follow the documentation for these tools for how to do this. **Note**: Enabling the write-back cache will result in faster formats during the installation process, but can be hazardous if there is a power failure. Refer to the ServeRAID documentation for more information about this subject.

The following sections describe the necessary preliminary steps and the differences from the basic installation covered in 2.3, "Basic Linux installation" on page 6.

2.4.1 Preparing the installation boot disk

To install the system with the latest driver available, you first have to download the respective boot disk image. You cannot boot directly from the CD-ROM in this case, since this boot image does not contain the newest ServeRAID driver.

You can get the boot floppy image from SuSE's FTP server:

```
ftp://ftp.suse.com/pub/suse/i386/update/6.2/disks/servraid
```

After downloading, you need to "dump" this image to a floppy disk. Because it is the actual raw image of the floppy, you cannot simply copy it to the diskette. If you already run Linux on another system, insert a blank floppy and use the following command line (assuming, that the downloaded image resides in the current directory):

```
dd if=./servraid of=/dev/fd0 bs=8192
```

This will write the image to the floppy disk. You can verify the success of this operation by taking a look at the directory of the disk (it contains a plain MSDOS filesystem) by using the mdir command from the mtools package.

```
SuSE:~ # ls -l servraid
-rw-r--r--   1 root      root       1474560 Oct 11 07:13 servraid
SuSE:~ # dd if=./servraid of=/dev/fd0 bs=8192
180+0 records in
180+0 records out
SuSE:~ # mdir a:
 Volume in drive A has no label
 Volume Serial Number is 6B7B-E2AB
Directory for A:/

ldlinux  sys       5860 07-19-1999   15:54
initdisk gz     729966 07-22-1999   14:43
message          2424 07-22-1999   14:43
syslinux cfg      107 07-22-1999   14:43
linux          676711 10-01-1999    5:17
        5 files           1 415 068 bytes
                            41 472 bytes free


SuSE:~ # _
```

Figure 53. Dumping a floppy image using Linux

If you do not have a possibility to use Linux to create the boot floppy, you can also use another PC running MS-DOS or Windows. There is a DOS tool called rawrite on the first CD-ROM of SuSE Linux. Download the floppy image and insert the SuSE CD-ROM in your drive. Here is an example session (assuming that the floppy image is located in C:\temp and the CD-ROM is in drive F:):

```
C:\>f:\dosutils\rawrite\rawrite
RaWrite 1.2 - Write disk file to raw floppy diskette

Enter source file name: c:\temp\servraid
Enter destination drive: a:
Please insert a formatted diskette into drive A: and press -ENTER- :
Number of sectors per track for this disk is 18
Writing image to drive A:.  Press ^C to abort.
Track: 79  Head: 1 Sector: 16
Done.

C:\>dir /w a:
 Volume in drive A has no label.
 Volume Serial Number is 6B7B-E2AB

 Directory of A:\

LDLINUX.SYS    LINUX         INITDISK.GZ   MESSAGE       SYSLINUX.CFG
               5 File(s)     1.413.101 bytes
                                43.520 bytes free

C:\>_
```

Figure 54. Creating a boot floppy image with rawrite

You can now start the installation by booting the installation system from this floppy disk.

2.4.2 Notes about the Installation procedure

The installation process will now be performed as described in the previous chapter. The ServeRAID adapter should be detected on bootup; you do not need to install a special driver. Make sure to add the right network driver before you proceed to the hard drive partitioning. The different logical drives you defined in the ServeRAID system will appear as separate SCSI hard disks. You can partition them like a regular hard disk. Please follow the guidelines about partitioning in 2.10, "Partitioning for experts" in the SuSE manual.

You can now follow the installation steps as described in the previous chapter.

When you get prompted for the kernel to install (see Figure 31 on page 27), select **SCSI Kernel IBM ServeRAID**. We will replace this image later on with the newer one from the boot floppy, but we need to install a kernel image in order to be able to configure LILO, the Linux Loader. Now complete the installation as described above. You should end up with the login prompt as shown in Figure 52 on page 40. Log in as the root user to perform the following post-installation steps.

> **Stop**
>
> Do not reboot the system before you have executed the following steps! You will not be able to boot the installed system without executing them!

The kernel image that has been installed during the installation process is using an older version of the IBM ServeRAID driver. We will now install the kernel image from the boot floppy as our new boot kernel.

To do this, insert the boot floppy in the floppy drive. Issue the command:

```
mcopy a:linux /boot/vmlinz
```

This will install the updated boot kernel image from the floppy disk in the /boot directory.

You also need to install a modified LILO from the first CD (below /unsorted/lilo), because the currently installed LILO is not able to boot from the ServeRAID (the Expanded BIOS Data Area will be overwritten). Insert the first CD-ROM and mount it using the command:

```
mount /cdrom
```

To update the installed package, type:

```
rpm -Uhv --force /cdrom/unsorted/lilo/lilo.rpm
```

Unmount the CD with the `umount /cdrom` command afterwards.

You now have to run LILO again by typing `lilo`. This will write the new boot manager code to the boot sector of your hard disk.

This will give you the following output "added Linux *" (or however you named your boot configuration during the installation).

The system can now be safely rebooted and you should be able to boot the system directly from the ServeRAID adapter.

For more information about how to administrate your ServeRAID adapter using the ServeRAID utilities, see Chapter 4., "Using the ServeRAID utilities" on page 75.

2.5 XFree86 configuration

After the initial installation, the system will only boot up on the text console. While this is fine if you want to use Linux only as a server operating system, many people prefer a window-based user interface. If you want to use a graphical desktop environment like KDE or GNOME, you first have to configure the X-Windows system to fit your configuration. Unfortunately, many IBM Netfinity systems use the S3 Trio3D video chipset, which is only partly supported by the version of XFree86 that is in cluded on the SuSE Linux 6.2 CD-ROMs. You should downlad the latest version (3.3.5 at the time of writing) from the SuSE ftp Server first. You can find the current release at the following address:

```
ftp://ftp.suse.com/pub/SuSE-Linux/suse_update/XFree86-3.3.5-SuSE/SuSE-6
.2/xsvga.rpm
```

To configure XFree86, we recommend you use SaX, SuSE's advanced X configuration tool. For a more detailed documentation of SaX, see section 9.1, "Configuration using SaX" in the SuSE Linux manual. If SaX fails for some reason, you can still use XF86Setup or xf86config as a fallback solution. Both belong to the XFree86 tool collection and can also be used to configure XFree86. However, they are not as user friendly as SaX and you may need some more experience with XFree86 to use them.

To start SaX, just type `sax` on the command line after you have logged in as user root. If you already know, which X server (the "driver") is the correct one for your video card, you can also use `sax -s <servername>`, for example `sax -s svga`.

After SaX finishes loading its configuration data, you will be presented with the mouse configuration dialog shown in Figure 55.

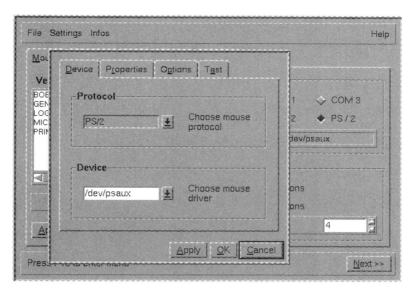

Figure 55. SaX: startup window

Because SaX is a graphical configuration tool, you first need to configure your mouse to be able to operate SaX more conveniently. If you configured your mouse during the initial system installation, you should already be able to move the mouse. If not, you have to use the keyboard by pressing the Tab key to move between the different input fields.

If your mouse is moving fine, click the folder named **Test** to test your mouse.

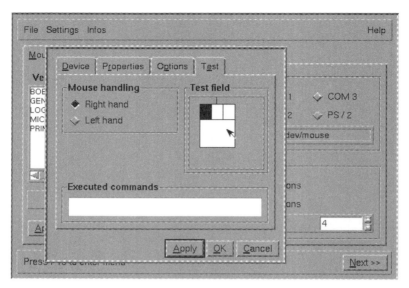

Figure 56. SaX: mouse test window

If your mouse has only two buttons, you can emulate the third (middle) mouse button by pressing the left and right button at the same time. To activate this emulation mode, Select the Options folder and check **Emulate 3 buttons**.

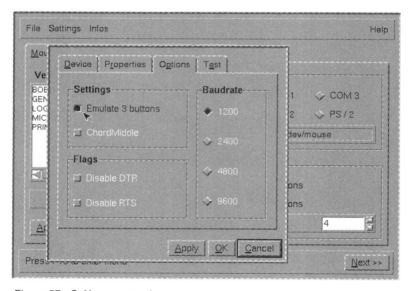

Figure 57. SaX: mouse options

Click **Apply** to apply the change. If your mouse is working fine, click **OK** to close the mouse configuration dialog. Click **Next >>** in the bottom right corner to continue to the keyboard configuration window.

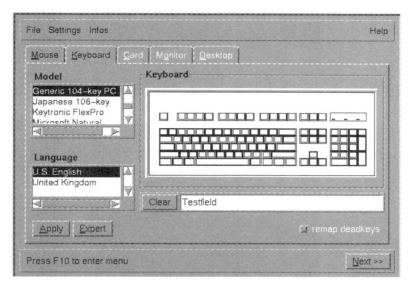

Figure 58. SaX: Keyboard configuration

By default, SaX adopts the keyboard configuration from the initial installation. Select the keyboard model and language, if necessary. You can use the test field to enter some text for testing purposes. If you keyboard is working fine, click **Next >>** to continue to the video card configuration window.

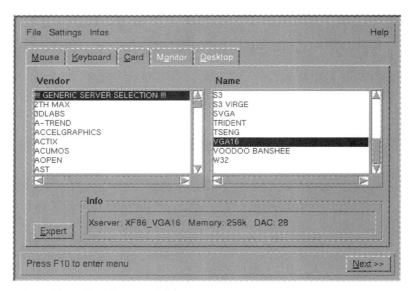

Figure 59. SaX: X Server selection

If SaX was able to detect your video card, you will see the word Autodetect in the Name field. You can then proceed to the monitor configuration window immediately. If your video card has not been detected, you can either select it from the Vendor list, or choose **Generic Server Selection** and select the correct X server for your video card. Some cards require additional configuration options. Click **Expert** to open the advanced configuration options dialog. Click **Next >>** to select your monitor.

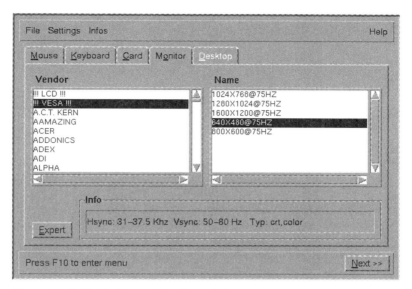

Figure 60. SaX: Monitor configuration window

In order to create an optimized screen resolution and refresh rate, SaX needs to know the capabilities (the horizontal and vertical frequency range) of your monitor.

Select your monitor vendor and name from the list. If you cannot find your model, you can either choose a generic VESA model, or enter the correct frequency range in the Expert Mode. Please see the technical documentation of your monitor for the correct values.

Stop

Please make sure to enter the correct frequency range in the expert mode! You can severely damage your monitor by choosing a frequency range that is too high for your model, if your monitor does not have a self-protection circuit.

Click **Next >>** to advance to the window.

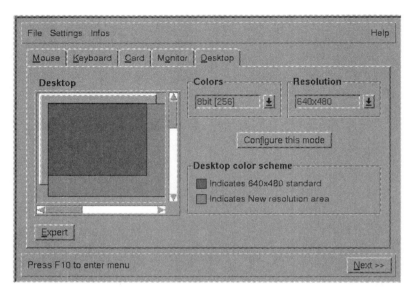

Figure 61. SaX: Screen selection window

The screen selection dialog gives you the opportunity to select the desired color depth and resolution. SaX will only display those resolutions and color depths that will fit into your video card's memory. After choosing the correct values, click **Next >>** to test this screen resolution.

SaX will now compute the best refresh rate for this resolution and switch to the display. If you do not see a picture, your monitor powers off, or begins to flicker, press Ctrl+Alt+Backspace, to return to SaX. If your monitor displays the higher resolution ok, you can now make some fine adjustments to this resolution. Click **Save** if you are satisfied with the result.

Chapter 3. Basic system administration

This chapter will give you an overview of how to perform the most common administrative tasks on a SuSE Linux system. Most of these tasks can be done with YaST, SuSE's configuration and administration tool. However, you may still edit the different configuration files manually, if you wish. YaST will detect manual changes and will not overwrite them.

3.1 Adding and removing software packages using YaST

SuSE Linux uses the RPM package manager to manage software packages of the distribution. RPM uses a database to store information about all files that belong to a certain package, including some additional information about the package. RPM itself is a command-line program. You can use it from the command line to add, remove or obtain information about software packages and system files. See 3.2, "Package management using RPM" on page 56 for more details. YaST, SuSE's administration and configuration tool, can act as a user-friendly front end to RPM.

To install or remove software packages, insert the first CD-ROM and start SuSE's installation and configuration tool YaST by typing `yast` at the command line (as user root). YaST will start up and you will see YaST's main menu.

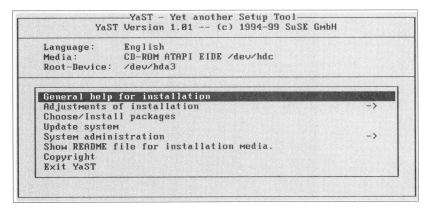

Figure 62. YaST: main menu

Highlight the menu entry **Choose/Install packages** and press Enter. Alternatively, you can invoke YaST with the following parameters:

```
yast --mask install --autoexit
```

51

This will automatically open the installation main menu and will return to the command line on exit.

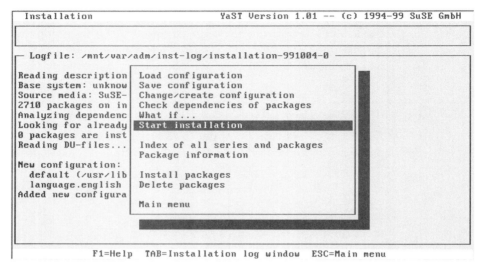

Figure 63. YaST: package installation main menu

SuSE Linux offers a choice of software configurations. These contain a list of selected software packages to fit a certain need. Select **Load configuration** to load a predefined configuration.

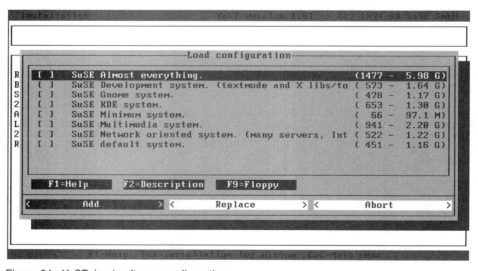

Figure 64. YaST: load software configuration

You can now Add the files from a configuration to your current configuration, or you can Replace it by one of these configurations. If you replace a configuration, all currently installed packages that are not part of the selected configuration will be marked for deletion! Press Esc to return to the main menu.

To add packages to or remove packages from your current configuration, select **Change / create configuration**. This will open the Series selection window shown in Figure 65.

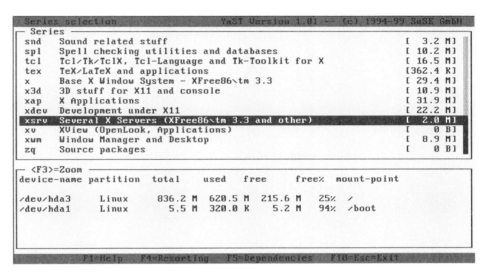

Figure 65. YaST: series selection

All software packages are categorized ito different series. Choose your category and press Enter to see all packages belonging to this series.

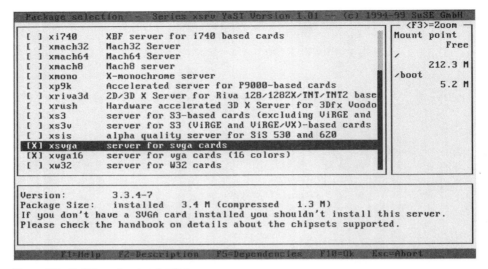

Figure 66. YaST: package selection

To select a package for installation/removal/update, press the Spacebar or Enter. This will toggle the status of the selected package. The indicator in the first column displays the current status:

Table 1. Package selection indicators

Indicator	Package status
[ ]	Package is not installed and not selected for installation
[X]	Package is marked for installation
[i]	Package is already installed
[R]	Package is installed and will be replaced / reinstalled
[D]	Package is installed and marked for deletion

If you want to change the package status of multiple packages at once, press Shift+A (see Figure 67).

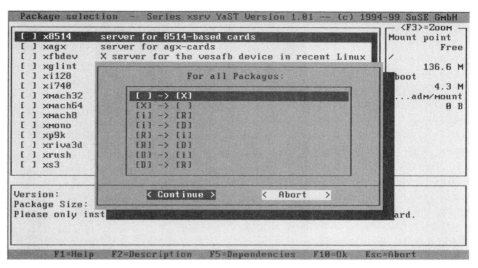

Figure 67. YaST: apply changes to all packages

After you have made your choice, press F10 to return to the series selection. You can now select or remove packages from other series, or press F10 once more, to return to the software configuration main menu. If you made any modifications to your current software configuration, you can start the actual installation or removal of packages by selecting **Start Installation**. If you want to verify what packages will be installed, removed or replaced, select **What if...**

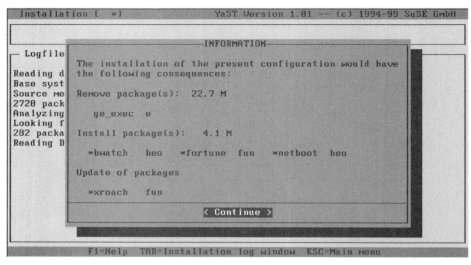

```
Installation [ *]              YaST Version 1.01 -- (c) 1994-99 SuSE GmbH

┌──────────────────────────────INFORMATION──────────────────────────────┐
─ Logfile│
         │ The installation of the present configuration would have
Reading d│ the following consequences:
Base syst│
Source me│ Remove package(s):  22.7 M
2728 pack│
Analyzing│   ge_exec  e
Looking f│
282 packa│ Install package(s):   4.1 M
Reading D│
         │   *bwatch   beo   *fortune  fun   *netboot  beo
         │
         │ Update of packages
         │
         │   *xroach   fun
         │
         │                    < Continue >
         └────────────────────────────────────────────────────────────┘

          F1=Help   TAB=Installation log window   ESC=Main menu
```

Figure 68. YaST: what if...

Click **Continue** to return to the main menu. If you are satisfied with your
selection, select **Start installation**. YaST will now check on which CD the
necessary packages are located and will prompt you for the respective CD.
After the packages have been installed, you will return to the main menu
shown in Figure 63 on page 52. You can now either add or remove additional
packages. If you want to save your current package selection (for example for
copying it to another system), select **Save configuration**.You will then be
prompted where you want to save the configuration to. Select **to floppy** or **to
hard disk**, depending on your needs. If you are saving to a floppy disk, make
sure that it does not contain valuable data! The diskette will be erased during
this process.

You can return to the YaST main menu by selecting **Main menu**.

3.2 Package management using RPM

Package management can also be done directly with the RPM package
manager on the command line. The following table shows some of the most
frequently used commands.

Table 2. Basic RPM commands

Command	Description
rpm -q <package>	If package is installed, check version and build number of installed package

Command	Description
rpm -qi <package>	Obtain some more information about an installed package
rpm -qa	List all installed packages
rpm -qf <filename>	Determine the (installed) package that <file> belongs to
rpm -Uhv <package.rpm>	Update/Install the file package.rpm showing a progress bar
rpm -F -v ./*.rpm	Update (freshen) all currently installed packages using the RPM files in the current directory
rpm --help	Get some help about the different options and parameters

Note

If you install packages using RPM on the command line, make sure to run the script SuSEconfig afterwards! Some packages require post-installation maintenace.

More information and options about RPM can be found in the manual page (man rpm), the RPM how-to (less /usr/doc/howto/en/RPM-HOWTO.txt.gz) and on the RPM home page at http://www.rpm.org. You can also display a short overview by running rpm --help.

3.3 User and group administration using YaST

Linux is a multi-user operating system. To differentiate between the various users, each user has to log in with a unique user name and password. Each user belongs to a primary user group, but he can also be a member of additional other groups as well (up to 16 groups). Each user name is associated with a user ID (UID), which is also unique throughout the system. The same applies to user group names and group IDs (GIDs).

Usually each user has a personal home directory. This is a piece of space on the file system (usually a directory below /home, for example /home/username) which belongs to him and where he can store his personal files (for example e-mail or text documents). Other users generally have no access to the files stored therein.

You should carefully consider adding user groups before adding users. Sometimes there are concerns about restricting access to some parts of the user filesystem. You can do this by creating separate user groups to control access to various files and filesystems. Also if you are going to be creating a system with many users, you should consider creating separate groups divided by what they are doing on the system. You can create an admin group for admins, a db2user group for DB2 users, and so forth. Linux allows you to control access to both files and directories by users, groups and everyone on the system.

Another concern in setting up users and groups is that you may want to share files with other systems. This can be done by the CD, tape, diskette or any similar device. You can use the network to share information with NFS, Samba, IPX and other network packages. If you use user and group names and characteristics that are not the same on all systems doing the sharing, then you can have file sharing and access problems.

If you are creating logins and groups on each box separately, it is often best to use a single system where all your IDs can be created. This system is then used as a reference. It is not necessary that everyone actually logs into the reference system. It only exists to coordinate ID and group creation and to prevent non-standard IDs and groups. A user also cannot log into the reference system if the password is not enabled. This will prevent unauthorized access to the system. If you want to administer lot of users on different machines, you should consider setting up NIS. See Chapter 12, "NIS - Network Information System" on page 189 for more information about this.

It is one of the root user's tasks to add and remove user or group accounts. With YaST, SuSE provides an easy-to-use tool for user and group administration. To use it, log in as the root user and type the command:

```
yast --mask user --autoexit
```

Alternatively you can invoke YaST by simply typing yast and choosing the menu **System administration -> User administration**. The following window will appear:

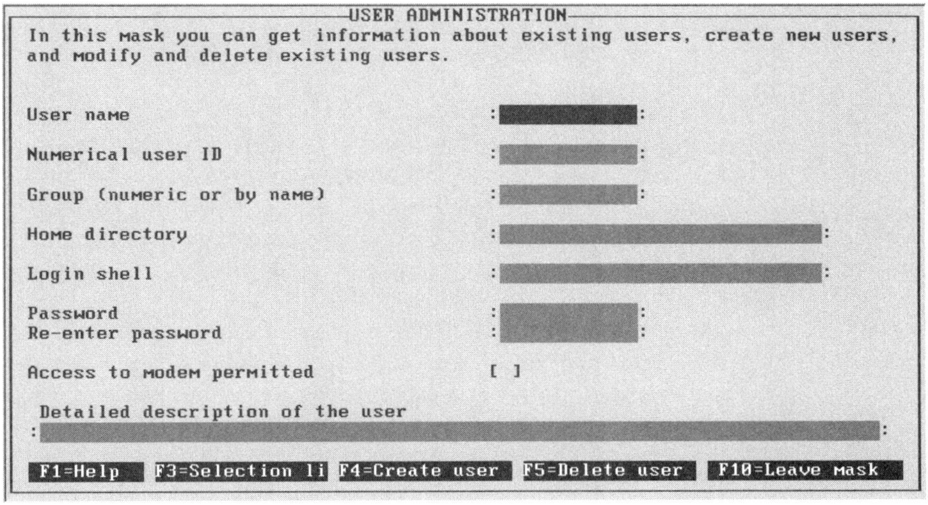

```
┌─────────────────────────USER ADMINISTRATION─────────────────────────┐
│ In this mask you can get information about existing users, create new users, │
│ and modify and delete existing users.                                 │
│                                                                        │
│ User name                         : ▓▓▓▓▓▓▓▓▓ :                        │
│                                                                        │
│ Numerical user ID                 : ▓▓▓▓▓▓▓▓▓ :                        │
│                                                                        │
│ Group (numeric or by name)        : ▓▓▓▓▓▓▓▓▓ :                        │
│                                                                        │
│ Home directory                    : ▓▓▓▓▓▓▓▓▓▓▓▓▓▓▓▓▓ :                │
│                                                                        │
│ Login shell                       : ▓▓▓▓▓▓▓▓▓▓▓▓▓▓▓▓▓ :                │
│                                                                        │
│ Password                          : ▓▓▓▓▓▓▓ :                          │
│ Re-enter password                 : ▓▓▓▓▓▓▓ :                          │
│                                                                        │
│ Access to modem permitted           [ ]                                │
│                                                                        │
│   Detailed description of the user                                     │
│ : ▓▓▓▓▓▓▓▓▓▓▓▓▓▓▓▓▓▓▓▓▓▓▓▓▓▓▓▓▓▓▓▓▓▓▓▓▓▓▓▓▓▓▓▓▓▓ :                      │
│                                                                        │
│  F1=Help   F3=Selection li  F4=Create user   F5=Delete user   F10=Leave mask │
└────────────────────────────────────────────────────────────────────┘
```

Figure 69. YaST: user administration main window

To add a new user, fill in the blanks. The user name should be short and in
lowercase (YaST will do some sanity check on the input). After you pressed
Tab or Enter to advance to the next input field, YaST will automatically look for
the next available user ID and will assign it to this user. The entries Group,
Home directory and Login shell will also be filled with default values, but you
are free to change them to fit your requirements.

Some information about the different shells:

- **/bin/bash** - This is the Bourne Again Shell, which is an extension to the
  Bourne Shell. This is the most popular shell for Linux.

- **/bin/sh** - This is the standard Bourne Shell that has been around since
  almost the beginning of UNIX.

- **/bin/ash** - This is another version of the Bourne Shell.

- **/bin/bsh** - This is the same as /bin/ash to which it is linked.

- **/bin/ksh** - This is the standard Korn shell that is the most popular shell
  for UNIX Administration.

- **/bin/tcsh** - This is a public domain extension of the C Shell.

- **/bin/csh** - This is the standard C Shell that was originated by the
  University of California at Berkeley.

- **/bin/zsh** - This is another extension of the Bourne Shell.

Your choice of shells is strictly a matter of preference, but generally UNIX admins prefer Bourne or Korn Shell programs whereas programmers tend to prefer C Shell-based programs.

If you want this user to be able to connect to the Internet using a modem, check **Access to modem permitted**. This will add this user to the user groups `dialout` and `uucp`, which have the necessary permissions to initiate a dial-up connection using the tool `wvdial`. The entry fields User name, Group and Login shell also provide a selection list where you can choose a previously defined value. Press F3 in the respective entry field.

After you have filled in all fields, press F4 to actually create the user. If the home directory of that user did not exist before, it will now be created and the contents of the directory /etc/skel will be copied into it. This skeleton directory contains a basic framework of configuration files for the user to start from.

If you want to remove a user account, just select the login name using F3 or enter the name manually in the user name input form. To delete this user, press F5 and confirm the following question with **Yes.** You will be prompted for a confirmation before the user's home directory will be removed, too.

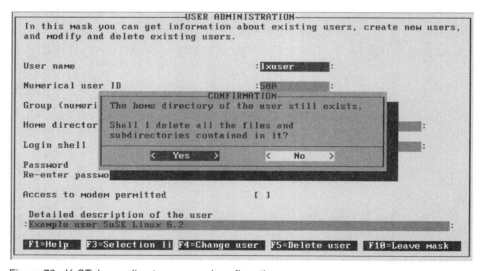

Figure 70. YaST: home directory removal confirmation

After you have finished the user administration, press F10 to return to the main menu.

3.4 Adding users on the command line

To add users to the Linux system you can also use the command `useradd`. In Linux you can find the options to `useradd` by typing the command by itself as in Figure 71. This is recommended only for commands that you know require an option. Otherwise, you may inadvertently execute a command you do not want to.

```
SuSE:~ # useradd
usage: useradd  [-u uid [-o]] [-g group] [-G group,...]
                [-d home] [-s shell] [-c comment] [-m [-k template]]
                [-f inactive] [-e expire ] [-p passwd] name
        useradd  -D [-g group] [-b base] [-s shell]
                [-f inactive] [-e expire ]
```

Figure 71. The useradd command

You can also use the `man` command to obtain more detailed information about the different parameters.

Other commands have information presented by using the `--help` option. This option is not implemented in all commands but in the case of the `useradd` command it will present basically the same information you see in Figure 71.

You can find out what your current default values are with the command `useradd -D` as shown in Figure 72.

```
SuSE:~ # useradd -D
GROUP=100
HOME=/home
INACTIVE=0
EXPIRE=10000
SHELL=/bin/bash
SKEL=/etc/skel
```

Figure 72. Default values for creating a user ID

The explanation of the options are as follows:

`-c comment`

This is a comment field about the user. It has been traditionally called the General Electric Comprehensive Operating System (GECOS) field and can include such information as office room numbers, phone numbers, etc. Any string of characters must be put into double quotes. For example, `-c comment "John Doe, rm. 45, x 78965"`.

`-d home_dir`

> The home directory location of the user. If this is not specified then the default is to append the login name to the end of the default value for HOME shown in Figure 72. For example, the home directory for jdoe will be /home/jdoe unless specified here.

`-e expire_date`

> This is the date on which the user account will be disabled. The date is specified in the format MM/DD/YY where MM is the month, DD is the date and YY is the two-digit format of the year. (Note that even though the date is represented in two digits, Linux converts the date to a format that is not Y2K dependent, so there are no Y2K worries here.) The default is the value of EXPIRE in Figure 72.

`-f inactive_time`

> This gives the status of the account. The value of 0 says to disable the account when the password expires. A value of -1 says not to disable it. The default is the value of INACTIVE in Figure 72.

`-g initial_group`

> The initial group that a user logs in with. This can be a name or number of a currently existing group. This is specified in the /etc/password file as the GID or Group ID value. The default group is given by the value of GROUP in Figure 72.

`-G group[,...]`

> This is a list of any additional existing groups the user may belong to. Each group is separated by a comma.

`-m [-k skeleton_dir]`

> The `-m` option says to create the user's home directory if it does not exist. The `skeleton_dir` is the location of files that are copied to a new user's directory. The default location, if you do not use the `-m` option, is the `/etc/skel` directory. The default is the value of SKEL in Figure 72.

> `-s shell`

> The is the shell that the user will first log in with. The default is the value of SHELL in Figure 72.

`-u uid [-o]`

> This is the numeric UID or user ID number that is used by Linux to distinguish one user from the other. All UIDs must be unique unless the `-o`

option is used. The -o option is often used for creating IDs that have the same access rights, but different logins and passwords. The system looks only at the UID and GID values for determining access rights.

-r

This is used to create a system account whose UID is lower than a certain number defined in /etc/login.defs. You will also need to specify the -m option if you want to create the home directory. Otherwise, it will not be created. System accounts generally have UID values between 0 and 99.

login

This is the login name that the user will log in with. This will need to be unique on the system.

3.4.1 Modifying users - the command line version

You can modify user logins with the usermod command.

```
# usermod
usage: usermod [-u uid [-o]] [-g group] [-G group,...]
               [-d home [-m]] [-s shell] [-c comment] [-l new_name]
               [-f inactive] [-e expire ] [-p passwd] name
```

Figure 73. The usermod command

The options to the usermod command are basically the same as those for the useradd command, so they will not be repeated except for those that are different. With the usermod command you need to observe the following options.

-d home [-m]

The -m option says to move the contents of the current home directory to the new home directory and create the directory if it does not exist.

-l new_name

This allows you to change the user's user name that he logs in with. The user cannot be logged in with this name when he does this.

-p passwd

This allows you to set the password of the user from the command line. This can be useful if you have a program that automates password creation since you can use a variable in the place of the passwd string.

3.4.2 Deleting users - the command line version

The command to delete users is `userdel`. You can see the options in Figure 74. This command is a lot simpler because there is not much choice you have when deleting a user.

```
# userdel
usage: userdel [-r] name
```

Figure 74. The userdel command

The only option that you can use is:

```
-r
```

This says for you to remove the home directory and its contents. Otherwise the home directory and its contents will not be deleted.

3.4.3 Group administration using YaST

To administer user groups, select **System Administration -> Group adminstration** from the YaST main menu. Alternatively, start YaST from the command line using the following parameters:

```
yast --mask group --autoexit
```

This will get you directly to the group administration window:

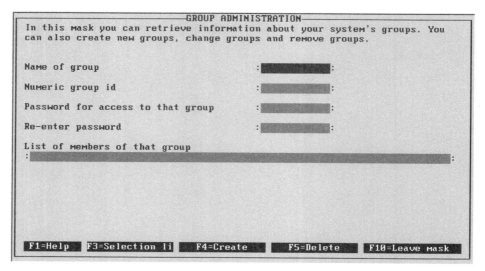

Figure 75. YaST: group administration window

Each user group has a unique name and ID. The default group for normal users is users. To create a new group, enter the name of the group and press Tab to advance to the next entry field. If you entered a new group name, YaST will automatically assign the next available group ID to this group. You can accept it or modify it to your needs. If this group is not intended to be a primary (default) user group, you can protect it with a password as well. All users that should be members of this group can be entered in the line **List of members of that group** (comma-separated). You can press F3 here to select them from the user list, or you can add them manually. Press F4 to create this group, F10 or Esc to leave this window.

If you want to delete a user group, select the group name with F3 or enter it manually and press F5 to delete it. Please note that this will not delete the user accounts belonging to this group! It will only remove the group information from the file /etc/groups. To leave the group administration window, press F10 or Esc.

3.5 Network configuration with YaST

A Linux system will in most cases be connected to one or more networks. YaST also offers configuration options to set up your network connection. If you need to connect your host to an Ethernet or token-ring network, you can use YaST to enter the correct networking parameters. If you did not define your network card during the initial installation, or if you added a new network card to your system, you first have to define the correct driver for this device. From the YaST main menu select **System administration -> Integrate hardware into system -> Configure networking device**. From the command line, type the following command to open the network device selection window shown in Figure 77 directly.

```
yast --mask netcard --autoexit
```

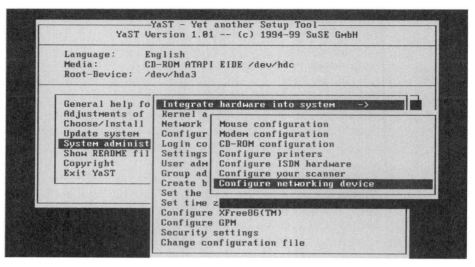

Figure 76. YaST: integrate hardware into system

```
                 ─────────SELECTION OF NETWORKING DEVICE─────────
           Here you may select your networking device.
           Your selections will be written to /etc/conf.modules



           Network type           :eth0_          :

           Networking device type    [AMD PCI PCnet32 (PCI bus NE2100)        ]

           Module options
           :                                                                  :


           F3=Selecti

                    <   Continue   >          <    Abort   >
```

Figure 77. YaST: network device selection

First enter the network type. The two most common ones are Ethernet (for example eth0, eth1, etc.) and token-ring (for example tr0, tr1, etc.). After entering the network type, select the correct driver for this card. Some drivers need additional options; please see Chapter 14, "Kernel parameters" in the SuSE Linux 6.2 manual for a detailed explanation of the possible values. Most modern PCI network cards do not need any additional parameters, so you can most likely skip this input field. Click **Continue** to finish this configuration dialog. YaST will now add this line to the kernel module configuration file /etc/conf.modules.

After you defined your network type, return to the YaST System administration menu.

Now you can define the networking parameters for this device. Select **System Administration -> Network configuration -> Network base configuration**. Alternatively, type the following command at the shell prompt to jump directly to the window shown in Figure 79:

```
yast --mask network --autoexit
```

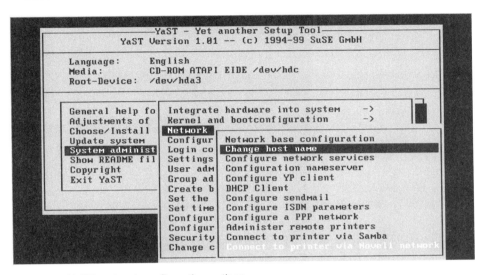

Figure 78. YaST: network configuration options

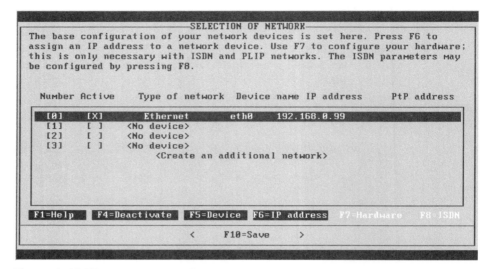

Figure 79. YaST: network base configuration

This configuration window allows you to assign IP addresses to network devices. If you did not configure your network device before, select the Type of Network first.

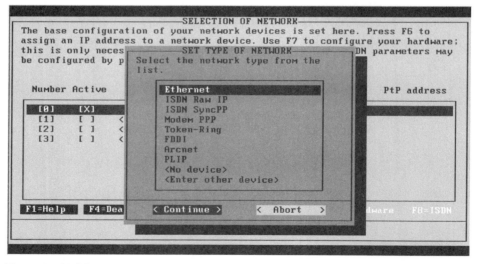

Figure 80. YaST: set type of network

Figure 80 shows the Set Type of Network selection box. Select the corresponding type for your network card and confirm the selection with **Continue**.

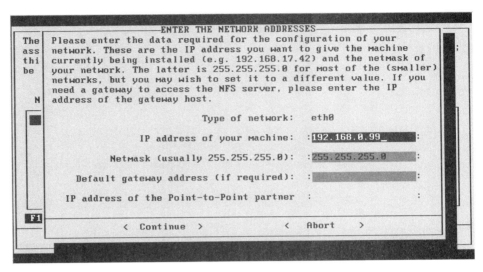

```
┌──────────────ENTER THE NETWORK ADDRESSES────────────────┐
│The│ Please enter the data required for the configuration of your  │
│ass│ network. These are the IP address you want to give the machine │
│thi│ currently being installed (e.g. 192.168.17.42) and the netmask of│
│be │ your network. The latter is 255.255.255.0 for most of the (smaller)│
│   │ networks, but you may wish to set it to a different value. If you │
│ N │ need a gateway to access the NFS server, please enter the IP   │
│   │ address of the gateway host.                                   │
│   │                                                                │
│   │                      Type of network:    eth0                  │
│   │                                                                │
│   │          IP address of your machine:  :192.168.0.99_        :  │
│   │                                                                │
│   │     Netmask (usually 255.255.255.0):  :255.255.255.0        :  │
│   │                                                                │
│   │    Default gateway address (if required): :               :   │
│   │                                                                │
│   │   IP address of the Point-to-Point partner  :             :   │
│F1 │                                                                │
│         <  Continue  >                    <  Abort  >              │
└────────────────────────────────────────────────────────┘
```

Figure 81. YaST: IP address configuration

After you have defined the network type, you can assign an IP address to this device. Press F5 to open up the dialog shown in Figure 81. Enter the IP address, Netmask and default gateway address, if necessary. Close the dialog box with **Continue**. If you configured a PLIP or ISDN device, you may also have to configure some additional hardware parameters by pressing F7.

If you have more than one network card, you can add it to the free lines below. If you need to add more than the predefined four lines, highlight **Create an additional network** and press Enter.

You can also use this dialog, if you want to assign more than one IP address to a single network card (IP aliasing). To do this, press F5 to select the type of network and choose **Enter other device**.

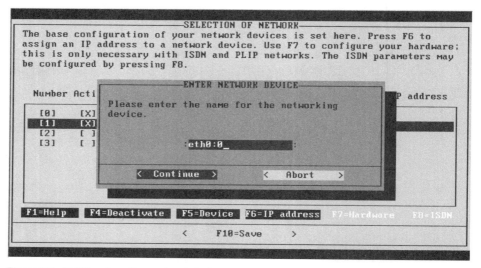

Figure 82. YaST: enter other networl device

You can add multiple IP addresses to one Ethernet card, by configuring it as eth0:0, eth0:1 and so on (IP aliasing support must be activated in the Linux kernel; the default SuSE kernel has been compiled with IP aliasing support).

After you have finished the network configuration, press F10 to save the current setup. YaST will now create the respective entries in /etc/rc.config and the network setup will be applied after the next reboot or after restarting the network and routing scripts.

3.6 Changing the configuration file with YaST

SuSE Linux utilizes a central configuration file /etc/rc.config to store most of the system configuration information. The contents of this file will be used by the init scripts on bootup, as well as for creating configuration files for the different services.

The format of this file is plain ASCII text. The configuration is stored in variables in the form VARIABLE=value. Additional comments are marked with a "#" at the beginning of the line. Since rc.config contains most of the configuration information, you do not need to edit the original configuration files for most services. It is sufficient to make the change in this single file; YaST (in combination with the SuSEconfig script collection) will take care of the correct creation of these files. However, if you are used to modifying the separate configuration files directly, you may still do so. SuSEconfig will detect the manual change and will not overwrite them. Instead you will receive a notification that SuSEconfig has detected a manual change and will create its version of this file in <filename>.suseconfig. You are free to manually implement the changes from SuSEconfig to your file.

If you want to edit variables in rc.config, you can open it in a normal text editor. Each variable has some lines of comments above its definition to give you an overview of the meaning of it. These variables are also covered in section 17.6 "The variables in /etc/rc.config" in the SuSE manual. After you have modified entries in rc.config, you have to run the script SuSEconfig afterwards to apply the changes to the different configuration files.

Alternatively, you can use YaST as a comfortable front end to edit this variables. From the YaST main menu, select **System administration -> Change configuration file**. To go directly to this dialog from the command line, invoke YaST with the following parameters:

```
yast --mask rcconfig --autoexit
```

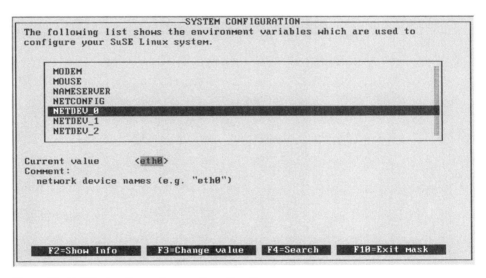

Figure 83. YaST: view the system configuration file

Use the cursor keys to highlight the desired variable. F2 gives you a description of the currently highlighted option.

To search for a certain keyword (case-sensitive), press F4 and enter the desired search term.

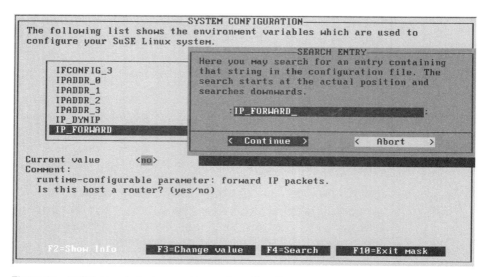

Figure 84. YaST: search for keyword in configuration file

To modify the selected entry, press F3 and enter the new value in the dialog box.

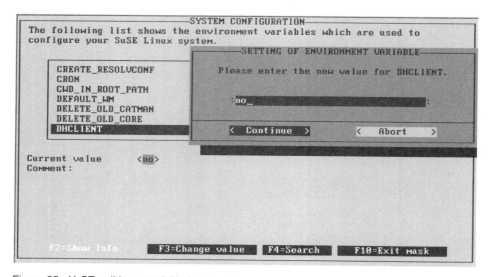

Figure 85. YaST: editing a variable in rc.config

Press F10 to finish the editing and return to the main menu after saving the changes in /etc/rc.config.

3.6.1 Finding Linux commands

You may want to run a Linux program from the command line prompt. If so, there are several directories that contain commands that you can run. You can run these without needing to know where they are because your search path includes a number of directories that will be searched whenever you try to execute a command. The search path is given by the environment variable $PATH. You can view the content of this variable by running the following command:

```
echo $PATH
```

If you want to find out where a command is located, execute the command:

```
whereis command_name
```

where `command_name` is the command you are looking for. If you want to find the command `yast` you can execute:

```
whereis yast
```

This will give you the following results:

```
yast: /sbin/yast
```

You notice that this command is located in the /sbin directory. Many of the major administrative commands will be found in the /sbin and /usr/sbin directories.

Another helpful command for finding files on your system is `locate`. The `locate` command will also list files that match the search name, if they are not in your current search path. To search for all README documents on SuSE Linux run the following command:

```
locate README
```

Since this will be a huge amount of output, you might want to redirect the ouput to a text pager like `less` or `more`:

```
locate README | less
```

This will enable you to look at the output page by page. Press q to leave `less` and return to the command line.

> **Note**
>
> SuSE Linux automatically runs `updatedb` once every 24 hours. If you cannot find what you are looking for run `updatedb` from a command line.

Chapter 4. Using the ServeRAID utilities

In this chapter we describe how to use and administer the IBM ServeRAID high-performance RAID adapter. The current version of the Linux driver supports all ServeRAID adapter versions. Before you start the installation of SuSE Linux on a RAID array, you need to define the RAID arrays and the logical drives. The logical drives will appear as physical disk drives to the operating system.

For more information about RAID and RAID levels, see Appendix A, "RAID levels" on page 235.

All SuSE Linux distributions from Version 6.2 and up support the ServeRAID SCSI adapter. To install the operating system follow the installation procedure described in 2.3, "Basic Linux installation" on page 6 and note the particularities about installing on a ServeRAID in 2.4, "Installation with ServeRAID" on page 40.

After you have installed and configured the system, get the RAID administration utilities from the following IBM Web site:

```
http://www.developer.ibm.com/welcome/netfinity/serveraid.html
```

The following files are available for download on this site:

- ips-100.tgz - this file contains the kernel patch for the 2.2.x kernel, which enables support for IBM ServeRAID adapters in those kernels.

- ipsutils.rpm - this file contains the Linux command line utilities for administrating the IBM ServeRAID SCSI adapter

- 009n012.exe - this file contains the WIN32 Administration Client, which can be used to remotely configure and monitor the ServeRAID adapter used in a Linux installation

4.1 Installing ipsutils.rpm

To successfully install the ipsutils package you have to be logged in as user "root". After you have downloaded the ipsutil.rpm package you need to install it using RPM. The ipsutil package is a standard RPM package. SuSE Linux uses RPM for installing the packages, so the RPM utility is already installed on your system. See 3.2, "Package management using RPM" on page 56 for more information on RPM. To install the package, use the following command:

```
rpm -Uhv ipsutil.rpm
```

This assumes that your current directory is where the ipsutil.prm file resides. After you finished reading the copyright notice, press q to quit the text viewer. After you have accepted the license agreement with y, the necessary files will be installed on your system. To check if the utilities work, type the following command in a terminal window or on the console:

```
ipssend
```

You will see output similar to Figure 86.

```
Licensed Material - Property of IBM Corporation
IBM ServeRAID Command Line Interface v3.50.17
Copyright (C) IBM Corporation 1996 - 1999
All Rights Reserved
US Government Restricted Rights - Use, Duplication, or Disclosure
Restricted by GSA ADP Schedule Contract with IBM Corporation


Usage: IPSSEND <Command> <Param 1> ... <Param N>
Help : IPSSEND <Command> for specific help on any command.
       Command    | Param 1   | Param 2       | Param 3   | Param 4     | Param 5
       ---------- | --------- | ------------- | --------- | ----------- | ----------
       AUTOSYNC   | Controller| Logical Drive | NOPROMPT  |             |
       BACKUP     | Controller| Filename      | NOPROMPT  |             |
       DEVINFO    | Controller| Channel       | SCSI ID   |             |
       DRIVEVER   | Controller| Channel       | SCSI ID   |             |
       ERASEEVENT | Controller| Options       |           |             |
       GETCONFIG  | Controller| Options       |           |             |
       GETEVENT   | Controller| Options       |           |             |
       GETSTATUS  | Controller|               |           |             |
       HSREBUILD  | Controller| Options       |           |             |
       INIT       | Controller| Logical Drive | NOPROMPT  |             |
       INITSYNC   | Controller| Logical Drive | NOPROMPT  |             |
       REBUILD    | Controller| Channel       | SCSI ID   | New Channel | New SCSI ID
       RESTORE    | Controller| Filename      | NOPROMPT  |             |
       SETSTATE   | Controller| Channel       | SCSI ID   | New State   |
       SYNCH      | Controller| Scope         | Scope ID  |             |
       UNATTENDED | Controller| Options       |           |             |
       UNBLOCK    | Controller| Logical Drive |           |             |
```

Figure 86. Ipssend command output

As you can see, ipssend supports quite a lot of commands for dealing with the IBM ServeRAID adapter. In the following sections we will cover the ones that are necessary in order to use the ServeRAID adapter efficiently.

4.2 ipssend commands

In this section we cover the different options of the ipssend command.

4.2.1 getconfig command

This command is used to get configuration information about the IBM ServeRAID controller, the logical drives and the physical drives. The getconfig command has the following syntax:

```
ipssend getconfig <Controller> <Options>
```

The parameters are explained in Table 3.

Table 3. getconfig command parameters

Parameter	Description
Controller	Number of controller (1 to 12)
Options	AD for controller information
	LD for logical drive information
	PD for physical device information
	AL (default) for all information

To get all information about the first ServeRAID controller, execute the following command:

```
ispsend getconfig 1
```

You will see a window similar to Figure 87.

```
Found 1 IBM ServeRAID Controller(s).
Read Configuration has been initiated for Controller 1...
------------------------------------------------------------------------------
Controller Information
------------------------------------------------------------------------------
   Firmware Version              : 2.88.10
   Boot Block Version            : 97139
   Date of Configuration Written : 6/25/1999
   Controller Configuration ID   : Null Config
   SCSI Channel Description       : 3 parallel SCSI wide
   Host Interface Description     : 1 32 bit PCI
   Initiator IDs (Channel/SCSI ID): 1/7  2/7  3/7
   Maximum Physical Devices       : 30
   Defunct Disk Drive Count       : 0
   Logical Drives/Offline/Critical: 2/0/0
   Rebuild Rate (Low/Medium/High) : High
   Read Ahead                     : Adaptive
   Unattended Mode (Yes/No)       : No
   Concurrent Commands Supported  : 128
   Configuration Update Count     : 14
------------------------------------------------------------------------------
Logical Drive Information
------------------------------------------------------------------------------
  Logical Drive Number 1
   Status of Logical Drive       : Okay (OKY)
   Raid Level                    : 5
   Size (in MB)                  : 100
   Write Cache Status            : Write Through (WT)
   Number of Chunks              : 3
   Stripe Unit Size              : 16K
   Access Blocked                : No
   Part of Array                 : A
  Logical Drive Number 2
   Status of Logical Drive       : Okay (OKY)
   Raid Level                    : 5
   Size (in MB)                  : 17256
   Write Cache Status            : Write Through (WT)
   Number of Chunks              : 3
   Stripe Unit Size              : 16K
   Access Blocked                : No
   Part of Array                 : A

   Array A Stripe Order (Channel/SCSI ID)  : 1,0 1,4 1,3
------------------------------------------------------------------------------
Physical Device Information
------------------------------------------------------------------------------
   Channel #1:
       Initiator at SCSI ID 7
       Target on SCSI ID 0
           Device is a 16 bit, Fast SCSI, tag queuing Hard Disk
           SCSI ID                 : 0
           PFA (Yes/No)            : No
           State                   : Online (ONL)
```

Figure 87. Executing ipssend getconfig 1

In this output you can see detailed information about your ServeRAID
configuration. If you want information only about the controller itself, then
execute this command:

```
ispsend getconfig 1 ad
```

You will see output similar to Figure 88.

```
[root@nf5500 /root]# ipssend getconfig 1 ad

Found 1 IBM ServeRAID Controller(s).
Read Configuration has been initiated for Controller 1...
--------------------------------------------------------------------------------
Controller Information
--------------------------------------------------------------------------------
   Firmware Version              : 2.88.10
   Boot Block Version            : 97139
   Date of Configuration Written : 6/25/1999
   Controller Configuration ID   : Null Config
   SCSI Channel Description       : 3 parallel SCSI wide
   Host Interface Description      : 1 32 bit PCI
   Initiator IDs (Channel/SCSI ID): 1/7  2/7  3/7
   Maximum Physical Devices       : 30
   Defunct Disk Drive Count       : 0
   Logical Drives/Offline/Critical: 2/0/0
   Rebuild Rate (Low/Medium/High) : High
   Read Ahead                     : Adaptive
   Unattended Mode (Yes/No)       : No
   Concurrent Commands Supported  : 128
   Configuration Update Count     : 14
Command Completed Successfully.
```

Figure 88. Executing ipssend getconfig 1 ad

To get information about logical drives, execute this command:

```
ipssend getconfig 1 ld
```

You will see output similar to Figure 89.

```
[root@nf5500 /root]# ipssend getconfig 1 ld

Found 1 IBM ServeRAID Controller(s).
Read Configuration has been initiated for Controller 1...
--------------------------------------------------------------------------------
Logical Drive Information
--------------------------------------------------------------------------------
  Logical Drive Number 1
     Status of Logical Drive       : Okay (OKY)
     Raid Level                    : 5
     Size (in MB)                  : 100
     Write Cache Status            : Write Through (WT)
     Number of Chunks              : 3
     Stripe Unit Size              : 16K
     Access Blocked                : No
     Part of Array                 : A
  Logical Drive Number 2
     Status of Logical Drive       : Okay (OKY)
     Raid Level                    : 5
     Size (in MB)                  : 17256
     Write Cache Status            : Write Through (WT)
     Number of Chunks              : 3
     Stripe Unit Size              : 16K
     Access Blocked                : No
     Part of Array                 : A

   Array A Stripe Order (Channel/SCSI ID)  : 1,0 1,4 1,3
Command Completed Successfully.
```

Figure 89. Executing ipssend getconfig 1 ld

- From this output you can get all information about the logical drives:

- Drive status

- RAID level

- Size

- Write cache status

- Number of chunks

- Stripe unit size

- Access

- Array

To get detailed information about a physical drive, execute this command:

```
ipssend getconfig 1 pd
```

You will see output similar to Figure 90.

```
[root@nf5500 /root]# ipssend getconfig 1 pd

Found 1 IBM ServeRAID Controller(s).
Read Configuration has been initiated for Controller 1...
------------------------------------------------------------------------------
Physical Device Information
------------------------------------------------------------------------------
    Channel #1:
        Initiator at SCSI ID 7
        Target on SCSI ID 0
            Device is a 16 bit, Fast SCSI, tag queuing Hard Disk
            SCSI ID                 : 0
            PFA (Yes/No)            : No
            State                   : Online (ONL)
            Size (in MB)/(in Sectors):    8678/17773888
            Device ID               : IBM-PCCODGHS09Y 035168164E69
        Target on SCSI ID 3
            Device is a 16 bit, Fast SCSI, tag queuing Hard Disk
            SCSI ID                 : 3
            PFA (Yes/No)            : No
            State                   : Online (ONL)
            Size (in MB)/(in Sectors):    17357/35548048
            Device ID               : IBM-PCCODGHS18Y 0351680EE209
        Target on SCSI ID 4
            Device is a 16 bit, Fast SCSI, tag queuing Hard Disk
            SCSI ID                 : 4
            PFA (Yes/No)            : No
            State                   : Online (ONL)
            Size (in MB)/(in Sectors):    8678/17773888
            Device ID               : IBM-PCCODGHS09Y 04206816F8A1
        Target on SCSI ID 15
            Device is a 16 bit, Fast SCSI, tag queuing Unknown Device
            SCSI ID                 : 15
            PFA (Yes/No)            : No
            State                   : Stand By (SBY)
            Size (in MB)/(in Sectors):      0/       0
            Device ID               : SDR    GEM200  2   1
    Channel #2:
        Initiator at SCSI ID 7
Command Completed Successfully.
```

Figure 90. *Executing ipssend getconfig 1 pd*

4.2.2 getstatus command

This command is used to retrieve the current status of the IBM ServeRAID controller. The `getstatus` command has the following syntax:

```
ipssend getstatus <Controller>
```

The parameters are explained in Table 4.

Table 4. getstatus command parameters

Parameter	Description
Controller	Number of controller (1 to 12)

To get the status of the first ServeRAID controller in your IBM Netfinity server, execute the command:

```
ipssend getstatus 1
```

You will see output similar to Figure 91.

```
[root@nf5500 /root]# ipssend getstatus 1

Found 1 IBM ServeRAID Controller(s).
Background Command Progress Status for controller 1...
    Current/Most Recent Operation  : Rebuild
    Source logical drive           : 1
    Target logical drive           : 1
    Rebuild Rate                   : High
    Status                         : Successfully Completed
    Logical Drive Size (in Stripes): 552192
    Number of Remaining Stripes    : 0
    Percentage Complete            : 100.00%
Command Completed Successfully.
```

Figure 91. Executing ipssend getstatus 1

If the ServeRAID controller is currently rebuilding a drive, you will see output similar to Figure 92.

```
[root@nf5500 /root]# ipssend getstatus 1

Found 1 IBM ServeRAID Controller(s).
Background Command Progress Status for controller 1...
    Current/Most Recent Operation  : Rebuild
    Source logical drive           : 1
    Target logical drive           : 1
    Rebuild Rate                   : High
    Status                         : In Progress
    Logical Drive Size (in Stripes): 3200
    Number of Remaining Stripes    : 2070
    Percentage Complete            : 35.31%
Command Completed Successfully.
```

Figure 92. Executing ipssend getstatus 1 during rebuilding of the drive

4.2.3 devinfo command

This command is used to retrieve the current status of the devices connected to the IBM ServeRAID controller. The `devinfo` command has the following syntax:

```
ipssend devinfo <Controller> <Channel> <SCSI ID>
```

The parameters are explained in Table 5.

Table 5. devinfo command parameters

Parameter	Description
Controller	Number of controller (1 to 12)
Channel	Channel of device (1 to 3)
SCSI ID	SCSI ID of device (0 to 15)

To get the status of a device with SCSI ID 0 on channel 1 on the first ServeRAID controller, execute the command:

```
ipssend devinfo 1 1 0
```

You will see output similar to Figure 93.

```
[root@nf5500 linux]# ipssend devinfo 1 1 0

Found 1 IBM ServeRAID Controller(s).
Device Information has been initiated for controller 1...
        Device is a 16 bit, Fast SCSI, tag queuing Hard Disk
        Channel               : 1
        SCSI ID               : 0
        PFA (Yes/No)          : No
        State                 : Hot Spare (HSP)
        Size (in MB)/(in Sectors):    8678/17773888
        Device ID             : IBM-PCCODGHS09Y 035168164E69
Command Completed Successfully.
```

Figure 93. Executing ipssend devinfo 1 1 0

If the ServeRAID controller is currently rebuilding a drive, you will see output similar to the one shown in .

```
[root@nf5500 /root]# ipssend devinfo 1 1 0

Found 1 IBM ServeRAID Controller(s).
Device Information has been initiated for controller 1...
        Device is a 16 bit, Fast SCSI, tag queuing Hard Disk
        Channel                 : 1
        SCSI ID                 : 0
        PFA (Yes/No)            : No
        State                   : Rebuild (RBL)
        Size (in MB)/(in Sectors):    8678/17773888
        Device ID               : IBM-PCCODGHS09Y 035168164E69
Command Completed Successfully.
```

Figure 94. Executing ipssend devinfo 1 1 0 during rebuilding of the drive

4.2.4 hsrebuild command

This command is used for setting the state of the Hot Swap Rebuild option. The hsrebuild command has the following syntax:

```
ipssend hsrebuild <Controller> <Options>
```

The parameters are explained in Table 6.

Table 6. hsrebuild command parameters

Parameter	Description
Controller	Number of controller (1 to 12)
Options	ON: Enable Hot Swap Rebuild
	?: Display status of Hot Swap Rebuild feature

This command is used to retrieve or set the Hot Swap Rebuild feature. If the Hot Swap Rebuild feature is set to ON, the rebuilding of a drive will start automatically, as soon as a failed drive in the RAID array has been replaced with a new one. This can improve the safety of your data.

> **Note**
>
> The Hot Swap Rebuild feature should not be confused with a hot spare drive. A hot spare drive means that a drive is in a waiting state as long as the RAID array is in an Okay state. Once the RAID array becomes in a Critical state, the hot spare drive is enabled and the data from the defunct drive automatically get rebuilt onto the hot spare drive, disregarding the Hot Swap Rebuild setting.

To retrieve information about the Hot Swap Rebuild status on the first ServeRAID controller, execute the command:

```
ipssend hsrebuild 1 ?
```

You will see output similar to Figure 95.

```
[root@nf5500 linux]# ipssend hsrebuild 1 ?

Found 1 IBM ServeRAID Controller(s).
Set Hot Swap Rebuild has been initiated for controller 1...
Hot Swap Rebuild is ON for controller 1.
```

Figure 95. Executing ipssend hsrebuild 1 ?

To enable the Hot Swap Rebuild option, execute the command:

```
ipssend hsrebuild 1 on
```

You will see output similar to Figure 96.

```
[root@nf5500 linux]# ipssend hsrebuild 1 on

Found 1 IBM ServeRAID Controller(s).
Set Hot Swap Rebuild has been initiated for controller 1...
Hot Swap Rebuild is already ON for controller 1.
```

Figure 96. Executing ipssend hsrebuild 1 on

4.2.4.1 setstate command

The setstate command is used to redefine the state of a physical device from the current state to the designated state. The setstate command has the following syntax:

```
ipssend setstate <Controller> <Channel> <SCSI ID> <New State>
```

The parameters are explained in Table 7.

Table 7. setstate command parameters

Parameter	Description
Controller	Number of controller (1 to 12)
Channel	Channel of device (1 to 3)
SCSI ID	SCSI ID of device (0 to 15)

Parameter	Description
New State	EMP (Empty) RDY (Ready) HSP (Hot Spare) SHS (Standby Hot Spare) DDD (Defunct Disk Drive) DHS (Defunct Hot Spare) RBL (Rebuild) SBY (Standby) ONL (Online)

> **Stop**
>
> Extreme caution must be taken when executing this command! For example, redefining a defunct (DDD) device to online (ONL) without going through a rebuild is extremely dangerous.

Before changing the state of a physical device, you should check the current status with the following command:

```
ipssend getconfig 1 pd
```

This command will show you all physical devices except empty ones (they are not displayed) on the first IBM ServeRAID controller. For example, if you want to set the state of a device on the first ServeRAID controller, channel 1 and SCSI ID 1 to RDY (Ready), execute the following command:

```
ipssend setstate 1 1 1 rdy
```

You will see output similar to Figure 97.

```
[root@nf5500 /root]# ipssend setstate 1 1 1 rdy

Found 1 IBM ServeRAID Controller(s).
Set Device State has been initiated for Controller 1...
Command Completed Successfully.
```

Figure 97. Executing ipssend setstate 1 1 1 rdy

You can verify the change of the device state by executing the command:

```
ipssend getconfig 1 pd
```

4.2.5 synch command

This command is used to synchronize the parity information on redundant logical drives. If the parity information is inconsistent, it will automatically be repaired. The synch command has the following syntax:

```
ipssend synch <Controller> <Scope> <Scope ID>
```

The parameters are explained in Table 8.

Table 8. setstate command parameters

Parameter	Description
Controller	Number of controller (1 to 12)
Scope	DRIVE for a single logical drive
Scope ID	Number of logical drive (1 to 8)

Note

It is recommended that you use this command on a weekly basis (for example as a `cron` job.

4.2.6 unattended command

This command is used to alter the unattended mode of the ServeRAID controller. The `unattended` command has the following syntax:

```
ipssend unattended <Controller> <Options>
```

The parameters are explained in Table 9.

Table 9. unattended command parameters

Parameter	Description
Controller	Number of controller (1 to 12)
Options	ON: Enable unattended mode
	OFF: Disable unattended mode
	?: Display status of unattended mode feature

If you want to see the current status of your first ServeRAID controller, execute the following command:

```
ipssend unattended 1 ?
```

You will see output similar to Figure 98.

```
[root@nf5500 /]# ipssend unattended 1 ?

Found 1 IBM ServeRAID Controller(s).
Set Unattended Mode has been initiated for controller 1...
Unattended Mode is set off.
```

Figure 98. Executing ipssend unattended 1 ?

If you want to set unattended mode to ON, then execute this command:

```
ipssend unattended 1 on
```

4.2.7 rebuild command

The `rebuild` command starts a rebuild on the designated drive. This command has the following syntax:

```
ipssend rebuild <Controller> <Channel> <SCSI ID> <New Channel> <New SCSI ID>
```

The parameters are explained in Table 10.

Table 10. REBUILD command parameters

Parameter	Description
Controller	Number of controller (1 to 12)
Channel	Channel of defunct drive (1 to 3)
SCSI ID	SCSI ID of Defunct drive (0 to 15)
New Channel	Channel of new drive (1 to 3)
New SCSI ID	SCSI ID of new drive (0 to 15)

This operation is valid for disk arrays containing one or more logical drives in the Critical (CRT) state. For example, if you want to rebuild a defunct drive on SCSI ID 1 on channel 1 in the first ServeRAID controller to the new drive on SCSI ID 0 on the same channel, you would execute the command as follows:

```
ipssend rebuild 1 1 1 1 0
```

You will see output similar to Figure 99.

```
[root@nf5500 linux]# ipssend rebuild 1 1 1 1 0

Found 1 IBM ServeRAID Controller(s).
Rebuild Drive has been initiated for controller 1...
Rebuilding Logical Drive #1:
..........10% Done
..........20% Done
..........30% Done
..........40% Done
..........50% Done
..........60% Done
..........70% Done
..........80% Done
..........90% Done
..........Done Logical Drive #1
Rebuilding Logical Drive #2:
[]
```

Figure 99. Executing ipssend rebuild 1 1 1 1 0

4.2.8 Replacing a defunct drive

When a physical drive in the RAID array becomes defunct, you will be notified of the failure by a light signal on the drive. You can simulate a defunct drive by executing the following command:

```
ipssend setstate 1 1 4 ddd
```

In this case we are simulating that the drive with SCSI ID 4 on channel 1 on the first ServeRAID controller is defunct. The following steps should be taken to replace the defunct drive:

1. Physically replace the defunct drive with a good drive.

2. The IBM ServeRAID controller will start rebuilding the drive automatically.

Note

Automatically rebuilding will work only on ServeRAID II and III. Additionally, Enable Hot Spare Rebuild must be set to Enabled!

You can check the progress of rebuilding the logical drives on the first IBM ServeRAID controller with the command:

```
ipssend getstatus 1
```

You will see the output similar to Figure 92 on page 81.

If the rebuild is not completed successfully, you will see output similar to the following:

```
[root@nf5500 /root]# ipssend getstatus 1

Found 1 IBM ServeRAID Controller(s).
Background Command Progress Status for controller 1...
    Current/Most Recent Operation  : Rebuild
    Source logical drive           : 1
    Target logical drive           : 1
    Rebuild Rate                   : High
    Status                         : Drive Failed
        Channel Number is          : 1
        SCSI ID Number is          : 0
    Logical Drive Size (in Stripes): 552192
    Number of Remaining Stripes    : 302692
    Percentage Complete            : 45.18%
Command Completed Successfully.
```

Figure 100. Failed rebuild

4.2.9 Replacing a defunct drive with disabled Hot Spare Rebuild

When you have disabled the Hot Spare Rebuild function in the IBM ServeRAID controller configuration, the following steps should be taken to replace the defunct drive. In our example, the drive with SCSI ID 1 on channel 1 on the first ServeRAID controller is defunct.

1. Physically replace the defunct drive with a working one.

2. Execute the following command to start rebuilding the drive:

    ipssend setstate 1 1 1 rbl

    You will see output similar to this:

```
[root@nf5500 /root]# ipssend setstate 1 1 1 rbl

Found 1 IBM ServeRAID Controller(s).
Set Device State has been initiated for Controller 1...
Command Completed Successfully.
```

Figure 101. Forced rebuild of the defunct drive

You can check the progress of rebuilding the logical drives on the first IBM ServeRAID controller with the command:

    ipssend getstatus 1

You will see the output similar to Figure 92 on page 81.

4.2.10 Replacing a defunct drive with a hot spare drive installed

When you have configured the hot spare drive option in your IBM ServeRAID configuration, the defunct physical drive is automatically rebuilt on this hot spare drive. Follow these steps to replace the defunct physical drive and set it as a hot spare drive:

1. You find out that there is a defunct physical drive in your RAID array on the first ServeRAID controller. In our example, the physical drive on SCSI ID 1 on channel 1 was defined as the hot spare drive. You can check this by executing the command:

   ```
   ipssend getconfig 1 pd
   ```

   You will see output similar to Figure 102.

```
[root@nf5500 /]# ipssend getconfig 1 pd

Found 1 IBM ServeRAID Controller(s).
Read Configuration has been initiated for Controller 1...
--------------------------------------------------------------------------------
Physical Device Information
--------------------------------------------------------------------------------
   Channel #1:
      Initiator at SCSI ID 7
      Target on SCSI ID 0
         Device is a 16 bit, Fast SCSI, tag queuing Hard Disk
         SCSI ID                  : 0
         PFA (Yes/No)             : No
         State                    : Online (ONL)
         Size (in MB)/(in Sectors):    8678/17773888
         Device ID                : IBM-PCCODGHS09Y 035168164E69
      Target on SCSI ID 1
         Device is a 16 bit, Fast SCSI, tag queuing Hard Disk
         SCSI ID                  : 1
         PFA (Yes/No)             : No
         State                    : Rebuild (RBL)
         Size (in MB)/(in Sectors):    8678/17773888
         Device ID                : IBM-PCCODGHS09Y 04206816F8A1
      Target on SCSI ID 3
         Device is a 16 bit, Fast SCSI, tag queuing Hard Disk
         SCSI ID                  : 3
         PFA (Yes/No)             : No
         State                    : Online (ONL)
         Size (in MB)/(in Sectors):   17357/35548048
         Device ID                : IBM-PCCODGHS18Y 0351680EE209
      Target on SCSI ID 4
         Device is a 16 bit, Fast SCSI, tag queuing Hard Disk
         SCSI ID                  : 4
         PFA (Yes/No)             : No
         State                    : Defunct Hot Spare (DHS)
         Size (in MB)/(in Sectors):    8678/17773888
         Device ID                : IBM-PCCODGHS09Y 0420681924B4
      Target on SCSI ID 15
         Device is a 16 bit, Fast SCSI, tag queuing Unknown Device
         SCSI ID                  : 15
         PFA (Yes/No)             : No
         State                    : Stand By (SBY)
         Size (in MB)/(in Sectors):       0/        0
         Device ID                : SDR    GEM200  2   1
   Channel #2:
      Initiator at SCSI ID 7
Command Completed Successfully.
```

Figure 102. After failing the drive in RAID array

As you can see, the hot spare drive is already rebuilding and the defunct drive is in Defunct Hot Spare (DHS) state.

2. Remove the defunct drive from the server. In our example this is the drive with SCSI ID 4 on channel 1.

3. Set the state of the drive to Empty (EMP) with the command:

```
ipssend setstate 1 1 4 emp
```

You will see output similar to Figure 103.

```
[root@nf5500 /]# ipssend setstate 1 1 4 emp

Found 1 IBM ServeRAID Controller(s).
Set Device State has been initiated for Controller 1...
Command Completed Successfully.
```

Figure 103. Setting the DHS to EMP

You can check the result of this operation by executing the command:

```
ipssend getconfig 1 pd
```

You will see output similar to Figure 104.

```
[root@nf5500 /]# ipssend getconfig 1 pd

Found 1 IBM ServeRAID Controller(s).
Read Configuration has been initiated for Controller 1...
--------------------------------------------------------------------------------
Physical Device Information
--------------------------------------------------------------------------------
    Channel #1:
        Initiator at SCSI ID 7
        Target on SCSI ID 0
            Device is a 16 bit, Fast SCSI, tag queuing Hard Disk
            SCSI ID                 : 0
            PFA (Yes/No)            : No
            State                   : Online (ONL)
            Size (in MB)/(in Sectors):    8678/17773888
            Device ID               : IBM-PCCODGHS09Y 035168164E69
        Target on SCSI ID 1
            Device is a 16 bit, Fast SCSI, tag queuing Hard Disk
            SCSI ID                 : 1
            PFA (Yes/No)            : No
            State                   : Rebuild (RBL)
            Size (in MB)/(in Sectors):    8678/17773888
            Device ID               : IBM-PCCODGHS09Y 04206816F8A1
        Target on SCSI ID 3
            Device is a 16 bit, Fast SCSI, tag queuing Hard Disk
            SCSI ID                 : 3
            PFA (Yes/No)            : No
            State                   : Online (ONL)
            Size (in MB)/(in Sectors):    17357/35548048
            Device ID               : IBM-PCCODGHS18Y 0351680EE209
        Target on SCSI ID 15
            Device is a 16 bit, Fast SCSI, tag queuing Unknown Device
            SCSI ID                 : 15
            PFA (Yes/No)            : No
            State                   : Stand By (SBY)
            Size (in MB)/(in Sectors):      0/         0
            Device ID               : SDR    GEM200  2    1
    Channel #2:
        Initiator at SCSI ID 7
Command Completed Successfully.
```

Figure 104. After removing defunct drive

As you can see, there is no entry for the defunct drive anymore.

4. Insert the new drive into the server. In our example this will be inserted at the same place as the defunct drive.

5. Set the state of that drive to Ready with the command:

   ipssend setstate 1 1 4 rdy

   You will see output similar to Figure 105.

```
[root@nf5500 /]# ipssend setstate 1 1 4 rdy

Found 1 IBM ServeRAID Controller(s).
Set Device State has been initiated for Controller 1...
Command Completed Successfully.
```

Figure 105. Setting the new drive state to RDY

With setting the state to Ready (RDY), the drive is started.

> **Note**
>
> All new drives must be first set to ready (RDY).

You can check the result of this operation by executing the command:

ipssend getconfig 1 pd

You will see output similar to Figure 106.

```
[root@nf5500 /]# ipssend getconfig 1 pd

Found 1 IBM ServeRAID Controller(s).
Read Configuration has been initiated for Controller 1...
--------------------------------------------------------------------------------
Physical Device Information
--------------------------------------------------------------------------------
    Channel #1:
        Initiator at SCSI ID 7
        Target on SCSI ID 0
            Device is a 16 bit, Fast SCSI, tag queuing Hard Disk
            SCSI ID                : 0
            PFA (Yes/No)           : No
            State                  : Online (ONL)
            Size (in MB)/(in Sectors):    8678/17773888
            Device ID              : IBM-PCCODGHS09Y 035168164E69
        Target on SCSI ID 1
            Device is a 16 bit, Fast SCSI, tag queuing Hard Disk
            SCSI ID                : 1
            PFA (Yes/No)           : No
            State                  : Rebuild (RBL)
            Size (in MB)/(in Sectors):    8678/17773888
            Device ID              : IBM-PCCODGHS09Y 04206816F8A1
        Target on SCSI ID 3
            Device is a 16 bit, Fast SCSI, tag queuing Hard Disk
            SCSI ID                : 3
            PFA (Yes/No)           : No
            State                  : Online (ONL)
            Size (in MB)/(in Sectors):    17357/35548048
            Device ID              : IBM-PCCODGHS18Y 0351680EE209
        Target on SCSI ID 4
            Device is a 16 bit, Fast SCSI, tag queuing Hard Disk
            SCSI ID                : 4
            PFA (Yes/No)           : No
            State                  : Ready (RDY)
            Size (in MB)/(in Sectors):    8678/17773888
            Device ID              : IBM-PCCODGHS09Y 0420681924B4
        Target on SCSI ID 15
            Device is a 16 bit, Fast SCSI, tag queuing Unknown Device
            SCSI ID                : 15
            PFA (Yes/No)           : No
            State                  : Stand By (SBY)
            Size (in MB)/(in Sectors):        0/        0
            Device ID              : SDR    GEM200   2   1
    Channel #2:
        Initiator at SCSI ID 7
Command Completed Successfully.
```

Figure 106. After setting the state to RDY

As you can see, the new drive appears as a Ready (RDY) device, in our example under SCSI ID 4 on channel 1.

6. Change the state of the new drive to the Hot Spare (HSP) with the command:

```
ipssend setstate 1 1 4 hsp
```

You will see output similar to Figure 107.

```
[root@nf5500 /]# ipssend setstate 1 1 4 hsp

Found 1 IBM ServeRAID Controller(s).
Set Device State has been initiated for Controller 1...
Command Completed Successfully.
```

Figure 107. Changing the state to HSP

You can check the result of this operation by executing the command:

```
ipssend getconfig 1 pd
```

You will see output similar to Figure 108.

```
[root@nf5500 /]# ipssend getconfig 1 pd

Found 1 IBM ServeRAID Controller(s).
Read Configuration has been initiated for Controller 1...
--------------------------------------------------------------------------------
Physical Device Information
--------------------------------------------------------------------------------
   Channel #1:
      Initiator at SCSI ID 7
      Target on SCSI ID 0
         Device is a 16 bit, Fast SCSI, tag queuing Hard Disk
         SCSI ID                  : 0
         PFA (Yes/No)             : No
         State                    : Online (ONL)
         Size (in MB)/(in Sectors):    8678/17773888
         Device ID                : IBM-PCCODGHS09Y 035168164E69
      Target on SCSI ID 1
         Device is a 16 bit, Fast SCSI, tag queuing Hard Disk
         SCSI ID                  : 1
         PFA (Yes/No)             : No
         State                    : Rebuild (RBL)
         Size (in MB)/(in Sectors):    8678/17773888
         Device ID                : IBM-PCCODGHS09Y 04206816F8A1
      Target on SCSI ID 3
         Device is a 16 bit, Fast SCSI, tag queuing Hard Disk
         SCSI ID                  : 3
         PFA (Yes/No)             : No
         State                    : Online (ONL)
         Size (in MB)/(in Sectors):    17357/35548048
         Device ID                : IBM-PCCODGHS18Y 0351680EE209
      Target on SCSI ID 4
         Device is a 16 bit, Fast SCSI, tag queuing Hard Disk
         SCSI ID                  : 4
         PFA (Yes/No)             : No
         State                    : Hot Spare (HSP)
         Size (in MB)/(in Sectors):    8678/17773888
         Device ID                : IBM-PCCODGHS09Y 0420681924B4
      Target on SCSI ID 15
         Device is a 16 bit, Fast SCSI, tag queuing Unknown Device
         SCSI ID                  : 15
         PFA (Yes/No)             : No
         State                    : Stand By (SBY)
         Size (in MB)/(in Sectors):     0/        0
         Device ID                : SDR    GEM200  2   1
   Channel #2:
      Initiator at SCSI ID 7
Command Completed Successfully.
```

Figure 108. After setting the state to HSP

Congratulations! You have just installed a new hot spare drive and it is now ready to use.

4.2.11 Using the ipsmon command

The `ipsmon` command is part of the ipsutils.rpm package. It can be used to monitor the current status of your IBM ServeRAID controller. The `ipsmon` command has the following syntax:

```
ipsmon <-f:filename> <-s>
```

The parameters are explained in Table 11.

Table 11. ipsmon parameters

Parameter	Description
-f:filename	Specifies a filename to report messages default filename is ipsmon.log
-s	Specifies if messages should only be logged to the standard output device

If you want to monitor the IBM ServeRAID controller activity on the standard console execute the command

```
ipsmon -s
```

You will see the output similar to Figure 109.

```
[root@nf5500 /root]# ipsmon -s

Licensed Material - Property of IBM Corporation
IBM ServeRAID Controller Monitor v3.50.17
Copyright (C) IBM Corporation 1996 - 1999
All Rights Reserved
US Government Restricted Rights - Use, Duplication, or Disclosure
Restricted by GSA ADP Schedule Contract with IBM Corporation

Found 1 IBM ServeRAID Controller(s)
Oct 12 1999 12:14:04 EDT INF000:A1C-SID-- No controller errors detected

Oct 12 1999 12:14:09 EDT INF001:A1C-SID-- rebuild started
```

Figure 109. ipsmon command

4.2.12 Using the ipsadm command

Using the `ipsadm` command you can remotely administer your IBM ServeRAID controller from any WIN32 based workstation. The WIN32 client can be downloaded from the following site:

```
http://www.developer.ibm.com/welcome/netfinity/serveraid.html
```

From that site you can download the following files:

- ips-100.tgz

  This file contains the kernel patch for the 2.2.x kernel, which enables the support for IBM ServeRAID adapter in those kernels.

- ipsutils.rpm

  This file contains the Linux utilities for IBM ServeRAID SCSI adapter

- 009n012.exe.

  This file contains the WIN32 Administration Client, which can be used to remote configure and monitor the ServeRAID adapter used in Linux installation.

By starting the executable file on any WIN32-based workstation, you will create the installation diskette for the IBM ServeRAID Administration and Monitoring Program. After you have created the diskette, execute the file setup.exe from the diskette. This will install the IBM ServeRAID Administration and Monitoring Program on your WIN32-based workstation. You run the program by starting IBM ServeRAID administration. You will see a window similar to Figure 110.

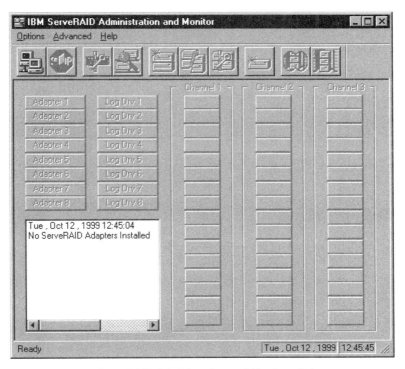

Figure 110. IBM ServeRAID Administration and Monitor window

To be able to remotely access the IBM ServeRAID controller of the IBM Netfinity server running Linux, you need to start the ipsadm utility on that server. ipsadm is basically a background process (daemon) listening for TCP/IP connections on port 1087 on one side and interacting with the IBM ServeRAID controller on the other side. So it basically accepts commands from the IBM ServeRAID Administration and Monitoring Program and passes them to the IBM ServeRAID controller. The ipsadm command has the following syntax:

```
ipsadm [-p:port#] [-f:filename] [-s:security file] [-d] [-er]
```

The parameters are described in Table 12.

Table 12. ipsadm parameters

Parameter	Description
-p:port#	Defines a port number for server communication
-f:filename	Specifies a filename to report messages
-s:security file	Specifies a filename to check for valid username:password
-d	Disables logging information to the display
-er	Displays all errors and warnings

In our example, we created a password file /etc/ips.pwd with the following entries:

```
nf5500:password
```

nf5500 is the user ID for accessing the IBM ServeRAID controller and the password is set to "password". To start the ipsadm utility, execute the command:

```
ipsadm -s:/etc/ips/pwd
```

In our example, we used the previously created password file. You will see output similar to Figure 111.

```
[root@nf5500 /root]# ipsadm -s:/etc/ips.pwd

Licensed Material - Property of IBM Corporation
IBM ServeRAID Administration & Monitoring Server Utility v3.50.17
Copyright (C) IBM Corporation 1996 - 1998
All Rights Reserved
US Government Restricted Rights - Use, Duplication, or Disclosure
Restricted by GSA ADP Schedule Contract with IBM Corporation

TCP/IP networking protocol initiated on port number 1087.
Using /etc/ips.pwd for username/password file.
Security enabled.
Not logging to a file.
Tue Oct 12 12:18:39 EDT 1999 --> IBM ServeRAID Administration Server started
Tue Oct 12 12:18:39 EDT 1999 --> Successfully created parent socket.
Tue Oct 12 12:18:39 EDT 1999 --> Bind to socket successful.
Tue Oct 12 12:18:39 EDT 1999 --> Listening for connection...
```

Figure 111. Starting IPSADM utility

To remotely connect to the IBM ServeRAID controller, follow these steps:

1. Start the IBM ServeRAID Administration and Monitoring Program and select **Options.** You will see a window similar to Figure 112.

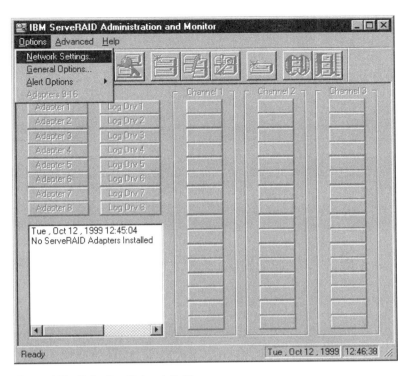

Figure 112. Selecting Network Settings

2. Select **Network Settings...** You will see a window similar to Figure 113.

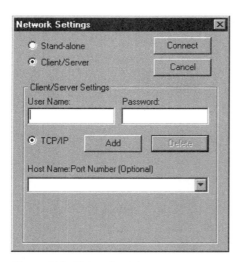

Figure 113. Network settings

3. Select the option **Client/Server** as you can see in Figure 113.

4. Enter the host name or the IP address of the IBM Netfinity server running the ipsadm utility in the Host Name:Port Number(Optional) field. The port number is optional and only needs to be supplied if you changed the default port on the server side. Click **Add** to add the host. You will see a window similar to Figure 114.

Figure 114. Host added

5. Click **OK** to return to the Network Settings dialog. You will see a window similar to Figure 115.

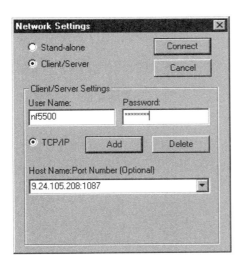

Figure 115. After the host is added

6. Enter the user name you defined in your password file in the User Name field and the respective password in the Password field. Click **Connect** to connect to the server with the IBM ServeRAID controller. You will see a window similar to Figure 116.

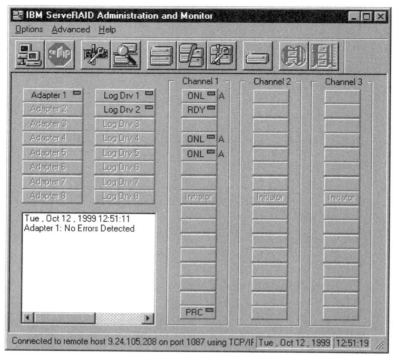

Figure 116. Connected to the server

Congratulations! You can now manage you IBM ServeRAID controller remotely.

If you want to automatically start up `ipsadm` at system bootup, you can add the following command line to the init script `/sbin/init.d/boot.local`. Open the file with a regular text editor, and add the following line at the end of the file:

```
ipsadm -d -s:/etc/ips/pwd &
```

The administration and monitoring server will now be started on system bootup without any manual intervention.

Chapter 5. DNS - Domain Name System

If you connect two or more computers to a network, they can share information and resources. However, these computers need to "talk in the same language" to be able to establish a connection. This "language" is called a network protocol. Today the most popular communication protocol is TCP/IP. This is the protocol that is being used on the Internet and in many local area networks as well.

Hosts in a TCP/IP network communicate with each other by using unique IP addresses. These addresses consist of four 8-bit numbers (octets) that are divided by dots. For example, host A has the address 192.168.99.1, while host B uses 122.68.29.5.

However, this addressing scheme is not very comprehensible to human beings and it is almost impossible to memorize a number of hosts by their IP addresses. Therefore a naming scheme has been invented.

Each host has a host name (for example fred) and belongs to a certain domain (for example snake-oil.com). Domains can be organized in a hierarchical fashion and can consist of different subdomains (for example marketing.snake-oil.com). The combination of a host name and its domain name is called a fully qualified domain name (FQDN) (for example fred.marketing.snake-oil.com). Since domains are hierarchical, it is possible to have more hosts with the same host name in different subdomains. Therefore, fred.marketing.snake-oil.com can be a different host from fred.management.snake-oil.com. If you want these hosts to be addressable from the Internet, you need to register your domain name with a central registry. There are several top-level domains, such as .com, .org or .net. In addition to these generic top-level domains, each country in the world has its own country code as the top-level domain. For example, Germany has .de, Denmark has .dk, and Finland uses .fi.

Since the hosts internally still use their IP addresses to communicate, there needs to be a mapping between host names and the corresponding IP address. There are two ways this can be implemented.

All host names of a network, including their IP addresses, are put into a static text file. This file has to be copied on each host that wants to communicate with the others by name. As soon as a host has been added or removed from the network, or an IP address or host name has changed, and the host files on all computers have to be adjusted accordingly. This can get very tedious, if the number of hosts reaches a certain amount.

This is where the Domain Name System (DNS) steps in. The following description of DNS is very simplified, but it should give you a rough picture of what DNS is all about.

Instead of maintaining a separate host file on each machine, there is a central server that carries a list of all hosts and IP addresses of its domain. All clients now send their host name resolution request to this central server instead of looking in a local table. The name server will look up the requested host name and return the respective IP address. The opposite is also possible: the client can also ask for a host name that belongs to a certain IP address. If a client asks for an IP address of another domain, the local domain name server will forward the request to the next name server above in its hierarchy, if it cannot answer the request by itself. Therefore changes to the table of host names have to be made at one central point only rather than on all participants of the network.

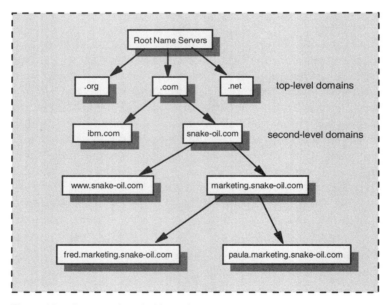

Figure 117. Internet domain hierarchy

This chapter will describe how to set up a name server for a local domain and how to maintain a host list for this domain.

5.1 Installation of software

The server that is supposed to be the DNS server needs to have a working TCP/IP network connection to the other hosts in its network first. The program that is responsible for this service is called named and belongs to the software package bind, which is coordinated by Paul Vixie for The Internet Software Consortium. There are two major versions of bind: bind4 and bind8. We will focus on the new version bind8, because it is more secure and is supposed to replace bind4 in the future. Most Linux distributions already contain a precompiled and preconfigured package for bind8.

Note

The package bind8 has been split up into two separate packages in SuSE Linux 6.3; bind8, which contains the actual server program, and bindutil, which contains the utilities such as nslookup, dig and host. We recommend that you install both on a server. A client needs only the bindutil package.

First make sure, that the package is actually installed. In SuSE Linux, you can use the RPM package manager to query the database of installed packages by entering the following command:

```
rpm -q bind8
```

If the package is already installed, RPM will return the version and build number of this package:

```
bind8-8.1.2-60
```

If it is not installed, you will receive the following message:

```
package bind8 is not installed.
```

You will then have to install this package first. Please refer to 3.1, "Adding and removing software packages using YaST" on page 51 for how to install software packages. The package bind8 is located in series n - Network-Support (TCP/IP, UUCP, Mail, News). Quit YaST to return to the command line after installing the package.

5.2 DNS sample configuration

Configuring DNS can be very complex, depending on the intended functionality. Covering this in depth is beyond the scope of this chapter. We will therefore focus on very a simplified example and recommend that you take a look at the very informative DNS how-to at:

```
http://www.linuxdoc.org/HOWTO/DNS-HOWTO.html
```

or at /usr/doc/howto/en/DNS-HOWTO.gz on your local filesystem for further info on DNS and bind.

We will construct a simple example: The company Snake Oil Ltd. wants to set up a local DNS server for their internal network (the internal IP address range is 192.168.99.xxx/24, a Class C network). They chose snake-oil.com as their local domain name. The network is also connected to the Internet. The name server will be configured to answer all requests about the local (internal) snake-oil.com domain and forward all other requests to the ISP's name server (ns.bigisp.com, fictional IP address 155.3.12.1) as a caching name server.

We begin with a simple example. At first the local DNS will be configured to act as a caching-only name server. This means that it forwards all requests to the ISP's name server(s) (forwarders) and caches all answers for further requests from its clients. This reduces the network traffic on the outside line.

Put the following lines in the /etc/resolv.conf file:

```
search snake-oil.com

nameserver 127.0.0.1
```

This will make sure that the server itself will use its local name server for host name resolution.

In SuSE Linux, you can use YaST to modify this entry. Choose **System administration -> Network configuration -> Configuration nameserver**. Enter the IP address 127.0.0.1 and your domain. To enter this dialog directly from the command line, enter the following command:

```
yast --mask nameserver --autoexit
```

The name server's main configuration file is /etc/named.conf. Most distributions ship with a very detailed example configuration file, you might want to save this for further reference. We will create a new file from scratch. Open up a text editor and create a new /etc/named.conf according to the following example:

```
options {
        directory "/var/named";
        pid-file "/var/named/slave/named.pid";
        listen-on { any; };
        forward only;
        forwarders { 155.3.12.1; };
        sortlist {
                { localhost; localnets; };
                { localnets; };
        };
};

logging {
        category lame-servers { null; };
        category cname { null; };
};

zone "localhost" IN {
        type master;
        file "localhost.zone";
        check-names fail;
        allow-update { none; };
};

zone "0.0.127.in-addr.arpa" IN {
        type master;
        file "127.0.0.zone";
        check-names fail;
        allow-update { none; };
};
```

Replace the IP address in the `forwarders` field with your ISP's name server IP address.

You also need to create the following /var/named/localhost.zone file:

```
$ORIGIN localhost.
@                       1D IN SOA       @ root (
                                        42              ; serial (d. adams)
                                        3H              ; refresh
                                        15M             ; retry
                                        1W              ; expiry
                                        1D )            ; minimum

                        1D IN NS        @
                        1D IN A         127.0.0.1
```

Furthermore, create a file /var/named/127.0.0.zone with the following content:

```
$ORIGIN 0.0.127.in-addr.arpa.

@                     1D IN SOA    localhost. root.localhost. (
                                   42               ; serial (d. adams)
                                   3H               ; refresh
                                   15M              ; retry
                                   1W               ; expiry
                                   1D )             ; minimum

                      1D IN NS     localhost.
1                     1D IN PTR    localhost.
```

Your network clients should all be configured to query the local DNS server's IP address instead of your ISP's name server.

You can now start the server with the command:

`rcnamed start.`

Check /var/log/messages for the startup messages. The name server should now resolve DNS queries from its clients by forwarding them to the ISP's name server. You can verify this with the commands host <somehostname> and nslookup.

If you want the name server to be started at the next system reboot, set the variable START_NAMED in /etc/rc.config to "yes". See 3.6, "Changing the configuration file with YaST" on page 70 for how to do this.

In the following step, this server should now also act as a primary name server for the local domain snake-oil.com. Stop the name server with rcnamed stop and edit the file /etc/named.conf so that it looks like the following example:

```
options {
        directory "/var/named";
        pid-file "/var/named/slave/named.pid";
        listen-on { any; };
        forward only;
        forwarders {9.24.106.15;};
        sortlist {
                { localhost; localnets; };
                { localnets; };
        };
};

logging {
        category lame-servers { null; };
        category cname { null; };
};

zone "." {
        type hint;
        file "root.hint";
};

zone "localhost" IN {
        type master;
        file "localhost.zone";
        check-names fail;
        allow-update { none; };
};

zone "0.0.127.in-addr.arpa" IN {
        type master;
        file "127.0.0.zone";
        check-names fail;
        allow-update { none; };
};

zone "snake-oil.com" {
        type master;
        file "snake-oil.zone";
};

zone "99.168.192.IN-ADDR.APRA" {
        type master;
        file "snake-oil.rev";
};
```

We have now added the zone files (the databases) needed for our local
domain "snake-oil.com". The file /var/named/snake-oil.zone is responsible for
the mapping of host names to IP addresses.

```
;
; Zone file for snake-oil.com
;
@       IN      SOA     ns.snake-oil.com. hostmaster.snake-oil.com. (
                        199910011       ; serial, todays date + todays serial #
                        8H              ; refresh, seconds
                        2H              ; retry, seconds
                        1W              ; expire, seconds
                        1D )            ; minimum, seconds
;
                NS      ns                      ; Inet Address of name server
                MX      10 mail                 ; Primary Mail Exchanger
                MX      20 mail.bigisp.com. ; Secondary Mail Exchanger
;
localhost       A       127.0.0.1
gw              A       192.168.99.1
ns              A       192.168.99.2
fred            A       192.168.99.3
mail            A       192.168.99.4
ftp             A       192.168.99.5
www             A       192.168.99.6
```

You should also create the zone file /var/named/snake-oil.rev. This is
necessary for reverse name lookups, for example, if you need to resolve an IP
address to its host name.

```
@       IN      SOA     ns.snake-oil.com. hostmaster.snake-oli.com. (
                        199910011 ; Serial, todays date + todays serial
                        8H      ; Refresh
                        2H      ; Retry
                        1W      ; Expire
                        1D)     ; Minimum TTL
                NS      ns.snake-oil.com.

1               PTR     gw.snake-oil.com.
2               PTR     ns.snake-oil.com.
3               PTR     fred.snake-oil.com.
4               PTR     mail.snake-oil.com.
5               PTR     ftp.snake-oil.com.
6               PTR     www.snake-oil.com.
```

Now let the name server reload its configuration again by running rcnamed
restart. Have a look at the messages in /var/log/messages. If everything went
well, you should see messages similar to the following:

```
Oct 26 18:03:20 ns named[14870]: starting
Oct 26 18:03:20 ns named[14870]: cache zone "" (IN) loaded (serial 0)
Oct 26 18:03:20 ns named[14870]: master zone "localhost" (IN) loaded (serial 42)
Oct 26 18:03:20 ns named[14870]: master zone "0.0.127.in-addr.arpa" (IN) loaded (serial
Oct 26 18:03:20 ns named[14870]: master zone "snake-oil.com" (IN) loaded (serial 199910
Oct 26 18:03:20 ns named[14870]: master zone "99.168.192.IN-ADDR.APRA" (IN) loaded (ser
199910011)
Oct 26 18:03:20 ns named[14870]: listening on [127.0.0.1].53 (lo)
Oct 26 18:03:20 ns named[14870]: listening on [9.24.105.210].53 (eth0)
Oct 26 18:03:20 ns named[14870]: Forwarding source address is [0.0.0.0].1041
Oct 26 18:03:20 ns named[14871]: Ready to answer queries.
```

Your name server should now correctly resolve host names for the snake-oil
domain as well.

5.3 Configuration tips

Use the listen-on directive in the options section of the named.conf file. For
each interface a name server listens on, a pair of filehandles is opened. On a
busy name server, saving every filehandle is a big win.

Check the /var/log/messages file from time to time for errors. Named is pretty
verbose in its error messages.

If you are constantly adding, removing or just making modifications to your
zone records, you might want to have a look at the nsupdate tool, which also
belongs to the bind8 package.

Chapter 6. Samba

If you look this word up in a dictionary, Samba is defined as a Brazilian dance, but Samba on Linux is something completely different. Samba is an implementation of a Server Message Block (SMB) protocol server that can be run on almost every variant of UNIX in existence. Samba is an open source project, just like Linux. The entire code is written in C so it is easily portable to all flavors of UNIX. Samba is a tool for the peaceful coexistence of UNIX and Windows on the same network on the level of file and print sharing over the NetBIOS protocol. It allows UNIX systems to show up in a Windows "Network Neighborhood" without causing a mess. With Samba, UNIX servers are acting like any other Windows server, offering their resources to the SMB clients. Recently SMB was renamed by Microsoft to Common Internet File System (CIFS).

6.1 What can you do with Samba?

- With Samba, a Linux server can act as a file/print server for Windows clients. It can replace expensive Windows NT file/print server in this role, creating a less expensive solution.

- Samba can act as a NetBIOS name server (NBNS) in a Windows world, where it is referred to as Windows Internet Name Service (WINS).

- Samba can participate in NetBIOS browsing and master browser elections.

- Samba can provide a gateway for the synchronizing of UNIX and Windows NT passwords.

- The Samba client software enables you to access any shared directory or printer on a Windows NT server or another Samba server and makes it possible for other UNIX machines to access Windows NT files.

- Using the Samba File System (SMBFS) you can mount any share from a Windows NT server or Samba server in your directory structure (this is only available on Linux).

6.2 Setting up Samba

You can check if the Samba package is installed by running the following rpm command on the command line or by using YaST as described in 3.1, "Adding and removing software packages using YaST" on page 51:

```
rpm -q samba
```

113

If Samba is not installed, please follow the instructions on how to install packages on SuSE Linux. The samba package is located in package series n - Network-Support (TCP/IP, UUCP, Mail, News). Quit YaST to return to the command line after installing the package.

6.2.1 Configuring Samba

In this section we will explain how to configure Samba so it can participate as a file/print server in an existing Windows network or just as a stand-alone file/print server for Windows and Linux clients.

Before you can start using Samba, you need to configure the smb.conf file. This file is the heart of the Samba server. When Samba is installed on SuSE Linux, this configuration file is installed here:

```
/etc/smb.conf
```

The Samba configuration file smb.conf is divided into two main sections:

1. Global Settings - these parameters affect the connection parameters.

2. Share Definitions - these define your shares. A share is a directory on the server that is accessible over the network and shared among users. This section has three subsections:

    a. Homes - in this subsection you define the user's home directories.

    b. Printers - in this subsection you define the available printers.

    c. Other Shares - this subsection can have multible entry. Create one for each share you want to define.

In the following sections we will describe how to modify smb.conf to efficiently and simply use Samba as a file/print server. We will cover only the basic parameters. See Chapter 8, "Samba PC Server" in the SuSE manual for more documentation about Samba.

Another good resource is the manual page for smb.conf(5) or the Web site of the Samba project:

```
http://www.samba.org
```

The preinstalled configuration file already contains a few commented examples. You can start off by modifying these to fit your needs.

6.2.1.1 Setting the NetBIOS parameters

The NetBIOS parameters are part of Global Settings. When you open your smb.conf file, you will see something similar to this:

```
#=================== Global Settings =========================
[global]
netbios name = NF5000
workgroup = LINUX
server string = Samba Server on SuSE Linux
```

Table 13 describes parameters that define the NetBIOS naming of your Samba server.

Table 13. NetBIOS parameters

Parameter	Description
netbios name	This is the name by which the Samba server is known on the network. This parameter has the same meaning as the Windows NT computer name. If you do not specify it, it will default to the server's host name.
workgroup	This parameter specifies in which Windows NT domain or workgroup the Samba server will participate. It is equivalent to the Windows NT domain or workgroup name.
server string	This is the description string of the Samba server. It has the same role as the Windows NT description field.

6.2.1.2 Global printing settings

In your smb.conf file ,you will see something similar to this:

```
load printers = yes
printcap name = /etc/printcap
printing = bsd
```

These parameters are described in Table 14.

Table 14. Printing parameters

Parameter	Description
load printers	This parameter defines if Samba should load all printers from the file /etc/printcap for browsing.
printcap name	This parameter lets you configure the location of the printcap file. The default value is /etc/printcap.
printing	This parameter tells Samba what printing style to use on your server. SuSE Linux uses the BSD printing style by default.

6.2.1.3 Global security settings

In your smb.conf you will see something similar to this:

```
security = user
;   password server = <NT-Server-Name>
encrypt passwords = yes
smb passwd file = /etc/smbpasswd
```

These parameters are described in Table 15.

Table 15. Security parameters

Parameter	Description
security	This parameter has four possible values: share, user, server, domain
password server	At the server or domain security level, this is the server that will be used for authorization. Enter the server's NetBIOS name here.
encrypt passwords	When setting this parameter to yes, you enable Samba to use the encrypted password protocol, which is used in Windows NT (starting with Service Pack 3) and Windows 98. This is needed to communicate with those clients.
smb passwd file	This parameter tells Samba where encrypted passwords are saved. By default, it will use /etc/smbpasswd.

The security modes are as follows:

1. Share - in this security mode, clients need to supply only the password for the resource. This mode of security is the default for the Windows 95 file/print server. It is not recommended to be used in UNIX environments, because it violates the UNIX security scheme.

2. User - user/password validation is done on the server that is offering the resource. This mode is most widely used.

3. Server - the user/password validation is done on the specified authentication server. This server can be a Windows NT server or another Samba server.

4. Domain - this security level is basically the same as server security, with the exception that the Samba server becomes a member of a Windows NT domain. In this case the Samba server can also participate in such things as trust relationships.

Because Windows NT 4.0 Service Pack 3 or later, Windows 95 with the latest patches, and Windows 98 use encrypted passwords for accessing NetBIOS resources, you need to enable your Samba server to use the encrypted passwords. Before you start the Samba server for the first time you need to create a Samba encrypted passwords file. This can be done with the mksmbpasswd.sh script. The recommended way is to first create the user accounts in Linux and then create the Samba password file with the command:

```
cat /etc/passwd | mksmbpasswd.sh > /etc/smbpasswd
```

This creates an empty Samba password file from the Linux password file. It contains all local users, but not their passwords.

Note

Use the same filename you specified for creating the Samba password file in the smb.conf configuration to tell the Samba server where the password file is.

By default the passwords for the Samba users are undefined. Before any connection is made to the Samba server, users need to create their passwords.

Now you need to specify the password for all users. If you are changing or specifying the password for the user, you can do this by executing the command:

```
smbpasswd -U username
```

You will see a window similar to the following:

```
[root@nf5000 /]# /usr/bin/smbpasswd -U user
New SMB password:
Retype new SMB password:
Password changed for user user.
[root@nf5000 /]# []
```

Figure 118. Specifying the password for Samba user

Note

Anyone with access to the /usr/bin/smbpasswd can change passwords for the Samba users.

Another way is to have each Samba user change the password for himself, by remotely connecting to the Samba server and executing the command:

```
smbpasswd
```

The output will be similar to Figure 118. If a Samba user already has defined a password, he will need to type in the old password before he can change it.

If you want to add a Samba server user later, you can do this with the following command:

```
smbpasswd -a username password
```

This will add a new user to the Samba password file.

> **Note**
>
> You have to be logged on as root if you want to manage other users. If you are logged on as a user, you can only change your own password. The smbpasswd utility uses the location of the password file from the smb.conf configuration file.

6.2.1.4 Global name resolution settings
In your smb.conf you will see something similar to:

```
name resolve order = wins lmhosts bcast
wins support = yes
;    wins server = w.x.y.z
```

The parameters are described in Table 16.

Table 16. Name resolution parameters

Parameter	Description
name resolve order	With this parameter you specify how Samba resolves NetBIOS names into IP addresses. The preferred value is wins lmhosts bcast.Refer to the manual page of smb.conf (5) for more information.
wins support	If this option is enabled, Samba will also act as a WINS server.
wins server	With this parameter, you tell Samba which WINS server to use.

> **Note**
>
> Samba can act as a WINS server or a WINS client, but not both. So only one of the parameters (`wins support` or `wins server`) can be set at the same time. If you specify the IP address of WINS server, then `wins support` must be set to "no".

6.2.1.5 Creating shares

In the previous sections we have explained how to prepare general configuration parameters. But a Samba server is useful only when it offers resources to the users. In this section we will explain how to create a share. A simple share definition section in smb.conf looks similar to this:

```
[redbook]
    comment = Redbook files
    path = /redbook
    browseable = yes
    printable = no
    writable = yes
    write list = @users
```

We explain the most important parameters for creating a share in Table 17.

Table 17. Share parameters

Parameter	Description
comment	This describes the function of this share.
admin users	This parameter is used to specify the users who have administrative privileges for this share. When they access the share, they perform all operations as user root.
path	Defines the path to the local directory you are sharing.
browseable	If this parameter is set to yes, you can see this share when you are browsing the resources on the Samba server. The value can be yes or no.
printable	This parameter specifies, if the share is a print share. The value can be yes or no.
write list	Users specified in this list have write access to the share. If the name begins with @, it refers to a group name.
writable	This parameter specifies if the share is writeable. The value can be yes or no.

Parameter	Description
read list	Users specified in this list have read access to the share. If the name begins with @ it refers to a group name.
read only	If this is set to yes, the share is read only. The value can be yes or no.
valid users	This parameter specifies which users can access the share.

You can easily set up a new share by using this basic set of parameters. Each share definition starts with the share name in square brackets "[]". You can specify the values for the share parameters below this name.

6.2.1.6 Share permissions

Although you can control the share permissions with share parameters, UNIX permissions are applied before the user can access files on the share. So you need to take care of the UNIX permissions, so that the user has access to the share directory under UNIX.

When a user creates a new file on the shared directory, the default create mask for files is 0744, and the default create mask for directories is 0755. If you can also force the use of a certain creation mask. The parameters necessary for this are explained in Table 18.

Table 18. Create mask parameters

Parameter	Description
create mask	This parameter assigns which permissions should be used when creating a new file.
directory mask	This parameter defines the permissions used for the creation of directories.

6.2.1.7 Creating shares for home directories

Samba has a special share section called [homes]. This share definition is used for all home directories, so you do not need to create separate shares for each user.

When a client requests a connection to a file share, existing file shares are scanned. If a match is found, that share is used. If no match is found, the requested share is treated as a user name and validated by security. If the name exists and the password is correct, a share with that name is created by cloning the [homes] section. The home share definition uses the same parameters as a normal share definition. The following is an example of a home share definition in the smb.conf configuration file:

```
[homes]
comment = Home Directories
path = %H
valid users = %S
browseable = no
writable = yes
create mode = 0700
directory mode = 0700
```

As you can see, we used some special variables in this definition, which are explained in Table 19.

Table 19. Variable description

Parameter	Description
%H	This variable represents the home directory of the current user.
%S	The name of the current service, which is equal to the user name in the case of home share.

As you can see in the example, we have used special creation masks for the creation of files and directories, by forcing all new files or directories to be accessible by the owner of this home directory only.

6.2.1.8 Creating a printer share

A Samba server uses the same procedure for printer shares as for the home shares. After all share definitions and user names are tested against the requested share name and the matched definition is still not found, Samba will search for a printer with that name (if the [printers] section exists). If the match is found in the printer definitions, that [printers] share section will be cloned with the name of requested service, which is really a printer name. The following is an example of a printer definition in the smb.conf configuration file:

```
[printers]
comment = All Printers
path = /var/spool/samba
browseable = no
# Set public = yes to allow user 'guest account' to print
guest ok = no
writable = no
printable = yes
create mask = 0700
```

As you can see, the [printers] section is just like any other share definition. When a user prints, he basically copies the data into a spool directory; after that, the data will be handled by the local printing system. The only difference between a printer share and other share definitions is, that the parameter printable is set to "yes". This means that a user can write a spool file to the directory specified in this share definition. If the share is printable, then it is also writable by default.

6.2.2 Starting and stopping the Samba server

You can start the Samba server by executing the command:

```
rcsmb start
```

As you can see in the process table, two daemons are started: smbd and nmbd. smbd is the actual Samba server and nmbd is WINS server.

Samba server can be stopped by executing the command:

```
rcsmb stop
```

Whenever you make modifications to the smb.conf configuration file, you need to restart the Samba server. This can be done by executing the following command:

```
rcsmb restart
```

6.2.3 Starting Samba as startup service

You can configure your boot process so that Samba will be started at bootup time.

To activate this feature, you simply have to set the variable START_SMB in /etc/rc.config to yes. You can either do this manually, or by using YaST as described in 3.6, "Changing the configuration file with YaST" on page 70.

The next time the Linux server is restarted, the Samba server will be started automatically.

6.2.4 Using SWAT

The Samba Web Administration Tool (SWAT) allows the remote configuration of the smb.conf configuration file through a Web browser. That means you can make configurations in a GUI-like environment, which makes it much easier for administrators who are not used to using a command line. SWAT itself is a small Web server and CGI scripting application that is designed to run from inetd to provide access to the smb.conf configuration file.

Authorized users with the root password can configure the smb.conf configuration file via Web pages. SWAT also places help links to all configurable options on every page, which help the administrator to understand the effect of the different parameters.

Before using SWAT you must check the following.

1. The file /etc/services should have the following line (this is the default in SuSE Linux):

```
swat 901/tcp
```

2. The file /etc/inetd.conf must contain the following line:

```
swat   stream  tcp      nowait.400      root    /usr/sbin/swat  swat
```

In SuSE Linux, this line already exists, but is deactivated with a comment sign (#). Just remove this sign from the beginning of the line and you are all set.

If you made any modifications to one of those files, you need to restart inetd. This can be done by executing the following command:

```
rcinetd restart
```

You are now ready to use SWAT. To start SWAT, point your favorite Web browser to the IP address of your Samba server on port 901, as you can see in Figure 119.

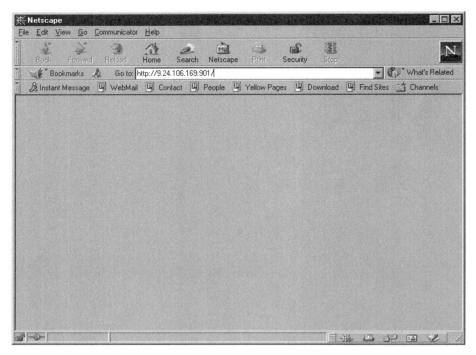

Figure 119. Starting SWAT

After you load the home page of SWAT, you will see a window similar to
Figure 120.

Figure 120. User authorization for SWAT

Type in the user name and password of a user defined on your Linux server.
Click **OK** to continue. You will see a window similar to Figure 121.

Stop

You can access SWAT using any regular user account, but you can make changes only when using the root user accpount.

Remember, when you are logging on to SWAT from a remote machine you are sending passwords in plain text. This can be a security issue, so we recommend that you do SWAT administration only over a trusted network connection.

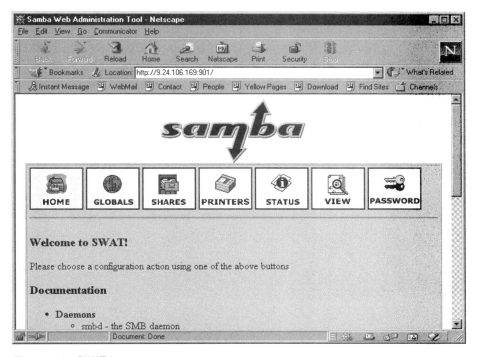

Figure 121. SWAT home page

As you can see in Figure 121, you have seven categories available:

1. Home - here you can find all the documentation you need about Samba.

2. Globals - display and modify global parameters from the smb.conf configuration file.

3. Shares - you can view, modify and add shares here.

4. Printers - to view, modify and add printers.

5. Status - check the current status of your Samba server here.

6. View - view the current configuration of the smb.conf configuration file.

7. Passwords - manage passwords for the Samba server.

In the following sections we will briefly describe the functions available in SWAT.

Note

After you made changes to the smb.conf configuration file, the Samba server must be restarted.

6.2.4.1 Globals
When you click the **Globals** icon in the main SWAT window, you will see a window similar to Figure 122.

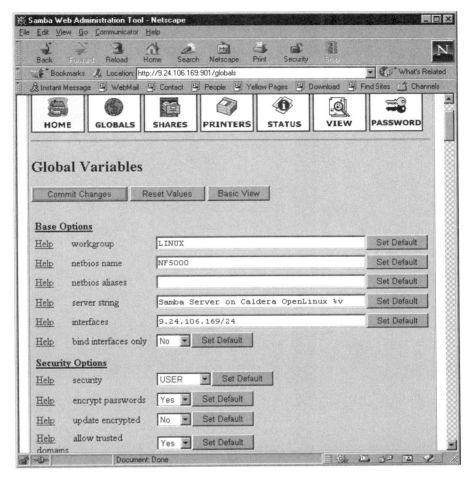

Figure 122. Global section in SWAT

This window enables you to modify the global parameters of your Samba server. By default you will see the Basic View. If you want to see the Advanced View, select **Advanced View**. In the Advanced View you have all options available, while the Basic View displays only the basic options. To return from the Advanced View to the Basic View select **Basic View.** After you have made your changes you can save them by clicking **Commit changes.** If you get a pop-up window similar to Figure 123, which warns you that you are sending nonsecure information over the network, you can easily select **Continue** if you are working locally or if you know that your network is secure.

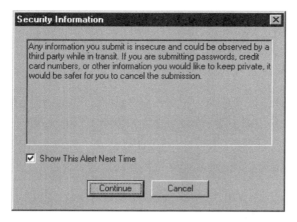

Figure 123. Security warning

6.2.4.2 Shares
When you click the **Shares** icon on any of the SWAT Web pages, you will see a window similar to Figure 124.

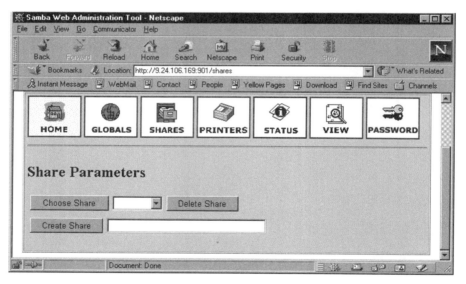

Figure 124. Shares section in SWAT

Here you can:

1. View the defined share
2. Delete a share

3. Create a new share

6.2.4.3 Viewing or modifying an existing share

To view an already defined share select the share from the field to the right of the **Choose Share** button, as shown in Figure 125.

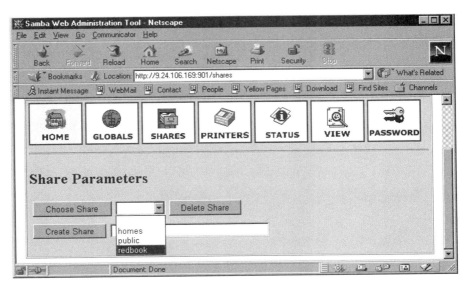

Figure 125. Choosing a share to view

After you have selected the share, click **Choose Share** to view the share properties. You will see a window similar to Figure 126.

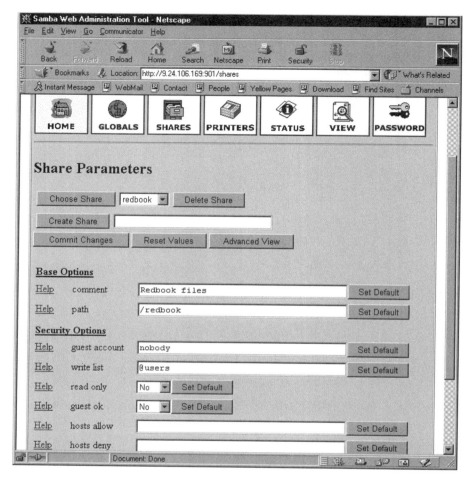

Figure 126. Share properties

If you want to see all available parameters, click **Advanced View.** You can also make changes and you can save them by clicking **Commit Changes**.

6.2.4.4 Deleting the existing share

To delete the existing share you must first select an already defined share similar to Figure 125. Then select **Delete Share.**

Stop

A share will be deleted immediately and without warning.

After you have deleted a share you must restart the Samba server.

6.2.4.5 Creating a new share

To create a simple share, do the following:

1. Create a directory that will be used for the share. You can do this by executing this command from a terminal session:

    ```
    mkdir /home/public
    ```

    In our example we created a "public" subdirectory below the "home" directory.

2. Make sure that the UNIX permissions are set correctly in that directory, so that only intended users have access permissions for it.

3. Type in the name of the share you are creating in the shares view of the SWAT Web pages displayed in Figure 127.

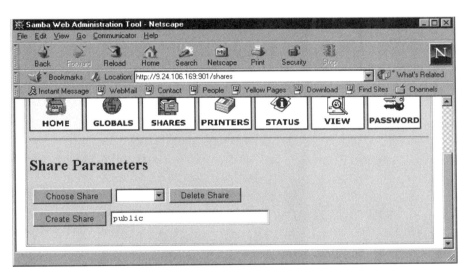

Figure 127. Entering the name for new share

4. Click **Create Share** to continue. You will see a window similar to Figure 128.

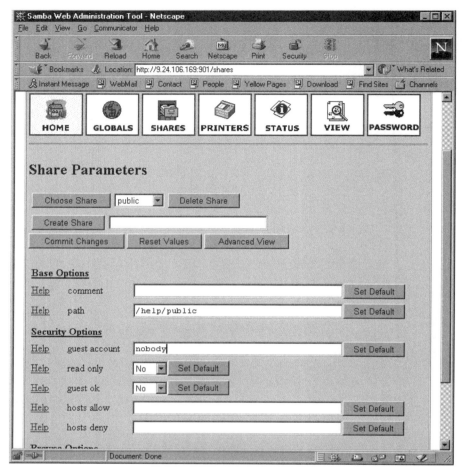

Figure 128. Entering the new share parameters

5. Fill in the necessary parameters. If you need to set some advanced parameters also, click **Advanced View** and you will see all available parameters. After you typed in all you want, click **Commit Changes** to save your new share.

6. You can see the changed smb.conf configuration file by selecting **View** from the SWAT Web page. You will see a window similar to Figure 129.

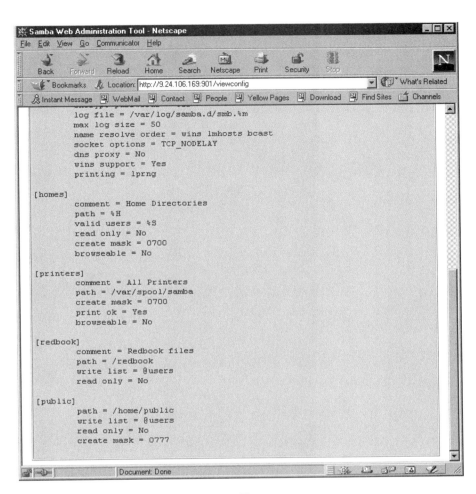

```
              log file = /var/log/samba.d/smb.%m
              max log size = 50
              name resolve order = wins lmhosts bcast
              socket options = TCP_NODELAY
              dns proxy = No
              wins support = Yes
              printing = lprng

[homes]
              comment = Home Directories
              path = %H
              valid users = %S
              read only = No
              create mask = 0700
              browseable = No

[printers]
              comment = All Printers
              path = /var/spool/samba
              create mask = 0700
              print ok = Yes
              browseable = No

[redbook]
              comment = Redbook files
              path = /redbook
              write list = @users
              read only = No

[public]
              path = /home/public
              write list = @users
              read only = No
              create mask = 0777
```

Figure 129. Viewing smb.conf configuration file

7. Restart the Samba server.

You have just created your first usable share on the Samba server. Be friendly and share it with other users!

6.2.4.6 Restarting the Samba server

The Samba server can be restarted from the **Status** section. To get to this section click the **Status** icon on any SWAT Web page. You will see a window similar to Figure 130.

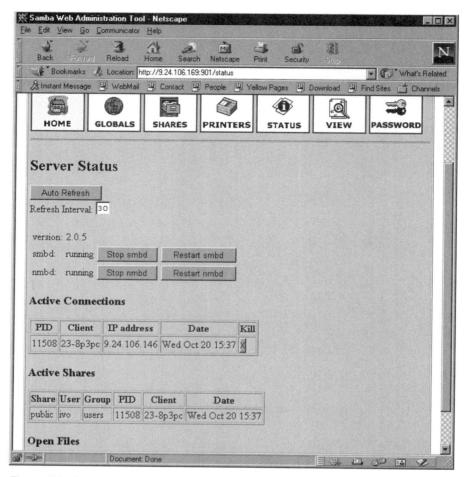

Figure 130. Restarting Samba server

To restart Samba server, simply click **Restart smbd.** On this page you can also restart just the WINS server by clicking **Restart nmbd.**

6.2.4.7 Printers

In the printers section you can view, modify, or add printers. The operations for handling printers are the same as for handling shares. You can access the printer settings by clicking the **Printers** icon on the SWAT Web page similar to Figure 131.

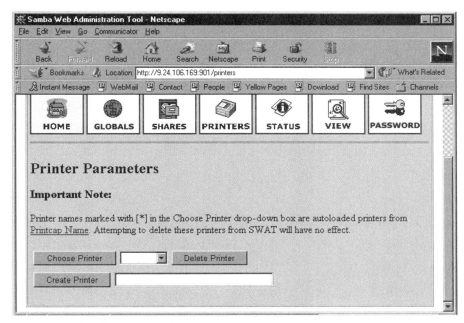

Figure 131. SWAT printers section

If you want to view the settings for a specific printer, then select the printer from the list as shown in Figure 132.

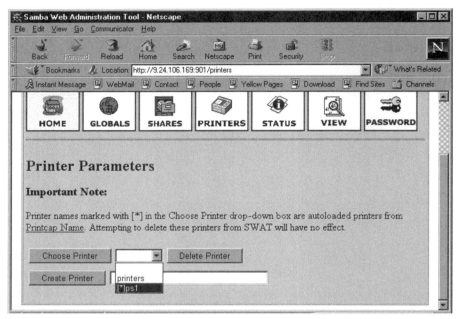

Figure 132. Selecting printer

After you have selected the printer click **Choose Printer** to view its properties. You will see a window similar to Figure 133.

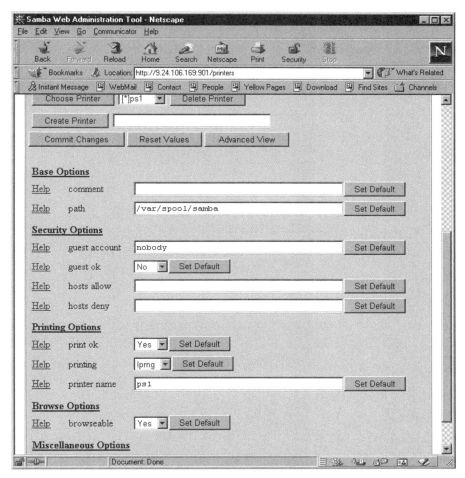

Figure 133. Printer properties

In this view you can also modify the printer properties. When you are done, save settings by clicking **Commit Changes.**

6.2.4.8 Status

In this section you can check the status of the Samba server. Here you can see all current connections and open files. You can also start or restart the Samba server or just its components. You can access the printer settings by clicking the **Status** icon on the SWAT Web page similar to Figure 134.

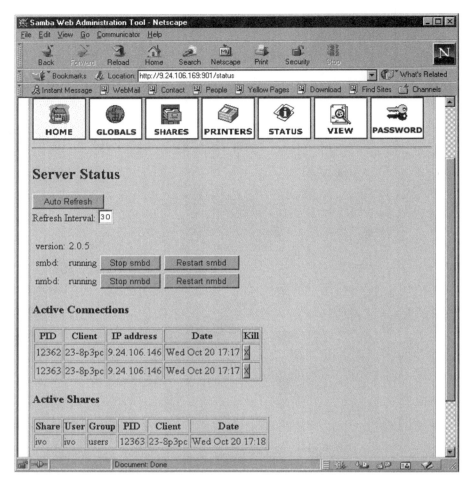

Figure 134. Status section

6.2.4.9 View

In this section you can see the current smb.conf configuration file. You can access printer settings by clicking the **View** icon on the SWAT Web page similar to Figure 135.

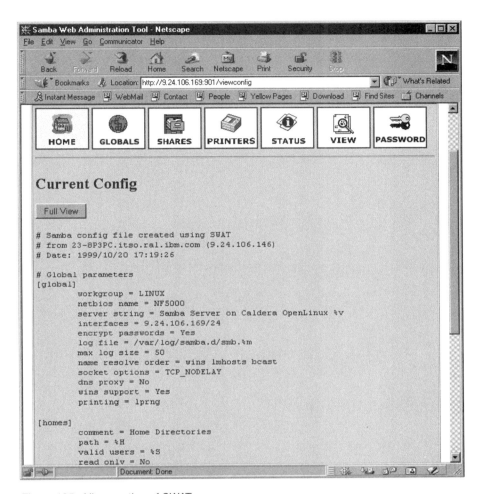

Figure 135. View section of SWAT

6.2.4.10 Password

In this section you can manage the passwords of your Samba users. You can access printer settings by clicking the **Password** icon on the SWAT Web page similar to Figure 136.

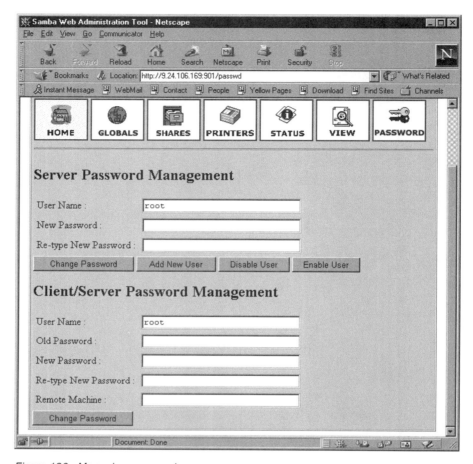

Figure 136. Managing passwords

6.3 Configuration and tuning hints

Try to play with the following socket options to your smb.conf file:

```
TCP_NODELAY IPTOS_LOWDELAY SO_SNDBUF=4096 SO_RCVBUF=4096
```

These options may increase the performance on local networks, but your mileage may vary. The documents

/usr/doc/packages/samba/textdocs/Speed.txt

and

/usr/doc/packages/samba/textdocs/Speed2.txt

will give you some more background about these and a few other tuning options.

6.4 Sources of additional information

Samba is very well documented. A wealth of document files can be found in the directory /usr/doc/packages/samba.

You can find more information at the official Web site of the Samba project:

```
http://www.samba.org
```

Using Samba by Robert Eckstein, David Collier-Brown and Peter Kelly, published by O'Reilly, is also a good book. It is available online at:

```
http://www.oreilly.com/catalog/samba/chapter/book/index.html
```

And there are always good how-to documents on the Linux Documentation project home page:

```
http://www.linuxdoc.org/HOWTO/SMB-HOWTO.html
```

Chapter 7. Apache and IBM HTTP Servers

The Apache Web server is the most popular Web server software on today's Internet. According to the NetCraft Web server survey at `http://www.netcraft.com/survey/`, more than 55% of all surveyed Web servers (more than 7.3 million) were running a version of Apache (as of the time of this writing). Apache is a very successful collaborative Open Source project. The Web site for Apache is `http://www.apache.org`. Because of the free availability of the full source code, it is a very flexible and powerful Web server solution. There are also a lot of additional modules, which can be used in combination with the Apache main program. Some popular examples are PHP (PHP: Hypertext Preprocessor, an embedded HTML scripting language), mod_perl (an embedded perl interpreter) and mod_ssl for secure transactions. More Apache modules can be downloaded from the Apache Module Registry at:

> `http://modules.apache.org.`

Some of key features of Apache are:

- Implements the latest protocols, including HTTP/1.1 (RFC2068).

- Is highly configurable and extensible with third-party modules.

- Can be customized by writing "modules" using the Apache module API.

- Provides full source code and comes with an unrestrictive license.

- Runs on most versions of UNIX (including Linux) without modification.

- DBM databases for authentication, which allow you to easily set up password-protected pages with enormous numbers of authorized user, without bogging down the server. A wide variety of SQL databases can be used for authentication too (using additional modules).

- Customized responses to errors and problems, which allow you to set up files, or even CGI scripts, which are returned by the server in response to errors and problems. For example, you can set up a script to intercept 500 server errors and perform on-the-fly diagnostics for both users and yourself.

- Multiple DirectoryIndex directives, which allow you to "say" `DirectoryIndex index.html index.cgi`, which instructs the server to either send back index.html or run index.cgi when a directory URL is requested, whichever it finds in the directory.

- Unlimited numbers of alias and redirect directives that may be declared in the config files.

- Content negotiation, the ability to automatically serve clients of varying sophistication and HTML level compliance, with documents which offer the best representation of information that the client is capable of accepting.

- Multi-homed servers, which allow the server to distinguish between requests made to different IP addresses (mapped to the same machine).

7.1 The IBM HTTP Server

The IBM HTTP Server powered by Apache is based on the Apache HTTP Server. In addition to Linux, this HTTP Server also runs on AIX, Solaris and Windows NT. See the home page at:

```
http://www-4.ibm.com/software/webservers/httpservers/
```

IBM HTTP Server for Linux offers the following additional features:

- Remote Configuration: a browser-based configuration tool to allow manipulation of the server configuration via a GUI.

- SNMP Support: Simple Network Management Protocol (SNMP) is a well-established protocol for managing and gathering information about servers remotely. This new support allows IBM HTTP Server to be managed by the SNMP protocol.

- LDAP: The IBM HTTP Server Lightweight Directory Access Protocol (LDAP) plug-in allows authentication and authorization (which is required when accessing a protected resource) to be performed by an LDAP server, thereby greatly decreasing the administrative overhead for maintaining user and group information locally for each Web server.

- Machine Translation Support: This new function, when used with an available IBM Machine Translation Engine, enables the IBM HTTP Server to translate English Web pages into other languages without human intervention. This permits a Web site visitor to read the page in his native language, effectively broadening the reach of your Web site. IBM Machine Translation Engines are included in the WebSphere Application Server 3.0 and include German, Simplified Chinese and Traditional Chinese. Additional languages will be available in the future.

- Support for SSL secure connections: The IBM HTTP Server powered by Apache supports both the SSL Version 2 and SSL Version 3 protocols. This protocol, implemented using IBM security libraries, ensures that data transferred between a client and a server remains private. Once your server has a digital certificate, SSL-enabled browsers such as Netscape Navigator and Microsoft Internet Explorer can communicate securely with your server using the SSL protocol. The IBM HTTP Server powered by

Apache supports client authentication, configurable cipher specifications, and session ID caching for improving SSL performance on the UNIX platforms.

- Fast Response Cache Accelerator: The Cache Accelerator can dramatically improve the performance of the IBM HTTP Server powered by Apache when serving static pages, for example, text and image files. Because the Cache Accelerator cache is automatically loaded during server operation, you are not required to list the files to be cached in your server configuration file. In addition, the server will automatically recache changed pages and remove outdated pages from the cache. The Cache Accelerator provides support for caching on Web servers with single and multiple TCP/IP adapters.

7.2 Apache HTTP Server installation

The Apache HTTP Server is installed and started by default on SuSE Linux, because it is used for the online help system. You can verify the installation by querying the RPM database:

```
rpm -q apache
```

This command will return either the version number of the installed package or an error message, if the package is not installed. Refer to 3.1, "Adding and removing software packages using YaST" on page 51 for how to install the package if it is missing. The package window is located in series n - Network-Support (TCP/IP, UUCP, Mail, News). Apache will be automatically started on bootup, if the variable START_HTTP in the central configuration file /etc/rc.config is set to yes. See 3.6, "Changing the configuration file with YaST" on page 70 for methods to modify this variable. To start, stop or reload window (after a configuration change), run the script:

```
/usr/sbin/rcapache (start|stop|reload).
```

This file is a symbolic link to the init script in:

```
/sbin/init.d/apache.
```

In the SuSE default installation, Apache will serve HTML documents from the directory /usr/local/httpd/htdocs and CGI scripts from /usr/local/httpd/cgi-bin. If you installed the PHP module (mod_php), it will also execute PHP code, if the file ends on .php3. The access log file is in /var/log/httpd.access_log, the error log file is /var/log/httpd.error_log. The Apache configuration files reside in the subdirectory /etc/httpd.

If you now point your browser to the server's IP address, you should see the following start page (/usr/local/httpd/htdocs/index.html), when the Apache HTTP Server is running:

Figure 137. Apache startup page on SuSE Linux

7.3 IBM HTTP Server installation

To install the IBM HTTP Server on SuSE Linux, you need to perform the following steps.

For the IBM HTTP Server and the remote administration capabilities, download the tar files from the Web page:

```
http://www-4.ibm.com/software/webservers/httpservers/download.html
```

The HTTPServer.linux.glibc21.server.tar file contains the following packages:

- IBM_HTTP_Server-1.3.6-2.i386.rpm - the IHS Web server

- IBM_Apache_Source-1.3.6-2.i386.rpm - the Apache 1.3.6 sources
- Readme.httpserver - Installation notes

The HTTPServer.linux.glibc21.admin.tar file contains the following packages:

- IBM_Admin_Server-1.3.6-1.i386.rpm - GUI Administration Server
- IBM_Admin_Server_Forms-1.3.6-1.i386.rpm - Web forms for the GUI

There are some additional packages such as SNMP and SSL modules, that also can be installed. However, these will not be covered in this chapter. Please see the installation instructions at:

```
http://www-4.ibm.com/software/webservers/httpservers/doc/v136/readme_ht
tpserver.htm
```

After you have downloaded the "tarballs", move them to the directory /tmp and extract them with the command:

```
tar xvf HTTPServer.linux.glibc21.server.tar
tar xvf HTTPServer.linux.glibc21.admin.tar
```

This will extract the above-listed RPM files from the tar archive into the subdirectory /tmp/IHS. You now need to become the root user (if you not already are). To avoid resource conflicts, you first have to shut down the currently running Apache Web server (if installed), by executing the following command:

```
rcapache stop
```

Also make sure, that it will not be started again after the next reboot by changing the variable START_HTTPD in /etc/rc.config to "no".

Now you need to install the packages with the following commands (assuming the packages reside in the current directory):

```
rpm -Uvh IBM_HTTP_Server-1.3.6-1.i386.rpm
rpm -Uhv IBM_Admin_Server-1.3.6-1.i386.rpm
rpm -Uhv IBM_Admin_Server_Forms-1.3.6-1.i386.rpm
```

The installation of the HTTP Server package will also attempt to start the server automatically. If this did not start, you might still have another HTTP Server running. Stop this one first, and try to restart the IBM HTTP Server with the following command:

```
/sbin/init.d/ibmhttpd start
```

If no errors are present on the command line or in the /opt/IBMHTTPServer/logs/error_log file, open the new HTTP Server's home page with your browser. You should see the following page:

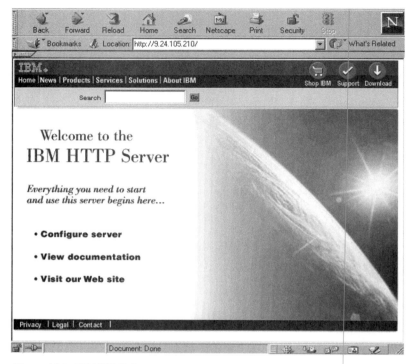

Figure 138. IBM HTTP Server startup page

If you still see the old Web server's startup page (see Figure 137), press Shift+Reload on the Netscape browser to force a reload of this page.

The basic installation of the IBM HTTP Server is now finished. In the default setup, it serves HTML pages from the directory /opt/IBMHTTPD/htdocs and CGI scripts from /opt/IBMHTTPD/cgi-bin. The log files reside in /opt/IBMHTTPD/logs.

7.3.1 Activating IBM HTTPD on system bootup

By default, the IBM HTTP Server has to be started manually after a system reboot. If you want to start it automatically, you have to add the startup script to the bootup procedure. Chapter 17, "The SuSE Linux boot concept" in the SuSE Linux 6.2 manual and the manual page init.d(7) give you a detailed description of these mechanisms.

If you want this server to be started on bootup, you have to create the correct symbolic links in the directory /sbin/init.d/rc2.d (if you start the system in runlevel 2, the default runlevel), or /sbin/init.d/rc3.d (If you use the graphical login, runlevel 3). You can do this manually with the following commands:

```
cd /sbin/init.d/rc2.d
ln -s ../ibmhttpd ./S67ibmhttpd
ln -s ../ibmhttpd ./K01ibmhttpd
```

This will start the IBM HTTP Server in runlevel 2 and make sure, that it will be properly shut down when switching into another runlevel (for example shutdown). Repeat the above last two steps in directory /sbin/init.d/rc3.d for runlevel 3.

SuSE Linux also ships with a runlevel configuration tool, called `rctab`, which can be used to configure the services to start in this runlevel. To add the script `ibmhttp` to this runlevel, run `rctab` with the following command line:

```
rctab -e -2
```

This will open an editor (vi by default, depending on the environment variable $EDITOR) that shows the sequence in which services will be started in this runlevel. Just move to the last entry in the list and add "ibmhttpd" at the first free slot (marked with a "-"). After saving this file, `rctab` will create the necessary symbolic links.

7.3.2 Setting up the Administration Server

You have to perform some preliminary steps before you can start using the Administration Server to be able to modify the configuration files of your IBM HTTP Server remotely.

The Administration Server tasks allow the Administration Server read/write/execute access to the necessary configuration files and one executable file. The Administration Server should obtain read/write access through a unique user ID and group, which must be created. The User and Group directives of the Administration Server's configuration file should be changed to the unique user ID and group. The Administration Server's configuration file's "group access permissions" should be changed to allow read/write "group access". In addition there is a utility program that should have "Group execute permissions" and "Set User ID Root permissions". This executable must run as root in order to request restarts for the IBM HTTP Server and the Administration Server.

To properly set up these prerequisites, these tasks can be performed by executing the script /opt/IBMHTTPserver/bin/setupadm. After the invocation, it will ask you a few questions and will give detailed information about each step it is performing. Enter the keywords marked in boldface in the following screens:

```
SuSE:/opt/IBMHTTPServer/bin # ./setupadm

****************************************************************
Please supply a User ID to run the Administration Server
We will create the USERID using System Administration tools
****************************************************************
[no default] -> wwwrun

****************************************************************
Please supply a GROUP NAME to run the Administration Server
We will create the Group using System Administration tools
****************************************************************
[no default] -> nogroup

****************************************************************
Please supply the Directory containing the files for
which a change in the permissions is necessary.
****************************************************************
[default: /opt/IBMHTTPServer/conf] -> [Enter]

****************************************************************
We will flag 'SetUserID for Root' as well as
update the Group, Group access permissions and
Group execute permissions, for file:
        /opt/IBMHTTPServer/bin/admrestart

This interface is necessary for Administration Server requests
to restart manage webservers
YES(default)-      ENTER 1
NO           -     ENTER 2
****************************************************************
[default: YES  - 1] -> [Enter]
```

```
****************************************************************
You may use WildCards (i.e *.conf)
Please supply a File Name for permission changes
Default will change file permissions for ALL files in directory
****************************************************************
[default: ALL FILES] -> [Enter]


These are the file(s) and directory for which we will be changing
Group permissions:

-rw-r--r--   1 root      root          4137 Jul 29 15:02 admin.conf
-rw-r--r--   1 root      root          4137 Jul 29 15:02 admin.conf.default
-rw-r--r--   1 root      root          6246 Jul 29 15:02 admin.msg
-rw-r--r--   1 root      root             1 Jul 29 15:02 admin.passwd
-rw-r--r--   1 root      root         30990 Oct 22 08:43 httpd.conf
-rw-r--r--   1 root      root         30989 Jul 29 14:58 httpd.conf.default
-r--r-----   1 root      root         46360 Jul 29 14:58 httpd.conf.sample
-rw-r--r--   1 root      root         12441 Jul 29 14:58 magic
-rw-r--r--   1 root      root         12441 Jul 29 14:58 magic.default
-rw-r--r--   1 root      root          7350 Jul 29 14:58 mime.types
-rw-r--r--   1 root      root          7350 Jul 29 14:58 mime.types.default
drwxr-xr-x   2 root      root          1024 Oct 22 08:43 /opt/IBMHTTPServer/conf

This is the file for which we will be adding 'set user ID' permission for Root:

-rwsr-x---   1 root      root         46807 Jul 29 15:02 /opt/IBMHTTPServer/bin/ad
mrestart


**************************************************
CONTINUE - Perform Changes ENTER 1
QUIT -      No Changes        ENTER 2
**************************************************
[default: QUIT - 2] -> 1
```

```
>>>Validating Group Name: 'nogroup'<<<
        Group Name: 'nogroup' already exists

>>>Validating UserID:wwwrun<<<
        UserID: 'wwwrun' already exists

>>>>>>>>>>>>>>>>>>>>>>>>>>>>>>>>>>>>>>>>>>>>>>>>>>>>>>>>>>>>>>
Changing Group:
CMD: 'chgrp  /opt/IBMHTTPServer/bin/admrestart'
<<<<<<<<<<<<<<<<<<<<<<<<<<<<<<<<<<<<<<<<<<<<<<<<<<<<<<<<<<<<<


>>>>>>>>>>>>>>>>>>>>>>>>>>>>>>>>>>>>>>>>>>>>>>>>>>>>>>>>>>>>>>
Change Group permissions and Add SetUserID permission for Root:
CMD: 'chmod  4750 /opt/IBMHTTPServer/bin/admrestart'
>>>>>>>>>>>>>>>>>>>>>>>>>>>>>>>>>>>>>>>>>>>>>>>>>>>>>>>>>>>>>>


>>>>>>>>>>>>>>>>>>>>>>>>>>>>>>>>>>>>>>>>>>>>>>>>>>>>>>>>>>>>>>
Changing Group:
CMD: 'chgrp  nogroup /opt/IBMHTTPServer/conf /opt/IBMHTTPServer/conf/* '
<<<<<<<<<<<<<<<<<<<<<<<<<<<<<<<<<<<<<<<<<<<<<<<<<<<<<<<<<<<<<


>>>>>>>>>>>>>>>>>>>>>>>>>>>>>>>>>>>>>>>>>>>>>>>>>>>>>>>>>>>>>>
Changing Group permissions:
CMD: 'chmod  g+rw /opt/IBMHTTPServer/conf /opt/IBMHTTPServer/conf/*'
<<<<<<<<<<<<<<<<<<<<<<<<<<<<<<<<<<<<<<<<<<<<<<<<<<<<<<<<<<<<<
Here are the new file(s) and directory permissions:

drwxrwxr-x  2 root     nogroup      1024 Oct 22 08:43 /opt/IBMHTTPServer/conf
-rw-rw-r--  1 root     nogroup      4137 Jul 29 15:02 admin.conf
-rw-rw-r--  1 root     nogroup      4137 Jul 29 15:02 admin.conf.default
-rw-rw-r--  1 root     nogroup      6246 Jul 29 15:02 admin.msg
-rw-rw-r--  1 root     nogroup         1 Jul 29 15:02 admin.passwd
-rw-rw-r--  1 root     nogroup     30990 Oct 22 08:43 httpd.conf
-rw-rw-r--  1 root     nogroup     30989 Jul 29 14:58 httpd.conf.default
-r--rw----  1 root     nogroup     46360 Jul 29 14:58 httpd.conf.sample
-rw-rw-r--  1 root     nogroup     12441 Jul 29 14:58 magic
-rw-rw-r--  1 root     nogroup     12441 Jul 29 14:58 magic.default
-rw-rw-r--  1 root     nogroup      7350 Jul 29 14:58 mime.types
-rw-rw-r--  1 root     nogroup      7350 Jul 29 14:58 mime.types.default

Here is a file with 'set user ID' permission for Root:

-rwsr-x---  1 root     nogroup     46807 Jul 29 15:02 /opt/IBMHTTPServer/bin/ad
mrestart
Changes Completed
```

```
********************************************************************
Configuration file: '/opt/IBMHTTPServer/conf/admin.conf'
will be saved as '/opt/IBMHTTPServer/conf/admin.conf.13:48:05_295'
Do you wish to update the Administration Server Configuration file
CONTINUE  enter 1
EXIT      enter 2
********************************************************************
[default: QUIT - 2] -> 1
USER DONE
GRoup  DONE
Successfully updated configuration file
Old configuration file saved as '/opt/IBMHTTPServer/conf/admin.conf.13:48:05_295
SuSE:/opt/IBMHTTPServer/bin #
```

To summarize the above steps: the Administration Server will be running under the user name "wwwrun" and the group "nobody."

The Administration Server is basically just another Web server, running in parallel with the main IBM HTTP Server(s). Therefore it has to be started separately and listens on another TCP port (8008 by default). By default, it has to be started manually. If you also want to start it on system bootup, you have to integrate the start script into the bootup procedure. Copy the file /opt/IBMHTTPServer/bin/adminctl to the directory /sbin/init.d and follow the steps described in 7.3.1, "Activating IBM HTTPD on system bootup" on page 148, using adminctl as the init script name instead of ibmhttpd this time.

The Administration Server is protected with a user name and password. You can create an entry in the password file /opt/IBMHTTPServer/bin/conf/admin.passwd by issuing the following command from inside the directory /opt/IBMHTTPServer/bin:

```
./htpasswd -m ../conf/admin.passwd <user name>
```

Enter the password for the required user name twice. It is possible to have more than one user name in this password file, if you need to differentiate between multiple administrators.

Now you can start the Administration Server by running the following command:

```
/opt/IBMHTTPServer/bin/adminctl start
```

After clicking **Configure Server,** shown in Figure 138 on page 148, you need to enter the user name and password you defined for the Administration Server user. If entered correctly, you will see the welcome page of the Administration Server:

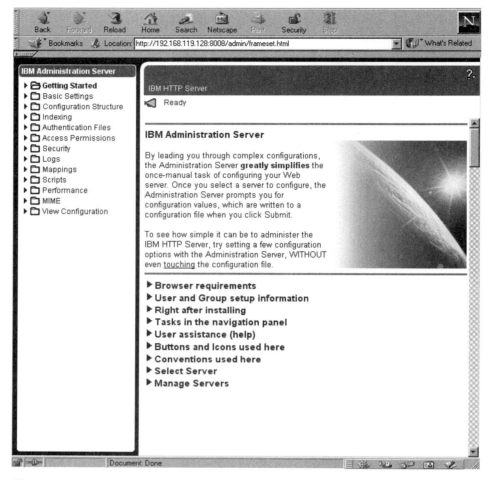

Figure 139. Administration Server startup window

You are now ready to start adjusting the configuration of your main Web server according to your needs. Please see the online documentation for help about the different configuration options.

7.4 General performance tips

Configuring Apache for maximum performance is dependent on many parameters. Apache is very flexible and gaining the best performance may require some research. A very informative document about Apache performance tuning can be found on the Apache Web site:

```
http://www.apache.org/docs/misc/perf-tuning.html
```

In short, experiment with the following options:

- Set FollowSymLinks option unless you really don't want it.
- Set AllowOverride to None unless you really need it.
- Explicitly list all DirectoryIndex file options from most to least commonly used.
- Tune KeepAliveTimeout starting with 3 ranging to 30 per content and connection types.
- Apache (and the IBM HTTP Server as well) use multiple processes to handle individual requests. Tune StartServers starting with 64 increasing in steps of 32 until performance drops off. Tune MaxClients starting with the value of StartServers. **Note:** Scaling performance can fall off dramatically if Max Clients is too large!
- For SMP systems listening on a single socket, try recompiling after defining SINGLE_LISTEN_UNSERIALIZED_ACCEPT.

A helpful utility to benchmark your Apache server is ab. In its simplest form, you can call it like this:

```
ab http://www.your-server.com/index.html
```

The following are ab options:

```
SuSE:/usr/src # ab -h
Usage: ab [options] [http://]hostname[:port]/path
Options are:
    -n requests     Number of requests to perform
    -c concurrency  Number of multiple requests to make
    -t timelimit    Seconds to max. wait for responses
    -p postfile     File containg data to POST
    -T content-type Content-type header for POSTing
    -v verbosity    How much troubleshooting info to print
    -w              Print out results in HTML tables
    -x attributes   String to insert as table attributes
    -y attributes   String to insert as tr attributes
    -z attributes   String to insert as td or th attributes
    -V              Print version number and exit
    -k              Use HTTP KeepAlive feature
    -h              Display usage information (this message)
```

Chapter 8. Packet filtering with IP Chains

Whenever you connect your computer to today's Internet, you are exposed to intruders from the outside. There are thousands of potential hackers just waiting to get into your computer to do damage or maybe to steal information. Therefore you schould set up some protective measures against them!

A very efficient way of blocking malicious attackers is IP packet filtering. The Linux kernel includes functions that enable it to analyze TCP/IP data packets by means of applying certain filter rules on them. This can be done for incoming as well as outgoing traffic.

8.1 What is a firewall?

As you can tell from the name, a firewall is a wall that protects what is on one side of the wall from fire on the other side. In the computer world a firewall protects you from the outside world, so nobody can set fire to your computer. Usually firewalls are used to protect an internal network from the outside world. You can also use a firewall on a single computer with a dial-up connection to the Internet. When you install a firewall to protect your internal network, every computer that wants to talk to a computer on the internal network must ask the firewall for permission. If the permission is not granted, access will be denied.

8.2 What can you do with Linux firewall?

With a Linux firewall, here are some of the possibilities:

- You can protect your internal network connected to the Internet from outside intruders.

- You can perform Network Address Translation (NAT), which allows local computers on your network to use Internet resources using unofficial IP addresses. This is also called IP masquerading.

- You can filter information going in or out of your internal network or just on one computer.

- You can use your Linux server as a gateway between two different types of networks, for example connecting token-ring and Ethernet worlds. This can be a cheap solution in comparison to buying an expensive router for this task.

- You can share your single dial-up Internet connection with others.

8.3 What do you need to run an IP packet filter?

To set up a packet filtering server with IP Chains, your Linux installation needs to meet some requirements:

1. You need a Linux kernel Version 2.2.x or higher. It is recommended that you use the latest available stable version. The kernel has to be compiled with appropriate modules for IP forwarding, IP masquerading, and IP firewalling. It is recommended that you compile all your networking options and available modules. The default kernel on SuSE Linux is already configured for this purpose.

2. Loadable kernel modules Version 2.1.121 or newer

3. IP Chains utilities 1.3.8 or newer

The default installation of SuSE Linux 6.2 meets all these requirements except that the kernel is not optimized to be used as a router. So if you want to increase the performance of the routing process you should recompile the kernel by choosing the option **IP - optimize as router not host**. However, this is only necessary on a high-bandwidth network. If your outside line to the Internet is only a 56 kbps modem connection, even an old 486 computer is sufficient for this task.

8.4 Network configuration for a firewall implementation

In this section we describe our lab network setup for implementing a firewall solution.

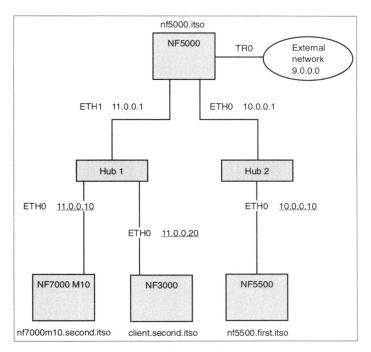

Figure 140. Lab network setup for firewall solution

You can see that our network setup contains from the following systems:

- Netfinity 5000 with three Network Interface Cards (NICs) acts as a gateway. The NICs have been configured with the following settings:

  a. eth0 - 10.0.0.1

  a. eth1 - 11.0.0.1

  a. tr0 - 9.24.104.202

- Netfinity 5500 with one NIC and the following settings:

  a. eth0 - 10.0.0.10, default gateway 10.0.0.1

- Netfinity 7000M10 with one NIC and the following settings:

  a. eth0 - 11.0.0.10, default gateway 11.0.0.1

- Netfinity 3000 with one NIC and the following settings:

  a. eth0 - 11.0.0.20, default gateway 11.0.0.1

As you can see, we have two separate networks, 10.0.0.0 and 11.0.0.0. These networks are connected to a Linux server that is acting as a gateway (router) between them. You see that our gateway is connected to the Internet

with a registered IP address. We enabled IP forwarding on the server that
was acting as the gateway.

8.5 How to permanently enable IP forwarding

On SuSE Linux, the network subsystem is started by executing the init script
during the server startup:

```
/sbin/init.d/network
```

For security reasons, IP forwarding is not enabled by default. To enable it
open the file /etc/rc.config in a text editor and look for the following line:

```
IP_FORWARD=no
```

and change it to:

```
IP_FORWARD=yes
```

You can also use YaST to modify the content of this variable. See 3.6,
"Changing the configuration file with YaST" on page 70 for information about
this.

IP forwarding will now be enabled on the next system bootup. If you want to
activate this feature immediately, enter the following command:

```
echo "1" > /proc/sys/net/ipv4/ip_forward
```

Now your server is ready to act as a router. You can try this by pinging to the
tr0 interface 9.24.104.202 from a machine on 11.0.0.0 network. If the ping is
successful, your router is working correctly. You will see a screen similar to
Figure 141.

```
[root@client /root]# ping 9.24.104.202
PING 9.24.104.202 (9.24.104.202): 56 data bytes
64 bytes from 9.24.104.202: icmp_seq=0 ttl=255 time=0.7 ms
64 bytes from 9.24.104.202: icmp_seq=1 ttl=255 time=0.3 ms
64 bytes from 9.24.104.202: icmp_seq=2 ttl=255 time=0.3 ms
64 bytes from 9.24.104.202: icmp_seq=3 ttl=255 time=0.3 ms
64 bytes from 9.24.104.202: icmp_seq=4 ttl=255 time=0.3 ms

--- 9.24.104.202 ping statistics ---
5 packets transmitted, 5 packets received, 0% packet loss
round-trip min/avg/max = 0.3/0.3/0.7 ms
[root@client /root]# []
```

Figure 141. Ping after enabling IP forwarding

8.6 Your first IP Chains success

It does not make sense to have a router without deploying it. In this section, we will set up IP masquerading manually on the gateway. To access the external network 9.0.0.0 from the internal network 11.0.0.0, use the IP masquerading function of IP Chains. Follow these steps on the gateway server to set up File Transfer Protocol (FTP) access from the internal network 11.0.0.0 to external network 9.0.0.0:

4. First load the kernel module for FTP masquerading:

   ```
   /sbin/modprobe ip_masq_ftp
   ```

   If you want to use other protocols, such as Real Audio and Internet Relay Chat (IRC), you can load these modules as well.

5. Setup the timeout for IP masquerading:

   ```
   /sbin/ipchains -M -S 8000 20 200
   ```

   The parameters have the following meaning:

   a. `8000` - timeout value for TCP sessions in seconds

   b. `20` - timeout value for TCP sessions after a FIN packet in seconds

   c. `200` - timeout value for UDP packets in seconds

   You can adjust these settings to meet your needs.

6. Change the built-in policy for forwarding by disabling it for all IP addresses:

   ```
   /sbin/ipchains -P forward DENY
   ```

7. Add the policy for enabling the forwarding with masquerading for your internal networks:

   ```
   /sbin/ipchains -A forward -s 10.0.0.0/24 -j MASQ
   /sbin/ipchains -A forward -s 11.0.0.0/24 -j MASQ
   ```

You are now ready to try your setup. Execute the following command from a computer on the 11.0.0.0 network:

```
/usr/bin/ftp <server>
```

Where `server` is an FTP server on the external network (in our example 9.0.0.0). You will see a screen similar to Figure 142.

```
[root@client /root]# ftp 9.24.106.49
Connected to 9.24.106.49.
220 TPIVO2 IBM TCP/IP for OS/2 - FTP Server ver 19:29:50 on Sep  2 1998 ready.
Name (9.24.106.49:root): ivo
331 Password required for ivo.
Password:
230 User ivo logged in.
Remote system type is OS/2.
ftp> █
```

Figure 142. FTP after IP masquerading setup

Congratulations! You have just enabled access from the internal network to the external network by using IP masquerading.

8.7 Setting up IP masquerading on SuSE Linux

SuSE Linux already contains preconfigured scripts to set up IP masquerading properly on system bootup. Make sure you installed the package firewall, which belongs to package series n - Network-Support (TCP/IP, UUCP, Mail, News) and the package ipchains. You can use YaST to install this package. See 3.1, "Adding and removing software packages using YaST" on page 51 for information about how to accomplish this task.

Note

The package firewall has been replaced with a newer version called firewalls in SuSE Linux 6.3. The configuration is done in the /etc/rc.firewall file and the documentation can be found in the user manual and in the /usr/doc/packages/firewalls/SuSEfirewall-technical.txt file.

If you want to configure IP masquerading, open the configuration file /etc/rc.config in a text editor or use YaST to modify the content of this file following the instructions in 3.6, "Changing the configuration file with YaST" on page 70.

The following variables are used for setting up masquerading on SuSE Linux:

Table 20. IP masquerading variables in /etc/rc.config

Variable	Description
MSQ_START="yes"	Start IP masquerading on system bootup.
MSQ_NETWORKS="10.0.0.0/24 11.0.0.0/24"	Space-separated list of local networks that should be masqueraded. You can specify an arbitrary number of single IP addresses or networks here.

Variable	Description
MSQ_DEV="tr0"	The networking device on which masquerading will take place. This is the device pointing to the outside network.
MSQ_MODULES="<list of modules>"	Kernel modules for masquerading special network protocols.

These options will be used by the init script /sbin/init.d/masquerade.

If you want to activate masquerading using the definitions in /etc/rc.config, run the following command:

```
rcmasquerade start
```

This will apply the IP chains rules to the masquerading device. If MSQ_START is set to yes, IP masquerading will be activated on the next system bootup.

8.8 How IP packets travel through the gateway

In this section we will explain how IP Chains basically works. You can see the path of an IP packet coming into your server in Figure 143.

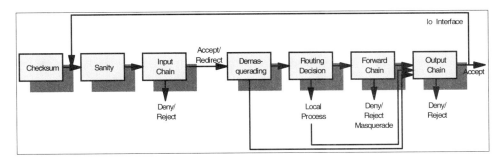

Figure 143. How the packet is travelling

The following are some short descriptions for each stage:

- Checksum - test, if the packet is corrupted or not.
- Sanity - Malformed packets are denied here.
- Input chain - This is the first real packet checking point. Packets can be rejected, denied or accepted.
- Demasquerade - If the packet is a reply to a previously masqueraded packet, it is demasqueraded and goes directly to the output chain.

- Routing decision - The routing code decides if this packet is for a local process or if it should be forwarded to a remote machine.

- Local process - a process running on the server can receive packets after this routing decision step, and can then send packets that will go through the routing decision step and the output chain afterwards.

- lo interface - if packets from a local process are destined for another local process, they will go through the output chain with interface set to "lo", then they will return to the input chain with interface "lo". The "lo" interface is usually called the loopback interface.

- Local - if the packet is not created by the local process, then the forward chain is checked.

- Forward chain - this is the checkpoint for all packets passing through this server to another.

- Output chain - this a checkpoint for all packets just before they are sent out.

As you can see from Figure 143, you have three places where you can check the packets following specific rules:

   a. Input chain
   b. Forward chain
   c. Output chain

Using the tool /sbin/ipchains you can set up your rules for packet checking.

Note

By default, all checking policies are set to ACCEPT. This means that all packets can come in, go through, or go out from your server without any restrictions.

You can see the current checking policies by executing:

```
/sbin/ipchains -L
```

You will see a screen similar to Figure 144.

```
[root@client /root]# ipchains -L
Chain input (policy ACCEPT):
Chain forward (policy ACCEPT):
Chain output (policy ACCEPT):
[root@client /root]# 
```

Figure 144. Listing the default IP Chains policies

8.9 Using IP Chains

With the `/sbin/ipchains` command you can create, change or delete your own policies for checking packets or you can modify built-in policies. You cannot delete the built-in chains, but you can append your rules to the existing chains or even create your own chains.

To manage whole chains you can use the parameters described in Table 21.

Table 21. Parameters for managing whole chains

Parameter	Description
-N	Create a new chain
-X	Delete an empty chain
-P	Change policy for a built-in chain
-L	List rules in a chain
-F	Flush the rules of a chain
-Z	Zero the packets and byte counters on all rules in a chain

For manipulating rules inside a chain, you can use the parameters explained in Table 22.

Table 22. Parameters for managing rules in the chain

Parameter	Description
-A	Append a new rule to a chain
-I	Insert a new rule in a chain at some position
-R	Replace a rule at some position in a chain
-D	Delete a rule at some position in a chain

And there are some more operations for managing masquerading. They are described in Table 23.

Table 23. Parameters for managing masquerading

Parameter	Description
-M -L	List the currently masqueraded connections
-M -S	Set masquerading timeout values

8.9.1 How to create a rule

The most common syntax for creating a new rule is:

```
/sbin/ipchains -A input -s source -p protocol -j action
```

The parameters are described in Table 24.

Table 24. IPChains parameters

Parameter	Description
-A	Append a new rule to the chain
source	IP address or host name of the source
protocol	Type of the protocol to which one a rule is applied
action	What will happen with the packet: 1) ACCEPT - packet will be accepted 2) REJECT - packet will be rejected 3) DENY - packet is dropped since it was not received 4) MASQ - packet will be masqueraded 5) REDIRECT - packet is redirected to local port 6) RETURN - fail off the chain immediately

---
Note

Redirecting packets to a local port using the REDIRECT action makes sense only in combination with masquerading for a transparent proxy server.

For example, if you want to create a rule for denying ICMP protocol packets (which are used when you execute the `ping` command) for a specific IP address, you will do this by executing the command:

```
/sbin/ipchains -A input -s IP_address -p icmp -j DENY
```

If you omit the protocol definition, all packet types will be denied. For example, if you want to block access to your machine from the network 11.0.0.0 with the subnet mask 255.255.255.0 you can do this by executing the following command:

```
/sbin/ipchains -A inout -s 11.0.0.0/255.255.255.0 -j DENY
```

or by typing:

```
/sbin/ipchains -A input -s 11.0.0.0/24 -j DENY
```

As you can see, the subnet mask can be specified with the number of used bits for that mask.

The command for not allowing any traffic from your server to the network 11.0.0.0 with subnet mask 255.255.255.0 will look like this:

```
/sbin/ipchains -A output -d 11.0.0.0/24 -j DENY
```

We used the "-d" parameter for specifying the destination address here.

8.9.1.1 Using the inversion flag

You can also use the inversion option "!" on some of the parameters. This means that this rule will be applied to everything else except for the parameters specified after "!". For example, if you want to deny packets coming from all IP addresses except from network 10.0.0.0 with subnet mask 255.255.255.0, you can do this by executing the following command:

```
/sbin/ipchains -A input -s ! 10.0.0.0/24 -j DENY
```

> **Note**
>
> The rules you entered at the command line are not permanent. They will be gone the next time you restart your server.

8.9.2 Making the rules permanent

There are two scripts available for making the rules permanent. To save all rules you created on the command line, you can execute the following command:

```
/sbin/ipchains-save > /etc/ipchains.conf
```

If you execute this command without a file name, the rules will be sent to the standard output.

You can then restore these saved rules by executing the following command:

```
cat /etc/ipchains.conf | /sbin/ipchains-restore
```

So if you want your saved rules to be enabled whenever you reboot your system, create a new init script using the template in /sbin/init.d/skeleton which runs the following command in its start section:

```
cat /etc/ipchains | /sbin/ipchains-restore
```

Now add the startup of this script to the bootup process using rctab. See 7.3.1, "Activating IBM HTTPD on system bootup" on page 148 for how to add init scripts to the bootup procedure. It should be started immediately after the network scripts have been executed.

8.10 Sources of additional information

You can find more information on the official Linux IP Firewall Chains page:

`http://www.rustcorp.com/linux/ipchains`

There is a special how-to about firewalling and masquerading on SuSE Linux:

`http://www.bb-zone.com/FWHowTo/index.html`

And there is a very good how-to document about firewalling on the Linux Documentation project Web site:

`http://www.linuxdoc.org/HOWTO/Firewall-HOWTO.html`

Chapter 9. DHCP - Dynamic Host Configuration Protocol

With the ever-decreasing number of available IP addresses along with the headache of maintaining static IPs, DHCP has become a necessity in most TCP/IP computing environments.

9.1 What is DHCP?

DHCP stands for Dynamic Host Configuration Protocol. When using TCP/IP, a computer system needs a unique IP address to communicate with other computer systems. Without DHCP, the IP address must be entered manually at each computer system. DHCP lets network administrators distribute IP addresses from a central location without having to actively manage each individual address.

With DHCP, IP addresses are distributed through pools, usually broken up by subnet. Leases are given out for a specific time period for each address. The process of managing leases is done by the DHCP server. Once a lease has expired, the DHCP server will try and contact the client or the client will contact the server to renew the lease. If the server cannot contact the client, the IP address is returned to the pool and will be available for the next client in need of an address.

9.2 Why should you use DHCP?

In the past, you had to have a static IP address for every device on a network. With the increasing number of computers accessing the Internet, the pool of available addresses is quickly diminishing. Network administrators can significantly reduce the number of IP addresses they need by using DHCP.

Even on smaller networks, keeping track of individual IP addresses can be a maintenance-intensive task. With DHCP, the server does all of the maintenance, mapping IP addresses to MAC addresses and tracking lease times. Administrators can adjust lease times, expand or reduce pools, and change gateways or DNS addresses, all from a central location.

9.3 Implementation on Linux

In this section we will discuss how to implement a DHCP server on Linux.

At first you have to install the DHCP server binaries, if they are not already installed. You can verify this with `rpm` on the command line or by using YaST.

169

See 3.1, "Adding and removing software packages using YaST" on page 51 for a description of this procedure. The package dhcp is available on the SuSE Linux CD set in the package series n (Network support).

After installing the package, use your text editor of choice to create the configuration file /etc/dhcpd.conf.

The following sample dhcpd.conf file is rather simple. We designate a default lease time of 600 seconds (10 minutes) but we will let clients request up to a 7200-second (2-hour) lease time. We include a recommended subnet mask of 255.255.255.0 and a broadcast address of 192.168.119.255. Other options we specify include a default gateway (router), a nameserver, and the domain name.

We are using a private 192.168.119.0 class C subnet for our subnet specifics. For our DHCP pool we will be giving out the addresses numbered from 15 to 100 for a total of 85 addresses. The rest can be used for static addresses.

```
default-lease-time 600;
max-lease-time 7200;
option subnet-mask 255.255.255.0;
option broadcast-address 192.168.119.255;
option routers 192.168.119.1;
option domain-name-servers 192.168.1.128;
option domain-name "ibm.com";

subnet 192.168.119.0 netmask 255.255.255.0 {
range 192.168.119.15 192.168.119.100;
}
```

Most options are pretty self-explanatory. The keyword range in the subnet section defines the range of IP numbers that are being leased to the clients. You are not limited to a single subnet. You are allowed to have shared network specific parameters, multiple subnet specific parameters, group parameters, and host-specific parameters. You can define multiple ranges, assign specific IP addresses based on the hardware address of the client, and specify a WINS server if needed.

More information is available from the dhcpd.conf(5) man page and in the README files below /usr/doc/packages/dhcp.

The DHCP server needs a place to keep track of already assigned leases. They are stored in the file /var/state/dhcp/dhcpd.leases.

To start the DHCP daemon type:

```
rcdhcp start
```

If you want to start the DHCP server on bootup, set the variable START_DHCPD in /etc/rc.config to "yes". You may also define a network interface, if you have multiple network interfaces and only want it to listen on one of them. Just set the variable DHCPD_INTERFACE to the desired value (for example eth0). See 3.6, "Changing the configuration file with YaST" on page 70 for instructions how to modify rc.config with YaST.

9.4 Setting up a DCHP relay agent

The dhcp package also contains a DHCP relay agent called dhcrelay. Since DHCP clients use network broadcasts to query a DHCP server for an IP address, the server usually has to reside on the same network as the client, because routers generally do not forward broadcasts. When a query is received, dhcrelay forwards it to the list of DHCP servers specified. When a reply is received, it is broadcast or unicast on the network from whence the original request came. The DHCP relay agent is preconfigured to run on SuSE Linux and also belongs to the DHCP package. If you want to use it, simply set the following two variables in /etc/rc.config:

```
START_DHCRELAY="yes"
DHCRELAY_SERVERS="102.234.2.1 110.23.4.32"
```

The first variable determines if the relay agent should be started on bootup. The second variable defines the IP addresses of the DHCP server to forward requests to. To start the DHCP relay daemon from the command line, run the following command

```
rcdhcrelay start
```

Chapter 10. Sendmail

Communicating with other people is one of the most desirable experiences in human history. Sending electronic mail is a way to communicate with people all over the globe. Electronic mail can be more reliable, cheaper and faster that ordinary mail.

10.1 What is Sendmail?

As you can tell from the name, Sendmail is used to send mail. However, Sendmail is not sending old fashioned mail, but electronic mail, which becomes more important every day. But in spite of that, Sendmail is basically acting as a post office. It receives mail from a sender and passes the mail on to the recipient post office. At the recipient post office, a local postman delivers mail to the recipient mailbox. Sendmail is a powerful Mail Transport Agent (MTA) and is used to pass the mail to another MTA, which can be Sendmail or some other application capable of handling electronic mail. If you are using electronic mail on your daily job, chances are high that every message you send or receive has been handled by a mail server running Sendmail at least once on its way through the Internet.

10.2 What can you do with Sendmail?

With Sendmail your Linux server can become a server for electronic mail. You can handle mail for users of a Linux server locally and users do not have to ask for mail accounts. The users on your Linux server will have their mailboxes locally and they will still be able to send mail to people anywhere. When you set up Sendmail, you can also offer mail service to the users who have accounts on other network servers that do not provide Internet mail service.

10.3 Starting up Sendmail in SuSE LInux

Sendmail is part of the base installation of SuSE Linux and will be installed by default. You can verify this by querying the RPM database with the command `rpm -q sendmail`. Most likely, it is already running in the background, if you chose the respective Sendmail option during the initial installation (see Figure 42 on page 35). Sendmail will use much of the system values that are already set, so it can run with minimal configuration on your part.

> **Note**
>
> In SuSE Linux 6.3, all Sendmail configuration options except for
> STMP=[yes|no] have been moved from /etc/re.config to
> /etc/rc.config.d/sendmail.re.config. This is important only if you edit the
> configuration file via a text editor. If you use YaST to modify these
> variables, you will not notice any difference.

Standard mail setups require very little work. Once you set up more advanced
mail routing features and multiple servers, it can get a little more complicated.
Most Sendmail configuration can be done by editing variables in the
configuration file /etc/rc.config and by modifying the files in /etc/mail. See 3.6,
"Changing the configuration file with YaST" on page 70 for methods to do this.
Do not forget to run SuSEconfig, after you manually changed any
Sendmail-related variables in /etc/config. The different variables and their
meaning are described in section 7.5, "Let's write - configuration of e-mail" in
the SuSE Linux 6.2 manual.

You need to be sure that the Sendmail process is running before you try
sending any mail. This can be done with the command:

```
rcsendmail status
```

If Sendmail is not running, check the variable SMTP in /etc/rc.config; it should
be set to "yes". Now start Sendmail with the following command:

```
rcsendmail start
```

10.4 Sending mail to local users

In the SuSE Linux default configuration, you should already be able to send
mail to local users on the system. You can test this by using a mail program
like pine or the mail command.

```
mail -s TESTMAIL lxuser
```

This command will send an e-mail to the local user lxuser with the subject
TESTMAIL. You can now enter the message text line by line. To finish the
message, enter a single dot on a new line and press Enter. If you now log in
as user lxuser, you should receive the message You have new mail. You could
now use any mail client to open this message locally or run the mail
command without parameters on the command line. Just press Enter to open
the first message for reading. Local-running mail clients will directly open the
mail spool file, which resides at /var/spool/mail/<username>. If you want to

track the processing of messages on your server, have a look at /var/log/mail, which is Sendmail's log file. This is the first place to check if any errors occur.

10.5 Setting up a simple mail server for a local net

This section explains how to set up a mail server for exchanging mail between users on a local net using a central mail server without a connection to the Internet.

Sendmail is closely related to a functional DNS setup. You should first set up a local name server that knows all participating hosts by host name. See Chapter 5, "DNS - Domain Name System" on page 103 for an example configuration. Alternatively, you can add all hosts to the mail server's /etc/hosts files.

Sendmail on SuSE Linux 6.2 does not allow remote hosts to use the local mail server for sending or relaying mail by default. This is a security feature to reduce the abuse of the mail server for sending out mass e-mail (spam). To allow hosts of your local domain to send mail via this server, you have to add them to the file /etc/mail/access:

```
my1dom.com RELAY
my2dom.com RELAY
```

This would allow all hosts from the domains my1dom.com and my2dom.com to use this mail server.

You need to run SuSEconfig and restart Sendmail by running rcsendmail restart to make these changes effective.

Alternatively you can add your local nets to the file /etc/mail/relay-domains:

```
192.168.0
192.168.1
```

This will allow all host from the Class C Networks 192.168.0.0/24 and 192.168.1.0/24 to use the mail server. You will also need to run SuSEconfig and restart Sendmail after modifying this file.

Now your clients should be able to use the IP address or host name of the mail server to send mail using the SMTP protocol. Each user needs to have a user account on the mail server. Your users can now send mail to other users by using their login names as e-maile-mail addresses. You can also create aliases for user names, if the login names are too cryptic. See 10.6, "Using the /etc/aliases file" on page 176 for information about this subject.

However, sending out mail messages is only one part of the story. Your clients need to be able to retrieve the mail from the mail server. The most popular method for retrieving mail from a mail server is the Post Office Protocol (POP). Linux can act as a POP server for your clients; you just have to install the package pop from package series n. This package also includes an IMAP deamon. IMAP is another popular method for remote mail retrieval and processing. After installing the package, configure your clients to use your mail server's IP address as their POP3 server and they should be able to retrieve the messages after providing the user name and password defined on the mail server.

10.6 Using the /etc/aliases file

By using the aliases file you can create aliases for users or groups that you send mail to. They do not even have to be on your system. This way when someone changes their name, their job, or e-mail address you just have to make changes in one place. The file has the format:

```
alias_name: name1, name2, ...
```

An example is shown in Figure 145.

```
dev_group: bjones, susegroup, mygroup@anywhere.not.org
susegroup: jsprat, fdown, jbgood
```

Figure 145. A sample /etc/aliases file

In the above example, an e-mail sent to susegroup will be delivered to the local user accounts of jsprat, fdown and jbgood. This is a simple way to set up small mailing lists.

You can also include commands in the /etc/aliases file so that when e-mail is sent to an alias it runs a program that will carry out some function.

Once you have created the file /etc/aliases, you need to run the command:

```
newaliases
```

This will update the /etc/mail/aliases.db file as seen in Figure 146. What is really happening is that mail uses a database, not a flat file for mail names and data. This allows much quicker processing of information.

```
# newaliases
/etc/mail/aliases: 14 aliases, longest 10 bytes, 152 bytes total
```

Figure 146. Running newaliases

10.7 Advanced Sendmail configuration in SuSE Linux

The configuration of Sendmail is highly automated by using YaST and
SuSEconfig and should cover the most common purposes. Here is an excerpt
of the relevant configuration variables in /etc/rc.config and their description:

```
# do you want to generate a sendmail-configuration /etc/sendmail.cf from
# parameters given in /etc/rc.config ("yes") or do you want to generate
# your /etc/sendmail.cf yourself ("no") ?
# (you could also use /etc/mail/linux.mc to do so.)
#
SENDMAIL_TYPE="yes"
#
# smarthost - this host gets all outgoing email from us
# normally used for uucp-connected sites or for dialup connections
# use "uucp-dom:server.uucp.com" to deliver all email to
# "server.uucp.com"
#
SENDMAIL_SMARTHOST="relay.suse.de"
#
# sendmail assumes the following space-separated host-names to be
# the local host (this must just be used for names differrent to the
# hostname, for e.g. aliases like www.nowhere.com)
#
SENDMAIL_LOCALHOST="localhost hurwitz hurwitz.suse.de"
#
# do not deliver any email locally, but send all email to another host
# this can just be used with another system that has the same users on it
# and you probably also want to set the FROM_HEADER to the other host
#
SENDMAIL_RELAY="relay.suse.de"
#
# with what parameters should sendmail be started?
# normal sites use "-bd -q30m -om". if you set SENDMAIL_EXPENSIVE and
# you have a dialup ISDN connection, you probably want to set this to
# "-bd -om" and run "sendmail -q" from your crontab.
#
SENDMAIL_ARGS="-bd -q30m -om"
#
# sendmail will only queue email in /var/mqueue and will only start
```

```
# to deliver it if "sendmail -q" is run
#
SENDMAIL_EXPENSIVE="no"
#
# sendmail will not try to canonify hostnames in your email
# so much less DNS-queries are send
# you probably want to enable this on a SENDMAIL_EXPENSIVE system
#
SENDMAIL_NOCANONIFY="no"
#
# have mail daemon on SMTP port? ("yes" or "no")
# needed, if you receive email from other hosts via tcp/ip
# not needed, if you have a uucp-only host or only out-going email.
# If set to "yes", sendmail will be started as daemon.
# As uucp site, you can get along with "SMTP=no", if you make
# a "sendmail -q" call after each poll.
# (As rmail is queuing the mail only and not delivering it...)
#
SMTP="no"
#
# From:-Line in email and News postings
# (otherwise the FQDN is used)
#
FROM_HEADER="suse.de"
```

The following features and configuration files are automatically handled by SuSEconfig:

- User aliases: /etc/aliases

- Access control: /etc/mail/access

- Address-rewriting outgoing: /etc/mail/genericstable

- Address-Rewriting incoming: /etc/mail/virtusertable

- Mail transport: /etc/mail/mailertable

- Rewriting In-/Out: /etc/mail/userdb

10.8 Sources of additional information

There are some helpful readme documents on your local filesystem:

```
/usr/doc/packages/sendmail/README.linux
/etc/mail/README
```

You can find more information on the official Web site of the Sendmail project at:

```
http://www.sendmail.org
```

There are also good how-to documents on the Linux Documentation project Web site at:

```
http://www.linuxdoc.org/HOWTO/Mail-User-HOWTO.html
http://www.linuxdoc.org/HOWTO/Mail-Administrator-HOWTO.html
```

We would also like to mention a very good alternative to Sendmail called Postfix, which has been written by Wietse Venema while working at the IBM T.J. Watson Research Center. Postfix is fast, easy to administer, and secure, while at the same time being Sendmail-compatible enough not to upset your users. The Web site can be found at:

```
http://www.postfix.org
```

SuSE Linux also ships Postfix as an RPM package to give you an alternative to Sendmail. Its configuration can also be done by YaST and SuSEconfig and it is very well documented. So, if you are looking for a fast and secure alternative to Sendmail, give Postfix a try.

Chapter 11. NFS - Network File System

Network File System (NFS), developed by Sun Microsystems, allows you to share directories across the network. The directory mounts become transparent to you. You access the mounted directories just like you do with any other directory or filesystem on your computer. The mounting process is the same as for any filesystem or partition that you want to mount on your system. The basic foundation of this is the `mount` command.

In order to share directories across the network you will need two basic things:

- The system sharing the data must allow you to have access

- The system that is using the data must originate the request and allow the mount to happen

Both concepts will be discussed in this chapter. As usual, we will only cover the basic concepts of NFS. For a more detailed description, see the NFS how-to at `http://www.linuxdoc.org/HOWTO/NFS-HOWTO.html`

11.1 Software installation

Before you can start setting up your NFS server, first you need to verify that the necessary RPM packages have been installed. You can query the RPM database for the required packages with RPM on the command line:

```
rpm -q nkita nkitb linuxnfs
```

Package nkita includes the user-level NFS server; it should have been installed by default when you first installed the system. Package nkitb includes the RPC portmapper, and package linuxnfs includes kernel-based NFS server support. Kernel-based NFS is the new NFS implementation on Linux that offers advanced NFS functionality and is multi-threaded. We recommend you use the kernel-based NFS server, and will cover its configuration and installation in this chapter. If one of these packages has not been installed, please install them by following the instructions in 3.1, "Adding and removing software packages using YaST" on page 51. They are located in package series n - Network-Support (TCP/IP, UUCP, Mail, News).

NFS makes use of several daemons (background processes) that need to be started on the server side. These daemons are:

portmap   This is the process that converts RPC (remote procedure call) program numbers into DARPA protocol port numbers. When a client wishes to make an RPC call to a given program number (for example the NFS server), it will first contact portmap on the server machine to determine the port number where RPC packets should be sent.

rpc.kmountd   This handles the exporting of NFS filesystems. It looks in the /etc/exports file to figure out what to do with mount requests from the connecting clients.

nfsd   This is the user level part of the actual NFS server process that delivers data to the clients. Multiple instances of this process can be run in parallel to speed up the service for multiple clients.

rpc.kstatd   This process implements the Network Status Monitor (NSM) RPC protocol. It is used by the NFS file-locking service to implement lock recovery when the NFS server machine crashes and reboots.

11.2 Allowing NFS access to data - the server side configuration

You can give NFS access to a filesystem by setting it up in the /etc/exports file. The file is set up on the exporting server and is the main configuration file for NFS. You can create a sample file entry by opening the /etc/exports file with your favorite editor. Then you can add an entry like:

```
/usr/local/share        myserver.mydomain.com(ro)
```

This says that the directory /usr/local/share is only accessible to the server `myserver.mydomain.com`.

> **Note**
>
> When exporting a filesystem you need to be sure that the exporting server can recognize and access the server that is in the /etc/exports file. You can verify this with the command
>
> ```
> ping server_name
> ```
>
> Where `server_name` is the name of the server you are trying to access. Otherwise the NFS commands may hang.

There are a number of options you can set up in the /etc/exports file. Some of them are explained in Table 25.

Table 25. Access options

Access options	
ro	Only permits read-only access to this share.
rw	Permits reading and writing. If both `ro` and `rw` are specified, `rw` takes priority.
root_squash	Accesses from the client's root user account will be mapped to the anonymous user (nobody by default) on the server.
no_root_squash	Accesses from the client's root account will not be mapped to the anonymous user on the server. Useful for diskless clients.
squash_uids and squash_gids	Specify a list of UIDs or GIDs that should be subject to anonymous mapping. A valid list of IDs looks like this: squash_uids=0-15,20,25-50
all_squash	Processes all requests for access as anonymous user.
anonuid=uid	When the options root_squash or all_squash are set, this user ID will be used to map an anonymous user request to.
anonuid=gid	When the options root_squash or all_squash are set, this group ID will be used to map an anonymous user request to.

A sample /etc/exports file is shown in the man pages for exports(5) and below in Figure 147.

```
# sample /etc/exports file
/               master(rw) trusty(rw,no_root_squash)
/projects       proj*.local.domain(rw)
/usr            *.local.domain(ro) @trusted(rw)
/home/joe       pc001(rw,all_squash,anonuid=150,anongid=100)
/pub            (ro,insecure,all_squash)
/pub/private    (noaccess)
```

Figure 147. A sample /etc/exports file

The lines in the sample /etc/exports file are explained as follows:

- `# sample /etc/exports file`

  This is just a comment. Any line or character string can be converted to a comment and disabled by entering a `#` symbol. Everything from that point to the end of the line is considered to be a comment.

- `/               master(rw) trusty(rw,no_root_squash)`

  This says that the root directory (/) is exported to the servers:

  `master` - whose rights are read-write

  `trusty` - whose rights are read-write and the access rights of the client's root user can be the same as the server's root

- `/projects       proj*.local.domain(rw)`

  The directory /projects is accessible read-write to all servers whose names match the pattern `proj*.local.domain`. This includes `proj.local.domain, proj1.local.domain,projprojproj.local.domain` and so forth.

- `/usr            *.local.domain(ro) @trusted(rw)`

  Any systems whose hostname ends in `.local.domain` is allowed read-only access. The `@trusted` netgroup is allowed read-write access.

- `/home/joe       pc001(rw,all_squash,anonuid=150,anongid=100)`

  The directory /home/joe is accessible to pc001 for read-write access; all requests for access are processed as an anonymous user. The anonymous UID number is set to 150 and the anonymous group ID is set to 100.This is useful when using a client that is running PCNFS or an equivalent NFS process on the PC. Since the PC IDs do not necessarily map to the UNIX IDs, this allows the proper file attributes to be set.

- /pub   (ro,insecure,all_squash)

    The directory /pub is accessible as read-only. It says that option in this entry also allows clients with NFS implementations that don't use a reserved port for NFS and process all requests as an anonymous user.

- /pub/private   (noaccess)

    The directory /pub/private does not allow any NFS access.

> **Note**
>
> NFS uses the numerical user and group IDs for the mapping of files between client and server. Make sure that you use identical user IDs on both systems. If this is not possible, you need to use the nfs.ugidd daemon to map on user names instead of their IDs. When you are using NFS with a lot of users, it is advisable to implement NIS as well to retain consistency of user IDs on the different hosts in your environment.

11.2.1 Starting the NFS server processes

After you have properly set up /etc/exports, you now need to start up the NFS server processes.

If the portmap daemon is not running, you will need to start it up first before you can start up the NFS daemons. You can do this with the following command:

```
rcrpc start
```

Once the portmap daemon is running you can start up the NFS daemons with the command:

```
rcnfsserver start
```

To stop the NFS server you can use the command:

```
rcnfsserver stop
```

You can restart the NFS process with the command:

```
rcnfs restart
```

You need to restart the NFS process if you have made changes to the configuration file /etc/exports.

If you want the NFS server to be started on system bootup, you need to activate the startup scripts for these processes. This can be either done by editing the configuration file /etc/rc.config manually with a text editor or by using YaST. This procedure is described in 3.6, "Changing the configuration file with YaST" on page 70.

The following variables have to be modified:

Table 26. Variables in rc.config for NFS server

Variable	Description
START_PORTMAP=yes	Start the portmapper. This is necessary when running an NFS server or NIS.
NFS_SERVER=yes	Start the NFS server on system bootup.
USE_KERNEL_NFSD=yes	Use the kernel-based NFS server instead of the user-mode process (recommended).
USE_KERNEL_NFSD_NUMBER=4	The number of parallel running NFS server threads (kernel-based NFS only).
REEXPORT_NFS=no	Enables you to reexport directories mounted via NFS from another server.

11.3 Accessing data remotely with NFS - the client side

To mount a remote filesystem on your local system, the mount point must exist. The mount process does not create the mount point automatically. To make the mount point, use the Linux mkdir command (a mount point is a regular directory). To make the /mnt/nfsserver mount point you would just do:

```
mkdir /mnt/nfsserver
```

Typically you do not need to worry about file attributes and ownerships when making an NFS mount point. The NFS access rights will usually supersede any permissions established for the directory.

Once you have created the mount point then you can use the mount command as follows:

```
mount -t nfs nfs_host:share_dir local_mount_dir
```

Where:

-t nfs says to do the mount as an NFS mount. On Linux, this parameter is now optional because if you explicitly specify the directory to be mounted as host:directory the mount command knows that it is an NFS mount.

nfs_host is the host that is exporting the filesystem to be shared.

share_dir is the actual directory that is to be shared.

`local_mount_dir` is the directory on the local host where the remote directory is going to be mounted. As mentioned earlier, this mount point must exist.

Chapter 12. NIS - Network Information System

In a distributed computing environment, maintenance of password, group, and host files can be a major task. Consistency is possibly the biggest difficulty here. For example, when a user changes his password on one machine, ideally it would be propagated to any other machines he has accounts on. When a network is composed of hundreds or thousands of machines, this convenience becomes a necessity. NIS is one way of addressing some of these problems.

12.1 What is NIS?

The Network Information System (NIS) is a service designed to provide a distributed database system for common configuration files. It was formerly known as Sun Yellow Pages (YP). NIS servers manage copies of the database files. NIS clients request the information from the NIS server instead of using their own configuration files.

NIS is designed after the client/server model. A NIS server contains data files called maps. These maps are owned by the NIS master and can only be updated by the master. There are NIS slave servers that replicate from the master. When there is a change to a master server's map, this change is then distributed to all the slave servers. Clients are hosts that request information from these maps but are not allowed to modify them locally.

NIS is commonly used in UNIX environments. However, it is also possible to integrate Windows NT clients in a NIS-based environment. NISGINA provides a NIS authenticated interactive logon for Windows NT 4.0 workstations. It supports changing UNIX passwords using a Windows NT dialog and some limited remote registry configuration.

12.2 How can I use NIS?

NIS is typically used to centrally manage commonly replicated configuration files. Examples of common configuration files are:

- /etc/hosts
- /etc/passwd
- /etc/group

NIS can also be used to distribute other files like /etc/hosts or /etc/services, but this will not be covered here.

12.3 Implementation on Linux

To introduce the concepts behind NIS, we will create a map of our password file kept on the NIS master server. This will allow users to log in to NIS clients without having to maintain a separate account on each system. Centralized administration is a key benefit of using NIS.

A note on security: Before deciding to put NIS in a production environment, please consider the security implications of passing sensitive data across the network. You may wish to take a look at NIS+, which has strong encryption as well as additional maintenance implications. The ypserv daemon on SuSE Linux has been compiled with TCP wrapper support. That means, you have to edit /etc/hosts.allow and /etc/hosts.deny to fit to your network environment. See section "TCP wrappers" in Chapter 18, "Security is a matter of trust" on page 356 in the SuSE Linux 6.2 manual for more information about these files.

At first, you have to make sure that the necessary software packages are installed.

Packages that need to be installed for a NIS server:

- ypserv.rpm
- nkitb.rpm

The following packages need to be installed for a NIS client:

- ypclient.rpm
- nkitb.rpm

You can use YaST to install these packages. See 3.1, "Adding and removing software packages using YaST" on page 51 for information about how to accomplish this task. The above-mentioned packages can be found in package series n - Network-Support (TCP/IP, UUCP, Mail, News).

12.3.1 Server side configuration

A key configuration file for the NIS master server is the /etc/ypserv.conf file. You do not need to modify anything in here for our example; it is listed for the sake of completeness. The following is a sample ypserv.conf we used:

```
#
# ypserv.conf   In this file you can set certain options for the NIS server,
#               and you can deny or restrict access to certain maps based
#               on the originating host.
#
#               See ypserv.conf(5) for a description of the syntax.
#

# Some options for ypserv. This things are all not needed, if
# you have a Linux net.

dns: no

# The following, when uncommented,  will give you shadow like passwords.
# Note that it will not work if you have slave NIS servers in your
# network that do not run the same server as you.

# Host                      : Map                  : Security  : Passwd_mangle
#
# *                         : passwd.byname        : port      : yes
# *                         : passwd.byuid         : port      : yes

# Not everybody should see the shadow passwords, not secure, since
# under MSDOG everbody is root and can access ports < 1024 !!!
*                           : shadow.byname        : port      : yes
*                           : passwd.adjunct.byname : port     : yes

# If you comment out the next rule, ypserv and rpc.ypxfrd will
# look for YP_SECURE and YP_AUTHDES in the maps. This will make
# the security check a little bit slower, but you only have to
# change the keys on the master server, not the configuration files
# on each NIS server.
# If you have maps with YP_SECURE or YP_AUTHDES, you should create
# a rule for them above, that's much faster.
*                           : *                    : none
```

The other key configuration file is the /var/yp/Makefile. The only map we want to create is the /etc/passwd file, so the others can be commented out if you wish. However, the default Makefile works just fine.

At first you have to define your YP domain. Open the central configuration file /etc/rc.config with your favorite text editor and edit the variable YP_DOMAINNAME="<domain>" to be your domain name. This domain name should not be confused with DNS domain names! The YP domain name can be any generic name.

You also have to define which hosts should be allowed to contact the NIS server. In our example, we will allow all hosts from the local Class C network 192.168.99.0/24 to connect to the server.

Open /etc/hosts.allow in a text editor and add the following line:

```
ypserv: 127.0.0.0/255.0.0.0 192.168.99.0/255.255.255.0
```

It is imperative that the local host also be allowed to connect to the ypserv process via the loopback interface (127.0.0.1).

Now add the following line to /etc/hosts.deny:

```
ypserv: ALL
```

NIS requires the RPC portmapper to be started. If it is not already running (you can check this with the command `rcrpc status`), start it with the command `rcrpc start` and set the variable START_PORTMAP in /etc/rc.config to yes to enable the automatic startup of the portmap on system bootup.

We are now ready to start the ypserv daemon:

```
rcypserv start
```

You should also start the YP password daemon yppasswdd, which enables you to change your user password remotely on the server by running yppasswd on the client:

```
rcyppasswdd start
```

To test our NIS setup we can use the `rpcinfo` command:

```
rpcinfo -u localhost ypserv
```

You should see:

```
program 100004 version 1 ready and waiting
program 100004 version 2 ready and waiting
```

We will now create our NIS maps:

```
/usr/lib/yp/ypinit -m
```

The fully qualified domain name (FQDN) of the local host will be selected as the master server.

```
<ctrl> d
```

Select **y** to confirm and begin building your maps.

Configure your machine as a client (see 12.3.3, "NIS Client configuration" on page 194) and use localhost as your YP server.

If you want to start the NIS server processes ypserv and rpc.yppasswd (used for changing passwords on the server by running `yppasswd` on the client side) on system bootup, you have to edit the following variables in /etc/rc.config:

```
START_YPSERV="yes"
START_YPPASSWDD="yes'
```

If you want to have slave servers, you have to change the variable NOPUSH=true to NOPUSH=false in /var/yp/Makefile and list the slave servers in /var/yp/ypservers. After you have made these modifications, run the following command to apply the changes:

```
cd /var/yp ; make
```

You should also start rpc.ypxfrd on the NIS master to have a faster transfer of your maps to the slave servers by running the following command:

```
rcypxfrd start
```

If you want to start this daemon on system bootup, you can do this by setting the variable START_YPXFRD in /etc/rc.config to "yes".

Table 27. YP server variables in /etc/rc.config

Variable	Description
YP_DOMAINNAME="nis.com"	Your NIS domain name. Do not confuse this with the DNS domain name!
START_YPSERV="yes"	Start the NIS server on bootup.
YP_SERVER="localhost"	The NIS server(s) space-separated IP addresses or host names (defined in /etc/hosts).
CREATE_YP_CONF="yes"	Create /etc/yp.conf automatically.
START_PORTMAP="yes"	Start the RPC portmapper (required for NIS).
START_YPBIND="yes"	Start the YP client process.
START_YPPASSWDD="yes"	Enables you to change your user password remotely from the client.
START_YPXFRD="yes"	Enables faster transfer of maps to the slave servers.

12.3.2 Installing a NIS slave server

Set up everything as would you do it for a normal client machine (see 12.3.3, "NIS Client configuration" on page 194). Add "localhost" at the end of YP_SERVERS in /etc/rc.config and run SuSEconfig, if you made the changes manually.

Now start ypbind with the command `rcypclient start` to have a working connection to the main YP server.

Now run `ypinit -s masterhost` to transfer all maps from the NIS master masterhost to the local server. You can now start the YP server with the command `rcypserv start` and restart ypbind to use localhost by running `rcypclient restart`.

On bootup you should first start ypserv and then ypbind. To check for new maps on a regular basis, add the following line to /etc/crontab:

```
51 * * * * root /usr/sbin/ypslave 2>/dev/null
```

Also add this host to /var/yp/ypservers on the YP server and enable pushing of new maps to this slave server as described in 12.3.1, "Server side configuration" on page 190. Whenever a new map is generated on the server, it will call yppush. yppush will connect all slave servers, which will in turn call ypxfr to update their maps.

12.3.3 NIS Client configuration

To test our NIS master server, we need to set up a client to run ypbind. For simplicity we can use the master server to verify our configuration. The same steps should be followed to set up a remote client.

We need to create a /etc/yp.conf file with our entries for the NIS domain and the NIS master server. You do not need to edit this file by hand; SuSEconfig will create this file for you according to your input in YaST or the variables in /etc/rc.config. For our test domain we used nis.com, and our master server name is nismaster.

Start up YaST on the command line and open the menu **System administration -> Network configuration -> Configure YP client.**

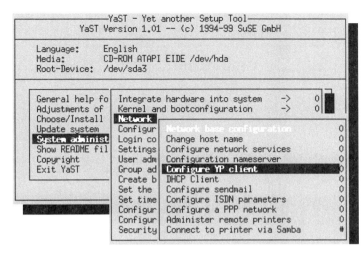

Figure 148. YaST: Configure YP client

Press Enter to open the following dialog box.

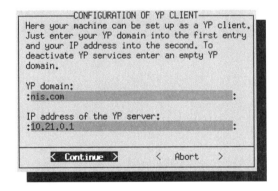

Figure 149. YaST: YP client configuration dialogue

Now enter your YP domain and the IP address(es) of your YP server and click **Continue**.

If you want to make these changes manually, you have to set the following variables in /etc/rc.config:

Table 28. YP client variables in /etc/rc.config

Variable	Description
YP_DOMAINNAME="nis.com"	Your NIS domain name. Do not confuse this with the DNS domain name!
YP_SERVER="nismaster"	The NIS server(s) space separated IP addresses or host names (defined in /etc/hosts).
CREATE_YP_CONF="yes"	Create /etc/yp.conf automatically.
START_PORTMAP="yes"	Start the RPC portmapper (required for NIS)
START_YPBIND="yes"	Start the YP client process

Make sure to run `SuSEconfig -quick` after making changes to these variables. If CREATE_YP_CONF is set to "yes", SuSEconfig will create the corresponding configuration file /etc/yp.conf and will add a single + sign at the end of /etc/passwd and /etc/group. This plus sign indicates that these files are managed by NIS.

If you are using host names instead of IP addresses for YP_SERVER, make sure that the NIS master's host name is listed in /etc/hosts or can be resolved by DNS.

If you do not want to reboot, run `domainname <your YP domainname>` now. If you need to change the YP domain name on an already running NIS client, it is safer to modify YP_DOMAINNAME in /etc/rc,config and reboot the system. Otherwise chances are high that already running processes might still use the old domain name.

NIS uses RPC for communication. Therefore, the RPC portmapper has to be started first:

    rcrpc start

We are now ready to start the ypbind daemon:

    rcypclient start

`ypwhich` will give you the name of the server ypbind is currently connected to. `ypwhich -m` will give you a list of all available maps. To test our NIS configuration we can also use the `ypcat` command:

    ypcat passwd

Please see the manual page for `ypcat` for more information about this tool.

You should see output similar to the following figure:

```
[root@test2 /root]# ypcat passwd
john:$1$Zx1Q62xM$XtP3v8/gPirZVQKK5/0hC1:501:501::/home/john:/bin/bash
ayne:$1$t/sEma1W$nLzLUZDsAUICeaXAg3f2z/:502:502::/home/ayne:/bin /bash
karri:$1$SZ5F27Vc$gI5Gc6.yDDjwLC42jSwCR1:507:510::/home/karri:/bin/bash
otto:$1$ctpEVbLK$W8Z9rX.SndoUTaqWyxCUu.:501:504::/home/otto:/bin/bash
bob:$1$NLcH9/fP$zbmyKDzEcH37ENu9hB22C.:502:505::/home/bob:/bin/bash
sammy:$1$HFgmti3X$H8d11enyorUkjl0Ba8/pm/:508:511::/home/sammy:/bin/bash
tina:$1$xow9ZBpk$CGD5jBgBy5Xe11.pnI2BQ1:504:507::/home/tina:/bin/bash
ivo:$1$OMaQooFS$Hp1C3BW8msWPbL65AT1YE.:505:508::/home/ivo:/bin/bash
nancy:$1$2Z9axj.Y$WZcW/evEbx63eMzhzvuwt/:506:509::/home/nancy:/bin/bash
korry:$1$SZ5F27Vc$gI5Gc6.yDDjwLC42jSwCR1:507:510::/home/korry:/bin/bash
steve:$1$YFNxznca$fOF2yRGDu/b83elC8UF8j.:503:506::/home/steve:/bin/bash
[root@test2 /root]# █
```

Figure 150. ypcat passwd

Now to really test the machine, log in to a NIS client using an account that is on the NIS master. When you log in, you might experience a successful login, but you will not see your home directory, since the home directory is located on nismaster. This can be fixed by creating a home directory for yourself on the client box as well. Another option would be to use NFS in conjunction with NIS to automatically mount the user's home directories. Using NIS in combination with NFS is common practice; see Chapter 11, "NFS - Network File System" on page 181 for information on how to set up NFS.

12.4 Sources of additional information

For further information or troubleshooting guidelines have a look at the following documentation:

The NIS how-to by Thorsten Kukuk is an excellent place to start:

http://www.linuxdoc.org/HOWTO/NIS-HOWTO.html

It can also be found on your local file system at:

/usr/doc/howto/en/NIS-HOWTO.gz.

The author's home page at http://www.suse.de/~kukuk/ contains some additional documents about NIS that are worth a read.

Managing NFS and NIS by Hal Stern is also a good resource.

Chapter 13. LDAP - Lightweight Directory Access Protocol

LDAP has become a buzzword in the IT world. The exciting thing about LDAP and directory services is that they can be used for so many purposes. This chapter will give you a brief explanation of what LDAP is, what it can be used for, basic structures, and simple implementation on the Linux OS. This chapter merely scratches the surface of what is actually possible with LDAP.

13.1 What is LDAP?

LDAP stands for Lightweight Directory Access Protocol. LDAP has become an Internet standard for directory services that run over TCP/IP. LDAP is a client/server protocol for accessing a directory service. Originally designed as a frontend for X.500 databases, LDAP is now commonly used in a stand-alone capacity. IBM, Netscape, Sun, Novell, Microsoft, and many other companies are incorporating LDAP into their directory structures.

13.1.1 Directory Services

A directory service is the collection of software, hardware, processes, policies, and administrative procedures involved in making the information in a directory available to the users of the directory.

A directory is similar to a database. However, directories and databases differ in the number of times they are searched and updated. Directories are tuned for being searched, while relational databases are geared toward maintaining data with a frequent number of updates.

Examples of directories would be the Yellow Pages, a card catalog, or an address book. Information is organized in a defined hierarchy and given attributes.

When we place a directory online, the data becomes dynamic in the sense that it can be easily updated and cross-referenced. Unlike printed material, any updates that occur are instantaneous for all users.

You can apply security to the directory so that only intended users can view, modify, or create data. This security can be based upon groups, individual users, or any other authentication scheme. The data can also be encrypted.

Directory services typically involve data distribution and replication. The advantages of distributing your directory services are performance, availability, and reliability. For a segmented network, distribution of servers containing the directory data improves performance by reducing network traffic and load on individual servers. By replicating your data on multiple servers you increase availability in case a single server should go down.

13.1.2 X.500

In the mid-1980s, the International Telecommunications Union (ITU, formerly the CCITT) and the International Organization for Standardization (ISO) merged their efforts on directory services standards and created X.500. The X.500 specifications consist of a series of recommendations on the concepts, models, authentication, distribution, attributes, objects, and replication that underlie an X.500 directory service.

Early X.500 implementations used a client access protocol known as DAP. DAP is thick, complicated, and difficult to implement for desktop computers. For all of these reasons other lighter-weight protocols were developed. As predecessors to LDAP, DIXIE and DAS were very successful. Out of this success a group from the Internet Engineering Task Force (IETF) began work on LDAP. The first Request for Comments (RFC 1487) describing LDAP was released in July 1993.

13.1.3 How you can use LDAP

LDAP allows system and network administrators to manage users, groups, devices, and other data from a central point. IT decision makers can avoid tying themselves to a single vendor for applications and operating systems. Developers can use LDAP-based standards to ensure cross-platform integration.

Some practical applications of LDAP-based directory services include:

- Corporate address book
- User administration
- Domain Name System

13.2 LDAP basics

The LDAP information model is based on objects. Objects can be people, printers, servers, or just about anything you can think of. The most basic unit of the LDAP model is the entry. An entry is a collection of information about an object. Each entry belongs to an object class that determines required and optional attributes. Each attribute has a type and one or more values. The type describes the kind of information contained in the attribute and the value contains the actual data.

13.2.1 LDIF files

An LDIF file is the standard way of representing directory data in a textual format. This format can typically be used for importing and exporting directory data. The following is a sample LDIF file for loading the LDAP directory and adding a user in the Netscape roaming profiles directory:

```
dn: o=ibm.com
objectclass: top

dn: ou=People,o=ibm.com
objectclass: top
objectclass: organizationalUnit

dn: cn=jhaskins, ou=People, o=ibm.com
objectclass: top
objectclass: organizationalUnit
cn: jhaskins
userpassword: secret

dn: ou=Roaming,o=ibm.com
objectclass: top
objectclass: organizationalUnit

dn: nsLIProfileName=jhaskins,ou=Roaming,o=ibm.com
objectclass: top
objectclass: nsLIProfile
nsliprofilename: jhaskins
owner: cn=jhaskins,ou=People,o=ibm.com
```

Each LDAP entry must have a DN or distinguished name. The distinguished name is a unique key that refers to that entry specifically.

> **Note**
>
> When importing LDIF files, watch for additional white space, spelling, and case. OpenLDAP will treat all of these differently. Authentication errors can usually be linked back to errors with the LDIF file.

13.3 Implementation on Linux

In our example, we will set up an LDAP server for roaming profiles with the Netscape Navigator Web browser. Although SuSE Linux includes an RPM package of OpenLDAP, we have to download a newer version and recompile it with an additional patch.

The patch addresses inconsistencies between OpenLDAP's and Netscape's LDAP implementation regarding the handling of modification time stamps on roaming entries. It is only needed for this special example using Netscape's roaming profiles and is generally not necessary for regular LDAP services.

The patch will not be incorporated into later releases of OpenLDAP. OpenLDAP's position is that their current implementation is more consistent with the LDAP precedent and the LDAP standards are not explicit on this issue.

Use YaST to install the OpenLDAP source RPM first. This will unpack the source package openldap-release.tgz and a patch file into /usr/src/packages/SOURCES. The directory /usr/src/packages/SPECS contains the specfile for this RPM. A specfile contains the building instructions for RPM to create the binary package. We will now apply the patch to the source file and rebuild the package afterwards. This makes sure that the files are registered in the RPM database.

Make sure that the package autoconf is installed as well before you continue.

Download the current OpenLDAP source archive from the FTP site:

```
ftp://ftp.OpenLDAP.org/pub/OpenLDAP/openldap-release.tgz
```

Copy it to the directory /usr/src/packages/SOURCES. This will overwrite the original source archive, but this is intentional.

Download the Netscape patch Albert-FitzPatrick-990519.gz from:

```
ftp://ftp.openldap.org/incoming/Albert-FitzPatrick-990519.tar.gz
```

Extract and rename it with the following command:

```
gunzip < Albert-FitzPatrick-990519.tar.gz > roaming.patch
```

Save it to the the directory /usr/src/packages/SOURCES afterwards.

Now enter the directory /usr/src/packages/SOURCES, extract the source package and apply the already included patch with the following commands:

```
cd /usr/src/packages/SOURCES
ln -s openldap-release.tgz ldap.tar.gz
pkgmake extract ldap
```

Apply this additional patch and add it to the already existing patch before installation with the following commands:

```
cd ldap/servers/slapd
ci -i -t-no-comment add.c
patch < ../../../roaming.patch
```

(answer the question "`Get file add.c from RCS with lock? [y]`" with `y`)

```
cd ../..
pgkmake diff
```

The roaming patch has now been added to the existing SuSE-applied changes. You can verify this by looking at the end of the ldap.dif file. It should now contain the patch for add.c.

Now we need to correct the version number of this package in the spec file. Open /usr/src/packages/SPECS/openldap.spec in your favorite text editor. Now look for the line beginning with Version: and correct the version number according to the current OpenLDAP release. Check the OpenLDAP Web site for this information (1.2.7 at the time of writing).

You can now rebuild the RPM package with the following command:

```
rpm --bb /usr/src/packages/SPECS/openldap.spec
```

After the RPM has been successfully built, you will find it in the directory:

```
/usr/src/packages/RPMS/i386/
```

Install it with `rpm` on the command line:

```
rpm -Uhv --force /usr/src/packages/RPMS/i386/openldap*.rpm
SuSEconfig -quick
```

The patched version of OpenLDAP is now installed.

13.3.1 Roaming Profiles for Netscape

In order to set up roaming profiles, we need the Netscape directory schema. You can download the roaming-073099.tar.gz file, which contains the files slapd.oc.conf, slapd.at.conf, and an excellent sample slapd.conf, from:

```
http://www.openldap.org/incoming/roaming-073099.tar.gz
```

Or make the following additions to slapd.oc.conf and slapd.ac.conf. Append the following lines to the end of the file /etc/openldap/slapd.oc.conf:

```
#from netscape to implement roaming access...
objectclass nsLIPtr
#        oid 2.16.840.1.113730.3.2.74
        requires
                objectclass
        allows
                nsLIPtrURL,
                owner

objectclass nsLIProfile
#        oid  2.16.840.1.113730.3.2.75
        requires
                objectclass,
                nsLIProfileName
        allows
                nsLIPrefs,
                uid,
                owner

objectclass nsLIProfileElement
#        oid  2.16.840.1.113730.3.2.76
        requires
                objectclass,
                nsLIElementType
        allows
                owner,
                nsLIData
                nsLIVersion

objectclass nsLIServer
#        oid  2.16.840.1.113730.3.2.77
        requires
                objectclass,
                serverhostname
        allows
                description,
                cn,
                nsServerPort,
                nsLIServerType,
                serverroot
```

Note

Make sure that you comment out the oid entries in the slapd.oc.conf.

Now add the following lines at the end of /etc/openldap/slapd.at.conf:

```
# ns-mcd-li-schema.conf
#
# Netscape Mission Control Desktop Roaming Access schema
#
attribute nsLIPtrURL        2.16.840.1.113730.3.1.399 ces
attribute nsLIPrefs         2.16.840.1.113730.3.1.400 ces
attribute nsLIProfileName   2.16.840.1.113730.3.1.401 cis
attribute nsLIData          2.16.840.1.113730.3.1.402 bin
attribute nsLIElementType   2.16.840.1.113730.3.1.403 cis
attribute nsLIServerType    2.16.840.1.113730.3.1.404 cis
attribute nsLIVersion       2.16.840.1.113730.3.1.405 bin
attribute nsServerPort      2.16.840.1.113730.3.1.280 cis
```

More information on the Netscape directory schema and roaming profiles can be found at:

```
http://help.netscape.com/products/client/communicator/manual_roaming2.h
tml
```

Modify your slapd.conf to support roaming profiles.

Now we will create the /etc/openldap/slapd.conf file. Replace `ibm.com` with the name of your organization.

```
#
# See slapd.conf(5) for details on configuration options.
# This file should NOT be world readable.
#
include /etc/openldap/slapd.at.conf
include /etc/openldap/slapd.oc.conf
schemacheck      off
lastmod          on
#referral ldap://ldap.itd.umich.edu

pidfile /var/run/slapd.pid
argsfile /var/state/slapd.args

###########################################################
# ldbm database definitions
###########################################################

database ldbm
suffix "o=ibm.com"
directory /var/tmp
rootdn "cn=root, o=ibm.com"
rootpw secret
# cleartext passwords, especially for the rootdn, should
# be avoid.  See slapd.conf(5) for details.
access to * by * write
access to * by * compare
access to * by * read
```

Stop

The permissions specified in the last three lines are extremely insecure and should only be used for testing purposes. See the slapd.conf(5) man page for more information about setting up appropriate permissions for your environment.

13.3.2 Start OpenLDAP

To start slapd, simply run `rcldap start` and check /var/log/messages for unusual warnings. If the start of `slapd` was successful, you should see a message similar to this:

```
ct 28 09:46:14 SuSE slapd[1193]: slapd starting
```

If you want OpenLDAP to be started on bootup, set the variable START_LDAP in /etc/rc.config to "yes". See 3.6, "Changing the configuration file with YaST" on page 70 for how to do this.

With `slapd` successfully running, we now need to load the initial database and create an LDIF file like the one on page 201. Replace `jhaskins` with your user name and `ibm.com` with your organization name.

Once you have created the entries.ldif file, load the LDAP server.

```
ldapadd -D "cn=root, o=ibm.com" -w secret -f entries.ldif
```

13.3.3 Configuring Netscape

The final step is to configure your Netscape browser.

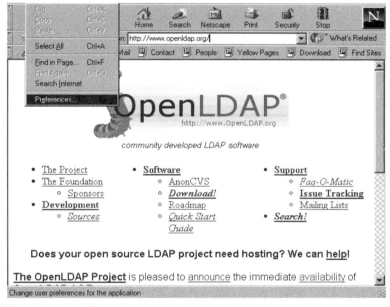

Figure 151. Configuring your browser

From the Edit drop-down menu, select **Preferences**.

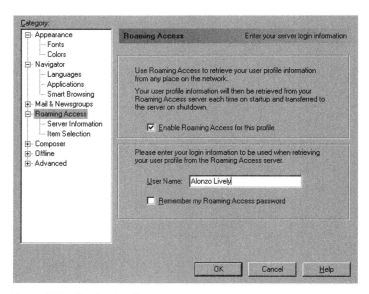

Figure 152. Configuring Netscape

Click the **Roaming User** (Netscape for Linux) or **Roaming Access** (Netscape for Windows) tab.

Click the **Enable Roaming access for this profile** check box.

Enter the user name.

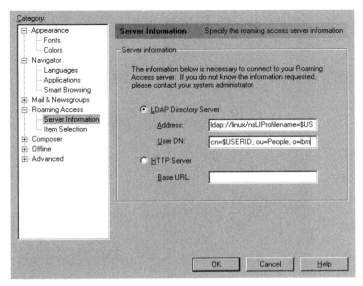

Figure 153. Configuring Netscape 2

Click **Server Information**.

Put the following into the LDAP Directory Server Address field:

    ldap://linuxbox/nsLIProfilename=$USERID, ou=Roaming, o=ibm.com

Replace `linuxbox` with the host name of the OpenLDAP server and `ibm.com` with the name of your organization (specified in the slapd.conf)

Enter the following into the LDAP Directory Server User DN field:

    cn=$USERID, ou=People, o=ibm.com

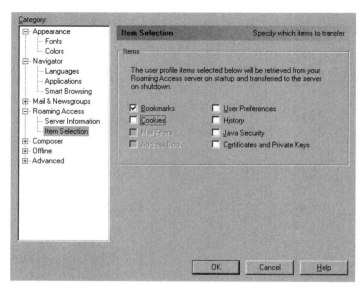

Figure 154. Configuring Netscape 3

Click **Item Selection**.

Select the items you would like to synchronize with the OpenLDAP server.

Restart Netscape and you are all set.

13.4 Sources of additional information

LDAP how-tos are available from the Linux Documentation project Web site at:

```
http://www.linuxdoc.org/HOWTO/LDAP-HOWTO.html
```

The OpenLDAP Web site is the key source of information about OpenLDAP, including a post from Phil Allred regarding Netscape Roaming Profiles and OpenLDAP.

```
http://www.OpenLDAP.org
```

Get "Don't make me LDAP you - Lightweight Directory Access Protocol: What it is, why you want it" from the LinuxWorld Web site at:

```
http://www.linuxworld.com/linuxworld/lw-1999-03/lw-03-uptime.html
```

Understanding and Deploying LDAP Directory Services, by Timothy Howes, Mark Smith, and Gordon Good, published by Macmillan, 1999.

Chapter 14. General performance tools in Linux

Linux offers a great variety of ways to optimize your system for maximum performance. Apart from the general fact that it is always good to have as much RAM and the fastest CPU as possible, there are some additional parameters to tune a Linux system. This section is intended as a collection of useful hints and tools, but without getting into too much detail about them. Please refer to the respective documentation and references. You should also note that using some of these hints may render your system unstable; use them at your own risk and only if you know what you are doing.

14.1 General configuration hints

These are some general tips for tweaking your system to maximize performance.

Recompile your programs and the Linux kernel with all available compiler optimization flags (for example, `-funroll-loops`, `-fomit-frame-pointer`, `-O6`) and all architecture-specific compiler options for your hardware architecture. This may increase the size of binaries or make them unable to run on some processors, but you can gain a lot of speed in comparison with the binaries shipped in the distribution. Alternatively you could use special compilers for your architecture (for example, pgcc), which offer even more sophisticated optimization options.

Create swap partitions of equal priority but different hard disk drives to allow load balancing. Please note that it need to be different devices! Using two different partitions on one hard disk will have the reverse effect. Even better, try to avoid swapping at all by adding more memory. A busy server should never need to swap, as this would severely degrade the overall performance.

If you are running a heavily loaded server with a lot of parallel processes, you might run into the Linux kernel's limit of running processes (512 by default). This maximum number of tasks is configurable in the kernel sources, so you have to recompile the kernel after changing this value. This value is defined in the file /usr/src/linux/include/linux/tasks.h:

```
#define NR_TASKS        512
```

You can increase this value up to 4090 processes, if necessary.

Linux offers a filesystem mount option that is called noatime. The atime is a timestamp of the last access time (reading and writing) for a certain file. This option can be added to the mount options in the /etc/fstab file. When a filesystem is mounted with this option, read accesses to files will no longer result in an update of the inode access time information. This information is usually not very interesting on a file or Web server, so the lack of updates to this field is not relevant. The performance advantage of the `noatime` flag is that it suppresses write operations to the filesystem for files that are simply being read. Since these write accesses add additional overhead, this can result in measurable performance gains. Instead of specifying this as a mount option that would apply to the whole filesystem, you can use the command `chattr` to set this flag on single files or directories. For example:

```
chattr -R +A /var/spool/news
```

This command would set the noatime flag recursively on all files below the news spool directory (a very common practice on busy news servers). See the manual page chattr(1) for more information.

You can use the hdparm tool to tune some hard disk drive parameters. Unfortunately most of them only work on IDE systems (which should be avoided in server systems, anyway), but the option `-a` works for SCSI, too. The manual page describes it as follows: "This option is used to get/set the sector count for filesystem read-ahead. This is used to improve performance in sequential reads of large files, by prefetching additional blocks in anticipation of them being needed by the running task. The default setting is 8 sectors (4 KB). This value seems good for most purposes, but in a system where most file accesses are random seeks, a smaller setting might provide better performance. Also, many drives have a separate built-in read-ahead function, which alleviates the need for a filesystem read-ahead in many situations." For example, to set the sector count read-ahead of your first SCSI disk to 4 sectors (2 KB), you would use the following command:

```
hdparm -a 4 /dev/sda
```

See the hdparm manual page for a complete list of available options.

The freely available tool Powertweak is a nice utility for tuning PCI chipset optimizations. It is expected to be extended to be a general performance tweaking tool similar to Powertweak on Microsoft Windows. See `http://linux.powertweak.com` for more information about it.

You should also disable all unused services and daemons, especially network-related services. This has several advantages: fewer open services need fewer system resources (file descriptors, memory) and the system is less vulnerable to external attacks against known security holes. A good starting point is the /etc/inetd.conf file. Comment out all services you do not need, or disable inetd completely.

The Linux /proc filesystem offers a lot of entry points for run-time optimization without recompiling the kernel. This directory does not physically exist on your hard drive; it is mapped as a virtual directory. Most of the files contained herein are readable and contain various system information. Other files can be edited with a regular text editor to set a certain kernel parameter. See /usr/src/linux/Documentation/sysctl/README in the Linux kernel sources for a detailed description of the tunable parameters (including filesystem, virtual memory, etc.).

There are some special TCP options that can be disabled in a local network with high signal quality and bandwidth, since they are mostly intended for lossy connections (see /usr/src/linux/net/TUNABLE in the Linux kernel sources for a detailed list):

To disable TCP timestamps, enter:

```
echo 0 > /proc/sys/net/ipv4/tcp_timestamps
```

To disable window scaling, enter:

```
echo 0 > /proc/sys/net/ipv4/tcp_window_scaling
```

To disable selective acknowledgments, enter:

```
echo 0 > /proc/sys/net/ipv4/tcp_sack
```

To tune the default and maximum window size (only if you know what you are doing), enter:

```
/proc/sys/net/core/rmem_default
```
- default receive window

```
/proc/sys/net/core/rmem_max
```
- maximum receive window

```
/proc/sys/net/core/wmem_default
```
- default send window

```
/proc/sys/net/core/wmem_max
```
- maximum send window

The following Web sites offer a lot of additional helpful hints about tuning and performance issues on Linux:

```
http://tune.linux.com
```

```
http://www.tunelinux.com
```

14.2 System monitoring and performance test tools

This section introduces a small collection of useful tools, among the many available, to monitor your Linux system or to gather system information.

To get an overview about all running processes and the system load, run the command `top` in a terminal session.

```
11:53am  up  3:57,  1 user,   load average: 0.00, 0.00, 0.00
34 processes: 33 sleeping, 1 running, 0 zombie, 0 stopped
CPU states:  0.0% user,  1.6% system,  0.0% nice, 98.4% idle
Mem:   62968K av, 59196K used,   3772K free,  17408K shrd,  15164K buff
Swap: 125996K av,      0K used, 125996K free               33768K cached

  PID USER      PRI  NI  SIZE  RSS SHARE STAT  LIB %CPU %MEM   TIME COMMAND
  515 root       20   0   792  792   628 R       0  1.6  1.2  0:01 top
    1 root        0   0   196  196   168 S       0  0.0  0.3  0:04 init
    2 root        0   0     0    0     0 SW      0  0.0  0.0  0:00 kflushd
    3 root        0   0     0    0     0 SW      0  0.0  0.0  0:00 kupdate
    4 root        0   0     0    0     0 SW      0  0.0  0.0  0:00 kpiod
    5 root        0   0     0    0     0 SW      0  0.0  0.0  0:00 kswapd
    6 root        0   0     0    0     0 SW      0  0.0  0.0  0:00 md_thread
   76 root        0   0   648  648   536 S       0  0.0  1.0  0:00 syslogd
   79 root        0   0   816  816   392 S       0  0.0  1.2  0:00 klogd
  116 at          0   0   552  552   456 S       0  0.0  0.8  0:00 atd
  121 root        0   0   452  452   376 S       0  0.0  0.7  0:00 gpm
  132 root        0   0  1592 1592  1488 S       0  0.0  2.5  0:00 httpd
  135 root        0   0   624  624   528 S       0  0.0  0.9  0:00 lpd
  137 wwwrun      0   0  1592 1592  1500 S       0  0.0  2.5  0:00 httpd
  138 wwwrun      0   0  1592 1592  1500 S       0  0.0  2.5  0:00 httpd
  139 wwwrun      0   0  1592 1592  1500 S       0  0.0  2.5  0:00 httpd
  140 wwwrun      0   0  1592 1592  1500 S       0  0.0  2.5  0:00 httpd
  141 wwwrun      0   0  1592 1592  1500 S       0  0.0  2.5  0:00 httpd
```

Figure 155. Example output of top

`Top` updates the process list in regular intervals. Press "?" to get an online help screen about the available parameters. To change the refresh interval, press "s" and enter the desired number of seconds between each update. If you want to sort the processes by memory consumption, press "m". To exit from top, press "q". This will bring you back to the command line.

Similar to `top`, `pstree` displays a hierarchical structure of all currently running processes:

```
SuSE:~ # pstree
init-+-atd
     |-cron
     |-dhclient
     |-gpm
     |-httpd---22*[httpd]
     |-httpd---httpd
     |-inetd-+-in.telnetd---login---bash---make---make---make---make---gcc-+-as
     |       |                                                              |-cc1
     |       |                                                              `-cpp
     |       `-in.telnetd---login---bash---pstree
     |-kflushd
     |-klogd
     |-kpiod
     |-kswapd
     |-kupdate
     |-login---bash
     |-lpd
     |-md_thread
     |-5*[mingetty]
     |-nmbd
     |-nscd---nscd---5*[nscd]
     |-sendmail
     |-smbd---smbd
     `-syslogd
```

If you are running a graphical desktop such as KDE, you can also use
window-based tools like KTop, the KDE Task Manager:

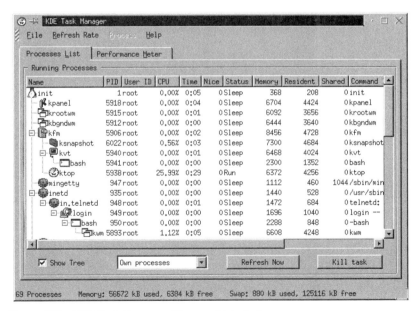

Figure 156. KDE Task Manager: Process List window

KTop offers two different views. It can either display a process list (similar to
`top` and `pstree`), or you can switch to the performance meter, which displays
the system load and memory usage over a longer time period.

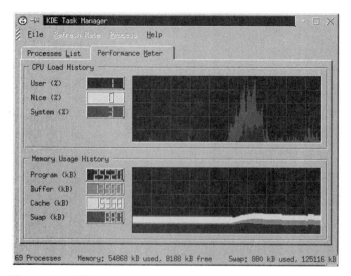

Figure 157. KDE task manager: performance meter

The Lothar project currently works on a very sophisticated hardware
detection and configuration tool. The Web site can be found at
`http://www.linux-mandrake.com/lothar/`. Figure 158 shows Lothar's graphical
front end.

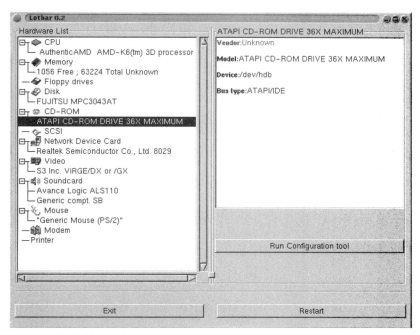

Figure 158. Lothar main screen

The KDE control center also gives you a lot of information about your system by reading a number of informative files in the /proc filesystem. They can also be displayed in a regular text viewer (for example `more`, `less` or `cat`).

The /proc/cpuinfo file contains information about your CPU (that is, vendor, Mhz, flags like mmx). For example:

```
SuSE:~ # cat /proc/cpuinfo
processor       : 0
vendor_id       : GenuineIntel
cpu family      : 6
model           : 5
model name      : Pentium II (Deschutes)
stepping        : 2
cpu MHz         : 513.953346
cache size      : 512 KB
fdiv_bug        : no
hlt_bug         : no
sep_bug         : no
f00f_bug        : no
coma_bug        : no
fpu             : yes
fpu_exception   : yes
cpuid level     : 2
wp              : yes
flags           : fpu vme de pse tsc msr pae mce cx8 sep mtrr pge mca cmov pat p
se36 mmx osfxsr
bogomips        : 313.75
```

The /proc/interrupts file lists all interrupts used by Linux. Note that this shows interrupts only from devices that have been detected by the kernel! If a device will not be detected because of a resource conflict, you have to resolve this conflict manually (for example, by changing the BIOS setup). For example:

```
SuSE:~ # cat /proc/interrupts
          CPU0
   0:     548029        XT-PIC  timer
   1:        557        XT-PIC  keyboard
   2:          0        XT-PIC  cascade
   8:          2        XT-PIC  rtc
   9:        371        XT-PIC  PCnet/PCI II 79C970A
  12:         68        XT-PIC  PS/2 Mouse
  13:          0        XT-PIC  fpu
  14:     198235        XT-PIC  ide0
  15:          3        XT-PIC  ide1
 NMI:          0
```

The /proc/ioports file contains all allocated device I/O ports. The same note as for interrupts applies here. Only devices that are actually detected by the kernel are listed here. For example:

```
SuSE:~ # cat /proc/ioports
0000-001f : dma1
0020-003f : pic1
0040-005f : timer
0060-006f : keyboard
0070-007f : rtc
0080-008f : dma page reg
00a0-00bf : pic2
00c0-00df : dma2
00f0-00ff : fpu
0170-0177 : ide1
01f0-01f7 : ide0
02e8-02ef : serial(auto)
02f8-02ff : serial(auto)
0376-0376 : ide1
03c0-03df : vga+
03e8-03ef : serial(auto)
03f6-03f6 : ide0
03f8-03ff : serial(auto)
1000-101f : PCnet/PCI II 79C970A
1020-1027 : ide0
1028-102f : ide1
```

The /proc/meminfo file displays info about memory (for example, memory
used, free, swap size). You can also use the `free` command to display this
information. For example:

```
SuSE:~ # cat /proc/meminfo
        total:     used:     free:  shared: buffers:  cached:
Mem:  64569344 62578688  1990656 54308864 18792448 27807744
Swap: 129019904   102400 128917504
MemTotal:      63056 kB
MemFree:        1944 kB
MemShared:     53036 kB
Buffers:       18352 kB
Cached:        27156 kB
SwapTotal:    125996 kB
SwapFree:     125896 kB
SuSE:~ # free
            total       used       free     shared    buffers     cached
Mem:        63056      61124       1932      53068      18352      27164
-/+ buffers/cache:     15608      47448
Swap:      125996        100     125896
```

The /proc/mounts file shows all currently mounted partitions. The `mount`
command without parameters will display similar information. For example:

```
SuSE:~ # cat /proc/mounts
/dev/root / ext2 rw 0 0
proc /proc proc rw 0 0
/dev/hda1 /boot ext2 rw 0 0
devpts /dev/pts devpts rw 0 0
SuSE:~ # mount
/dev/hda3 on / type ext2 (rw)
proc on /proc type proc (rw)
/dev/hda1 on /boot type ext2 (rw)
devpts on /dev/pts type devpts (rw,gid=5,mode=0620)
```

The /proc/partitions file displays all existing partitions on all devices. You can also use `fdisk -l` to display this information. For example:

```
SuSE:~ # cat /proc/partitions
major minor  #blocks  name

   3     0   1023907 hda
   3     1      6016 hda1
   3     2    126000 hda2
   3     3    891072 hda3
   3    64   1023907 hdb
   3    65   1023088 hdb1
  22     0 1073741823 hdc
SuSE:~ # fdisk -l

Disk /dev/hda: 32 heads, 63 sectors, 1015 cylinders
Units = cylinders of 2016 * 512 bytes

   Device Boot    Start       End     Blocks   Id  System
/dev/hda1   *        1         6       6016+  83  Linux
/dev/hda2            7       131     126000   82  Linux swap
/dev/hda3          132      1015     891072   83  Linux

Disk /dev/hdb: 32 heads, 63 sectors, 1015 cylinders
Units = cylinders of 2016 * 512 bytes

   Device Boot    Start       End     Blocks   Id  System
/dev/hdb1            1      1015    1023088+  83  Linux
```

The /proc/pci file gives information about all your PCI devices. You can also use the `lspci` command. Please note that /proc/pci is obsolete and will be replaced by /proc/bus/pci/* in the future. For example:

```
SuSE:~ # cat /proc/pci
PCI devices found:
  Bus  0, device   0, function  0:
    Host bridge: Intel 82439TX (rev 1).
      Medium devsel.  Master Capable.  No bursts.
  Bus  0, device   7, function  0:
    ISA bridge: Intel 82371AB PIIX4 ISA (rev 8).
      Medium devsel.  Master Capable.  No bursts.
  Bus  0, device   7, function  1:
    IDE interface: Intel 82371AB PIIX4 IDE (rev 1).
      Medium devsel.  Fast back-to-back capable.  Master Capable.  Latency=64.
      I/O at 0x1020 [0x1021].
  Bus  0, device  15, function  0:
    Display controller: Unknown vendor Unknown device (rev 0).
      Vendor id=15ad. Device id=710.
      Medium devsel.  Fast back-to-back capable.  Master Capable.  Latency=64.
      I/O at 0x1030 [0x1031].
      Non-prefetchable 32 bit memory at 0xfc000000 [0xfc000000].
      Non-prefetchable 32 bit memory at 0xfb000000 [0xfb000000].
  Bus  0, device  16, function  0:
    Ethernet controller: AMD 79C970 (rev 16).
      Medium devsel.  Fast back-to-back capable.  IRQ 9.  Master Capable.  Laten
cy=64.  Min Gnt=6.Max Lat=255.
      I/O at 0x1000 [0x1001].
      Non-prefetchable 32 bit memory at 0xfd000000 [0xfd000000].
SuSE:~ # lspci
00:00.0 Host bridge: Intel Corporation 430TX - 82439TX MTXC (rev 01)
00:07.0 ISA bridge: Intel Corporation 82371AB PIIX4 ISA (rev 08)
00:07.1 IDE interface: Intel Corporation 82371AB PIIX4 IDE (rev 01)
00:0f.0 Display controller: Unknown device 15ad:0710
00:10.0 Ethernet controller: Advanced Micro Devices 79c970 [PCnet LANCE] (rev 10
)
```

The /proc/swaps file displays information about all active swap partitions. For example:

```
SuSE:~ # cat /proc/swaps
Filename                  Type          Size    Used  Priority
/dev/hda2                 partition     125996  56    -1
```

The /proc/version file displays some version information about the Linux kernel. The command uname -a will display similar information. For example:

```
SuSE:~ # cat /proc/version
Linux version 2.2.10 (root@Mandelbrot.suse.de) (gcc version 2.7.2.3) #1 Tue Jul
20 16:32:24 MEST 1999
SuSE:~ # uname -a
Linux SuSE 2.2.10 #1 Tue Jul 20 16:32:24 MEST 1999 i686 unknown
```

If you want to obtain some more information about your SCSI devices, have a look at the files below /proc/scsi.

A tool that is also gathering system information from the /proc filesystem is vmstat. It reports information about processes, memory, paging, block IO, traps, and CPU activity. The first report produced gives averages since the last reboot. Additional reports give information on a sampling period of length delay. The process and memory reports are instantaneous in either case. vmstat is very helpful for logging CPU and memory usage over a longer period of time.

Apart from configuring numerous parameters of your hard drive, the command hdparm can also be used to perform hard disk performance tests with the command hdparm -tT <device>. For example:

```
SuSE:~ # hdparm -tT /dev/hda

/dev/hda:
 Timing buffer-cache reads:   64 MB in  0.68 seconds =94.12 MB/sec
 Timing buffered disk reads:  32 MB in 29.51 seconds = 1.08 MB/
SuSE:~ # hdparm -c1 /dev/hda

/dev/hda:
 setting 32-bit I/O support flag to 1
 I/O support  =  1 (32-bit)
SuSE:~ # hdparm -tT /dev/hda

/dev/hda:
 Timing buffer-cache reads:   64 MB in  0.67 seconds =95.52 MB/sec
 Timing buffered disk reads:  32 MB in 12.92 seconds = 2.48 MB/sec
```

Another popular hard disk performance test is bonnie, found at http://www.textuality.com/bonnie/ (an RPM package for SuSE Linux is included in the distribution). Note, however, that these tests are mostly useful for testing different parameter settings on one machine as a relative measure, not as a comparison between different systems.

To test the throughput of your network, you can either use netperf, found at http://www.netperf.org/netperf/NetperfPage.html or bing (included in SuSE Linux).

Chapter 15. Backup and recovery with BRU

It may seem obvious that backing up and restoring data quickly is critical, but many administrators leave this task at the end of the "to do" list until it is too late. With the ease of use of the commercially available BRU utility, there is no need to wait.

15.1 What is BRU?

BRU is a backup and restore utility with significant enhancements over other common utilities such as tar, cpio, volcopy and dump. BRU is designed to work with most backup devices, including cartridge, 4mm DAT, 8mm (Exabyte) and 9-track tape drives.

BRU includes incremental backups, full backups, multivolume archives, distribution and updates, error detection and recovery, random access capabilities, file comparisons, file overwrite protection, and increased speed over previous versions.

15.2 Installing BRU

Before we begin, we need to know:

1. The device name of our tape drive. Typically under SuSE Linux this will be /dev/st0.

2. The size of our backup media in megabytes.

To install BRU from the floppy drive with the `tar` command:

```
cd /tmp
tar xvf /dev/fd0
./install
```

Follow the prompts regarding readme files and licenses until you come to the following window:

```
##########################################################
Creating New /etc/brutab file.  This file will contain
information about devices on your system.
##########################################################


Please select backup devices from the following list
or enter Q when you are done.

a) 1/4 Inch Catridge Tape Drive
b) 4mm DAT Tape Drive
c) 8mm (Exabyte) Tape Drive
d) DLT (Digital Linear Tape)
e) Other
q) Quit


What is the type of this device: _
```

Figure 159. Selecting your backup devices

Select all of your backup devices and then enter Q when you are done.

You will now be asked to enter your BRU serial number.

When input correctly, you will be asked if you would like to install the X11 interface.

Select **Y**.

The installation program needs to create an xbru directory. You can select a path or accept the default /usr/local/.

The installation program will install executables in a user-specified directory. The default is /usr/local/bin.

Note

The key configuration file is: /etc/brutab. Consult the *BRU User's Guide* for advanced information. Do not edit unless you know what your doing.

BRU is now installed.

15.3 Basic commands

The basic command structure for BRU is:

```
bru modes [control options] [selection options] [files]
```

Where `bru` is the command or program followed by the mode specifying backup, restore, or various queries. `Control options` specify devices and buffer size. `Selection options` control which files or directories to work with. `Files` is the specified target of the `bru` command.

15.3.1 Basic backup

To back up the single file /home/ayne/.profile:

```
bru -c -vvvv -G /home/ayne/.profile
```

To back up the complete directory /home/ayne:

```
bru -c -vvvv -G /home/ayne
```

To back up the entire system:

```
bru -c -vvvv -G /
```

15.3.2 Basic restore

To restore the single file /home/ayne/.profile:

```
bru -x -vvvv -ua -w /home/ayne/.profile
```

To restore the complete directory /home/ayne:

```
bru -x -vvvv -ua -w /home/ayne
```

To restore the entire system:

```
bru -x -vvvv -ua -w /
```

15.3.3 Basic verification and listing commands

The `-i` mode can be used in conjunction with a backup command or by itself. The -i mode reads each block of data and verifies the checksum of the block. If used with the verbosity options (`-vvvv`), BRU will give a complete listing of the contents of an archive.

The `-G` mode displays the archive header block, which contains detailed information on the archive including the command used to create the archive. See the *BRU User's Guide* for more information.

The -gg mode displays the contents of the on-tape directory. This mode can only be used if the archive was created with the -G option.

15.4 X Interface

To use BRU's X interface, you will need to be in an X-Windows environment. Type:

```
xbru
```

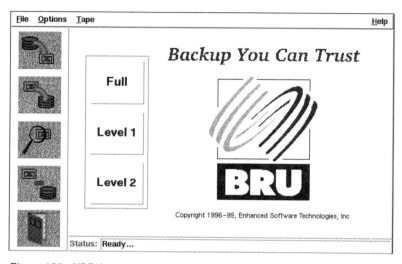

Figure 160. XBRU

You will see a figure similar to Figure 160.

From this interface you can:

- Create and restore backups.
- Create save, and load backup definitions.
- Schedule backups.
- List and verify the contents of archives.
- View the BRU log.

15.4.1 The big buttons

The three main buttons (Full, Level 1, and Level 2) are shortcuts to various levels of backing up your system, directories, or individual files.

- Select **Full** to back up all the files in the user's home directory, or if the user is root, the entire system.

- Select **Level 1** to execute a backup for the same files as listed above, on the condition that files have been modified since the previous full backup. If no previous full backup has been done, this will be considered a full backup.

- Select **Level 2** to execute a backup for the same files as listed above, on the condition that files have been modified since the previous level 1 backup. If no previous level 1 backup has been done, this will be considered a level 1 backup.

15.4.2 Creating archives

Creating archives with BRU's X interface is simple. Click the **Backup** button to bring up the Backup File Selection interface (Figure 161).

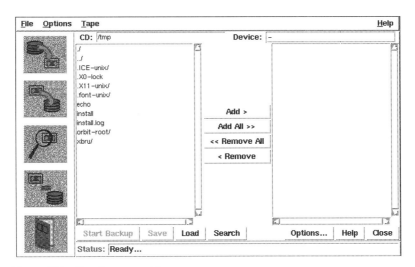

Figure 161. Creating an archive

The box on the left displays the contents of the current directory. You can change the current directory by clicking in the upper right-hand corner of the screen and editing the CD entry.

You can add or remove files and directories from the backup list by selecting them and clicking on the appropriate button.

BRU also provides a search function. Click the **Search** button to bring up a dialog box prompting you for a search string. This string can contain typical wildcards.

Backup Definitions are a way to define a set of commonly used backup options or preferences for use at a future time. You can create definitions for use with the backup scheduler or simply use the default selections.

After you have selected the files and directories that you wish to back up, click the **Continue** button. You will be led through a series of dialog boxes regarding your overwriting, appending, and labeling preferences for the archive. The backup will proceed by presenting you with an estimated time to completion and progress window.

15.4.3 Scheduling

To access the scheduling feature, select **File > Scheduler**.

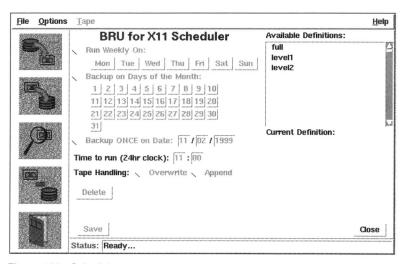

Figure 162. Scheduler

BRU provides a scheduling utility to automate the backup process for the busy administrator. There are three predefined definitions: Full, Level 1, and Level 2. These are the same definitions used in 15.4.1, "The big buttons" on page 226. You can create your own definitions in the creating archives interface.

From the BRU for X11 Scheduler interface, you can set scheduled backups based on weekly, monthly, or single dates. The scheduler is very flexible. In order to take advantage of the scheduling options, you must save your desired schedule configuration and verify that the scheduler is being run from cron. To verify or add the cron entry, log in as root and type:

```
crontab -e
```

Insert the following line:

```
0/5 * * * * /usr/local/bin/bruschedule
```

If you chose a different path for the binaries during installation, change the entry accordingly.

Save the crontab entry. You can now schedule backups.

15.4.4 Restoring files

Restoring files with BRU's X interface is simple. BRU will retrieve the contents of the archive when you click the **Restore** button. After scanning the archive, the Restore File Selection interface (similar to Figure 161) will appear.

> **Note**
>
> If the on-tape directory is not in the archive, then BRU must scan the entire archive to get a listing. This can be very time consuming. When creating an archive, use the -G option to create the on-tape directory.

The box on the left displays the contents of the current directory that is stored on the tape. You can change the current directory by clicking in the upper right-hand corner of the screen and editing the CD entry.

You can add or remove files and directories from the backup list by selecting them and clicking on the appropriate button.

When you have selected all of the files and directories that you wish to restore, click the **Restore** button. A progress window will show each file as it is restored.

15.4.5 Listing and verifying archives

For listing the contents of an archive, BRU gives you three options:

1. Header - This option shows the archive header record, which lists the label, creation date, version, and serial number. For more information on the Header, consult the *BRU User's Guide*.

2. Filenames only - This option displays the on-tape directory. If the archive was created without using the -G option, BRU will scan the entire archive to create a list of files. You will be prompted before this occurs, as this can be a lengthy process.

3. Full details - This option scans the entire archive for details such as file names, permissions, owners, size, modification times, etc. This process can be time consuming.

For verifying archives, BRU give you two options:

1. Checksum Verification - When archives are written, a checksum is calculated for each block of data. The checksum is stored in the header of each block. Checksum verification will read each bock, recalculate the checksum, and compare the checksum to the value in the header. Each file will be listed as it is verified, along with any errors found. If no errors are found, you know you have an accurate backup.

2. Differences Verification - BRU compares the files in the archive to the files on the hard drive. Any differences, such as modification times, size, or files in the archive that are nonexistent on the hard drive are noted. An end of differences notice will be listed when the verification is complete.

15.5 Summary

For information on advanced features consult your *BRU User's Guide* or the BRU Web site at:

```
http://www.estinc.com/
```

Chapter 16. Setting up a Beowulf cluster

For a long time, parallel computing has been a domain of commercial vendors. By using Linux, it is now possible to create a powerful supercomputer using regular PCs with off-the-shelf components that are networked together with fast Ethernet cards or by using special high-speed interconnections like SCI or Myrinet. Beowulf clusters offer high performance computing at a fraction of the cost of a regular parallel computer (the price/performance ratio is usually between three and ten times better than for a "regular" supercomputer).

Beowulf was "the son of Scyld in the Scandian lands", a character from one of the oldest English epic poems. The legend tells that he defeated a monster called "Grendel" (see `http://legends.dm.net/beowulf/index.html` and `http://www.lnstar.com/literature/beowulf/beowulf.html` for historical background).

The first Beowulf cluster was set up by Donald Becker and Tom Sterling at the NASA Goddard Space Flight Center in 1994. Don Becker is also well known in the Linux community for his work on network drivers in the Linux kernel.

To make use of the parallelism, your software needs to be distributable between the nodes of a cluster. One way is to use libraries like PVM (Parallel Virtual Machine) or LAM/MPI (Local Area Metacomputer/Message Passing Interface). Regular programs are not suitable for distributed computing. There is now a special load-sharing software called MOSIX, which allows transparent process migration in a cluster. MOSIX can be used by any software that spawns multiple processes or threads. MOSIX requires a special patched Linux kernel and will not be covered here.

This chapter will focus on how to set up PVM and how to demonstrate the parallel computing power using a special version of the famous raytracing software POVray, called PVMPOVray. Raytracing is a method to create realistic images of a scene that is only described by coordinates, light sources, textures and surface properties like reflectivity or opacity. The raytracer now computes the reflections, shadows and refractions of all light rays in the picture and generates the respective image of this scene. Further information about POVray can be found on the POVray Web site at `http://www.povray.org`.

To set up a simple Beowulf cluster, you need at least two PCs running Linux and a functional TCP/IP network connection between them. Regular Ethernet is fine for starters; however, it does not offer the best performance, since it has a rather high latency, which is crucial if you run applications that need to communicate a lot between nodes. To enable the communication between the nodes, PVM needs to be installed on all these machines as well. XPVM is a useful tool to monitor the communication and setup of the virtual machine, if the number of nodes is not too high (approx. 20-30). XPVM only needs to be installed on the master server.

When using SuSE Linux, make sure that the following packages are installed on all machines in the cluster. These packages can be found in the "beo" package series:

- pvm
- povray
- pvmpov

One machine acts as the master node that distributes jobs to the "slave" nodes. They should share a common work directory (NFS) and it should be possible to run a remote shell rsh from each node to another without being prompted for a password (edit the /etc/hosts.equiv file on each machine or create a ~/.rhosts file in the home directory of the user who wants to spawn jobs on remote machines). Start the PVM console by typing pvm on the command line. At the PVM command prompt pvm>, use the command add <Hostname> to add nodes to your virtual machine. PVM now attempts to start the PVM daemon process on the remote machine using rsh. If this fails, have a look at the log files on the remote machine. The command conf gives you a list of all nodes in your cluster that have successfully been added to PVM. Use quit to return to the shell. Alternatively, you can create a file that contains the names of all hosts that you want to use for your cluster (one on each line) and run pvm <hostfile>. This will automatically add all these hosts to the virtual machine. This is basically all you need to set up a basic Beowulf cluster. To make use of the parallel computing power, you now need to have a program that has been written using the PVM library. One example here is PVMPOVray.

To run XPVM, you first have to set the following environment variable:

```
export XPVM_ROOT=/usr/X11R6/lib/xpvm/
```

Now you can start xpvm by typing xpvm in a terminal window. Add the other nodes by clicking **Hosts... -> Other Hosts...** An icon should appear for each host that has been successfully added to the virtual machine. Click **Tasks... -> SPAWN** to start the distribution of a job. To give a demonstration, spawn the following command:

```
/usr/X11R6/bin/x-pvmpov +L/usr/lib/povray3/include
+I/usr/lib/povray3/povscn/level2/skyvase.pov +O skyvase.tga +D +W640
+H400 +N
```

Set NTasks to the number of hosts involved.

A window should now pop up, and the picture will be created tile by tile. The finished image can be found as "`skyvase.tga`" in your home directory.

Appendix A. RAID levels

This appendix has been included for the convenience of our readers who are unfamiliar with the disk subsystem technology known as RAID. We anticipate that this will be a small percentage of our readership as RAID is an important technology that most people implementing business-critical IT systems probably know about. RAID is mentioned in many places throughout this book and a basic understanding of its features and benefits will help you to understand why.

Even those who know about RAID already will be interested to hear about the new RAID-5E level supported by IBM's latest ServeRAID adapter.

A.1 What is RAID?

Although very commonly implemented using SCSI disks, RAID is independent of the specific disk technology being used. IBM Netfinity servers have RAID controllers that support SCSI, Fibre Channel, and SSA disk subsystems. In addition, Windows NT supports its own software-based RAID, though this is not often used, as much of the performance gained from having a dedicated hardware RAID controller is lost.

A typical RAID disk subsystem will have between two and six physical disks that are accessed by the processor by way of a specialized RAID controller adapter. The controller makes the array appear as a single large virtual disk to the processor. Because this disk has six completely independent head mechanisms for accessing data (in the case of a six-drive array), the potential for improved performance is immediately apparent. In an optimal situation, all six heads could be providing data to the system without the need for the time-consuming head-seeks to different areas of the disk, which would be necessary were a single physical disk being used.

However, the primary intent of a RAID implementation is to prevent the system served by the array from being affected by critical hard disk failures. Several different implementations of RAID have been defined and are referred to as levels. Each level has different characteristics and these levels allow a choice to be made to best meet the cost, security, and performance desired. The three most common implementations are levels 0, 1, and 5. These are the levels available with all of IBM's disk subsystems supported by Netfinity servers, namely SCSI, SSA, and Fibre Channel. The Netfinity ServeRAID-3HB Ultra2 SCSI adapter introduces a new enhanced RAID-5 described in A.1.5, "RAID-5 enhanced" on page 243.

A.1.1 RAID-0

RAID-0, sometimes referred to as disk striping, is not really a RAID solution since there is no redundancy in the array at all. The disk controller merely stripes the data across the array so that a performance gain is achieved. This is illustrated in Figure 163:

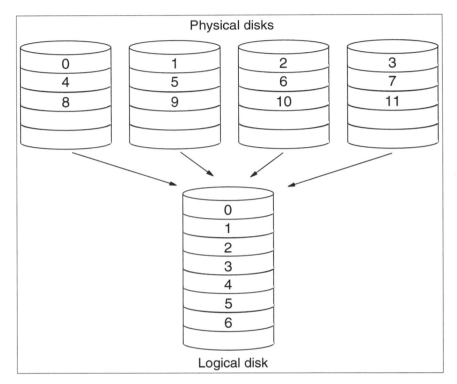

Figure 163. RAID-0 implementation

It is common for a striped disk array to map data in blocks with a stripe size that is an integer multiple of real drive track capacity. For example, IBM's ServeRAID adapters allow stripe sizes of 8 KB, 16 KB, 32 KB or 64 KB, selectable during initialization of the array. Applications get better performance if their data I/O size matches the stripe size of the array so it is recommended that you take this into consideration when defining your RAID sets.

Advantages:

- Performance improvement in many cases.
- All disk space available for data.

Disadvantages:

- No redundancy.

A.1.2 RAID-1 and RAID-1E

RAID-1, or disk mirroring, offers true redundancy. Each stripe is duplicated, or mirrored, on another disk in the array. In its simplest form, there are two disks where the second is a simple copy of the first. If the first disk fails then the second can be used without any loss of data. Some performance enhancement is achieved by reading data from both drives. Certain operating systems, including Windows NT, provide direct support for disk mirroring. There is a performance overhead, however, as the processor has to issue duplicate write commands. Hardware solutions where the controller handles the duplicate writes are preferred.

When more than two disks are available, the duplication scheme can be a little more complex to allow striping with disk mirroring, also known as Enhanced RAID-1. An example is shown in Figure 164:

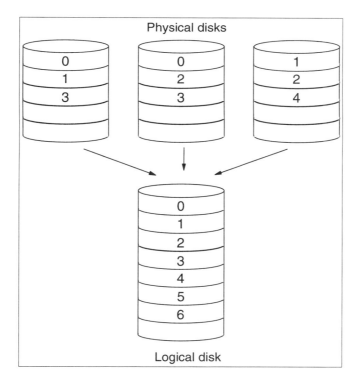

Figure 164. RAID-1E implementation

As you can see, any one disk can be removed from the array without loss of information because each data stripe exists on two physical disks. The controller detects a failed disk and redirects requests for data from the failed drive to the drive containing the copy of the data. When a drive has failed, the replacement drive can be rebuilt using the data from the remaining drives in the array.

When a disk fails, there is only one copy of the data that was on the failed disk available to the system. The system has lost its redundancy, and if another disk fails, data loss is the result. To avoid this, failed disks should be replaced as soon as possible. The controller then rebuilds the data that was on the failed disk from the remaining drives and writes it to the new disk, restoring the redundancy.

To avoid having to manually replace a failed disk, IBM's Netfinity ServeRAID controllers implement *hot spare* disks. A hot spare disk is held idle until a failure occurs, at which point the controller immediately starts to rebuild the lost data onto the hot spare, minimizing the time when redundancy is lost. The controller continues to provide data to the system while the rebuild takes place.

When you replace the failed drive, its replacement becomes the array's new hot spare.

Advantages:

- Performance improvement in many cases.
- Redundancy. A drive can fail without loss of data.

Disadvantages:

- Cost. The logical disk has only half the capacity of the physical disks.

A.1.3 RAID-10

As we have seen, RAID-1 offers the potential for performance improvement as well as redundancy. RAID-10 is a variant of RAID-1 that effectively creates a mirror copy of a RAID-0 array.

In large disk subsystems that require, for example, two external storage enclosures, it would be beneficial to ensure that mirrored data exists in both units. This would allow an entire unit, including its power supply or connecting cables, to fail without interrupting operation. RAID-10 does just this by allowing one RAID-0 array to be contained in one of the enclosures and its mirror copy in the other. A diagram of a RAID-10 configuration is shown below:

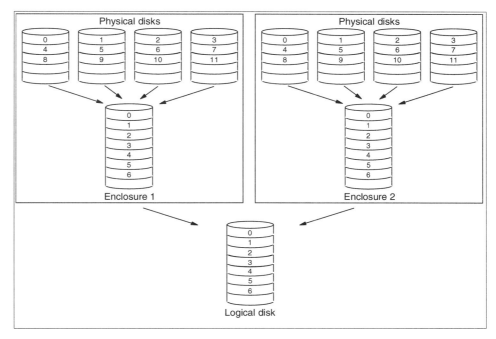

Figure 165. RAID-10 configuration

RAID-10 configurations are supported by the IBM Netfinity Fibre Channel RAID Controller Unit.

Advantages:

- Performance improvement in many cases.
- Redundancy. A drive can fail without loss of data.
- Provides fault tolerance for disk enclosures.

Disadvantages:

- Cost. The logical disk has only half the capacity of the physical disks.
- Slightly less flexible than RAID-1E (requires an even number of disks).

A.1.4 RAID-5

RAID-5 is one of the most capable and efficient ways of building redundancy into the disk subsystem. The way redundancy is implemented, capacity loss is equal to one of the drives in the array and data striping provides the read performance gains from RAID-0 and RAID-1. The principles behind RAID-5 are very simple and are closely related to the parity methods sometimes used for computer memory subsystems. In memory, the parity bit is formed by evaluating the number of 1 bits in a single byte. For RAID-5, if we take the example of a four-drive array, three stripes of data are written to three of the drives and the bit-by-bit parity of the three stripes is written to the fourth drive.

As an example, we can look at the first byte of each stripe and see what this means for the parity stripe. Let us assume that the first byte of stripes 1, 2, and 3 are the letters A, B, and G respectively. The binary code for these characters is 01000001, 01000010 and 01000111 respectively.

We can now calculate the first byte of the parity block. Using the convention that an odd number of 1s in the data generates a 1 in the parity, the first parity byte is 01000100 (see Table 29). This is called *even parity* because there is always an even number of 1s if we look at the data and the parity together. Odd parity could have been chosen; the choice is of no importance as long as it is consistent.

Table 29. Generation of parity data for RAID-5

Disk 1 "A"	Disk 2 "B"	Disk 3 "G"	Disk 4 Parity
0	0	0	0
1	1	1	1
0	0	0	0
0	0	0	0
0	0	0	0
0	0	1	1
0	1	1	0
1	0	1	0

Calculating the parity for the second byte is performed using the same method, and so on. In this way, the entire parity stripe for the first three data stripes can be calculated and stored on the fourth disk.

The presence of parity information allows any disk to fail without loss of data.

In the above example, if drive 2 fails (with B as its first byte) there is enough information in the parity byte and the data on the remaining drives to reconstruct the missing data. The controller has to look at the data on the remaining drives and calculate what drive 2's data must have been to maintain even parity. Because of this, a RAID-5 array with a failed drive can continue to provide the system with all the data from the failed drive.

Performance will suffer, of course, because the controller has to look at the data from all drives when a request is made to the failed one. However, that is better than losing the system completely. A RAID-5 array with a failed drive is said to be critical, since the loss of another drive will cause lost data. For this reason, the use of hot spare drives in a RAID-5 array is as important as in RAID-1.

The simplest implementation would always store the parity on disk 4 (in fact, this is the case in RAID-4, which is hardly ever implemented for the reason about to be explained). Disk reads are then serviced in much the same way as a level 0 array with three disks. However, writing to a RAID-5 array would then suffer from a performance bottleneck. Each write requires that both real data and parity data are updated. Therefore, the single parity disk would have to be written to every time any of the other disks were modified. To avoid this, the parity data is also striped, as shown in Figure 166, spreading the load across the entire array.

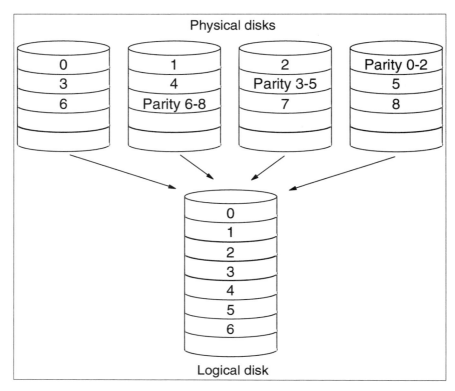

Figure 166. RAID-5 implementation

The consequence of having to update the parity information means that for every stripe written to the virtual disk, the controller has to read the old data from the stripe being updated and the associated parity stripe. Then the necessary changes to the parity stripe have to be calculated based on the old and the new data. All of this complexity is hidden from the processor, but the effect on the system is that writes are much slower than reads. This can be offset to a greater or lesser extent by the use of a cache on the RAID controller. IBM's ServeRAID controllers have cache as standard, which is used to hold the new data while the calculations are being performed. Meanwhile, the processor can continue as though the write has taken place. Battery backup options for the cache, available for some controllers, mean that data loss is kept to a minimum even if the controller fails with data still in the cache.

Advantages:

- Performance improvement in many cases.
- Redundancy. A drive can fail without loss of data.

- Storage overhead is equal to the size of only one drive.

Disadvantages:

- Overhead associated with writes can be detrimental to performance in applications where the write/read ratio is high. A controller cache can alleviate this.

A.1.5 RAID-5 enhanced

RAID-5 Enhanced (RAID-5E) puts hot spare drives to work to improve reliability and performance. A hot spare is normally inactive during array operation and is not used until a drive fails. By utilizing unallocated space on the drives in the array, a virtual distributed hot spare (DHS) can be created to improve reliability and performance. Figure 167 shows normal operation of a RAID-5E array. The data areas of the individual disks shown contain the application data and stripe parity data as for a normal RAID-5 array:

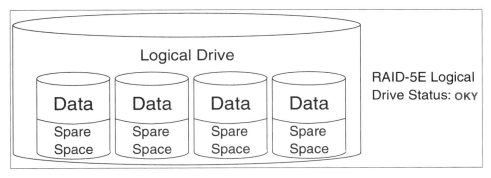

Figure 167. RAID-5E array: normal operation

In the event of a physical drive failing, its status will change to Defunct Disk Drive (DDD) and the ServeRAID adapter will start rearranging the data the disk contained into the spare space on the other drives in the array, provided there is enough space, of course.

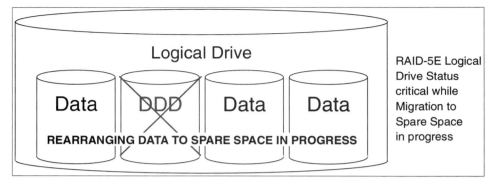

Figure 168. RAID-5E array: single physical disk failure

During the migration of data, the logical drive will be in a critical, nonredundant state. As soon as all the data is rearranged, the logical drive will be marked OKY (Okay) and have full redundancy again. This is illustrated in Figure 169.

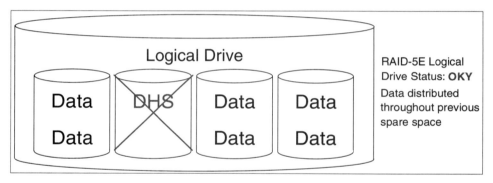

Figure 169. RAID-5E array: data distributed throughout previous spare space

In the event of a second physical disk failure before the previously failed disk has been replaced, illustrated in Figure 170, normal RAID-5 procedures will be taken to provide service to the system through the checksum calculations described in A.1.4, "RAID-5" on page 239.

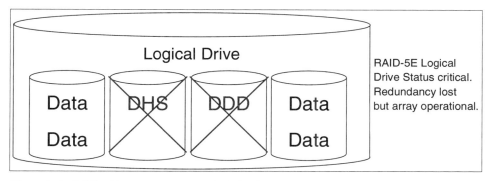

Figure 170. RAID-5E array: second physical disk failure

Advantages (compared to RAID-5):

- 15 - 20% performance improvement for smaller arrays with typical data transfer size.
- Protects data, even in the event of a two-drive failure.

Disadvantages:

- Migration time.

Design characteristics:

- One RAID-5E logical drive per array.
- Minimum of four physical drives in array configured for RAID-5E logical drive.

A.1.6 Orthogonal RAID-5

Orthogonal RAID-5 is an enhancement of RAID-5 in the sense that it is powered by more than one disk controller and hence improves both reliability and performance.

The performance of a disk subsystem depends on more than just the underlying performance of the disks. Multiple requests to one disk or across one adapter will typically take longer to satisfy than the same number of requests to multiple disks across multiple adapters.

In addition, the overall reliability of a standard RAID-5 system is dependent on the reliability of the one disk adapter to which all of the disks are connected. Orthogonal RAID-5 solves both of these concerns by grouping the disk arrays orthogonally to the disk adapters, SCSI buses, and power cables.

This would normally be implemented as a four-drive orthogonal RAID-5 array, where each disk would be connected to a different adapter and SCSI bus.

The result of this is that any one component of the disk subsystems, not just a disk drive, can fail with no loss of data and no interruption to system operation.

A.1.7 Performance

With different parameters affecting your RAID solution it is virtually impossible to find the perfect combination without measuring live throughput. Increasing redundancy also increases price and possibly lowers performance due to added overhead, which could be solved with more or faster controllers, again increasing the price.

As you can see in Figure 171 on page 247, speed is a significant issue when deciding on RAID level. The numbers shown in this figure and in Figure 172 on page 248 are based on benchmark testing performed by IBM's Netfinity server development team. Specific systems may not show precisely the same performance ratios but the figures are representative of typical performance data.

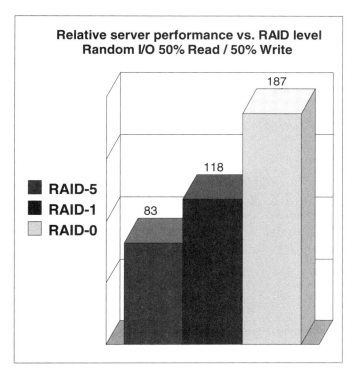

Figure 171. Relative server performance versus RAID strategy

It is important to point out that the speed difference in Figure 171 is mainly due to the same number of drives being used for all tests. Generally, the more drives you use in your array, the faster it gets, but it also requires your RAID controller to be able to attach more drives when using RAID-1 or RAID-5 to get optimal performance.

Using the same number of drives:

• RAID-0 gives up to 50% more throughput than RAID-1.
• RAID-1 gives up to 50% more throughput than RAID-5.

The above test was done using a worst-case scenario with 50% reads and 50% writes. A high write/read ratio adversely affects the performance of RAID-1 and RAID-5 arrays, so throughput improves with a higher percentage of reads, which is generally more common in a real-world environment.

• While increasing the number of drives boosts performance, it also increases the price. Figure 172 on page 248 shows what happens with I/O throughput when we add drives to a RAID-0 array.

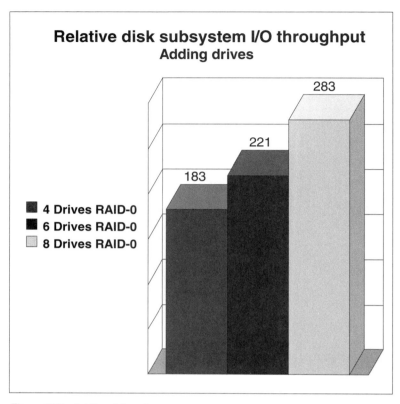

Figure 172. Adding drives to an array

Server throughput improves up to 50% when the number of drives is doubled for a RAID-0 and similar gains are shown for RAID-1 and RAID-5.

A.1.8 Recommendations

Before configuring your array you have to decide on a stripe size for the array. When configuring for maximum performance, Table 30 shows some rules of thumb:

Table 30. Recommended stripe configurations for ServeRAID adapters

Environment	Stripe size	Read-ahead
Groupware (Lotus Notes, Exchange)	16 KB	ON
Database Server (Oracle, SQL Server, DB/2)	16 KB	OFF
File Server (Windows NT 4.0, NetWare 4.1x)	16 KB	ON

Environment	Stripe size	Read-ahead
Web Server	8 KB	OFF
Other	8 KB	ON

A.1.9 Summary

RAID is an excellent and proven technology for protecting your data against the possibility of hard disk failure. IBM has a range of RAID controllers that bring the benefits of the technology to our Netfinity servers. As Intel-based servers become more and more critical to our customers' businesses, they are demanding the reliability provided by RAID.

Here is a quick summary of the different RAID levels we have covered in this appendix:

RAID-0: Block interleave data striping without parity

- Best performance of all RAID levels
- Drive seek times and latencies effectively reduced by parallel operation
- Significantly outperforms single large disk

RAID-1: Disk mirroring

- Fast and reliable but requires 100% disk space overhead
- Two copies of data maintained
- No performance degradation with a single disk failure
- Writes are slower than a single disk, reads are quicker

RAID-1E: Data stripe mirroring

- All the benefits of RAID-1
- Provides mirroring with an odd number of drives

RAID-10: Mirrored RAID-0 arrays

- All the benefits of RAID-1
- Can provide fault tolerance for entire storage enclosures

RAID-5: Block interleave data striping with distributed parity

- Best for random transactions
- Poor for large sequential reads if request is larger than block size
- Block size is the key to performance; must be larger than typical request size

- Performance degrades in recovery mode, that is, when a single drive has failed

RAID-5E: RAID-5 with distributed hot spare

- All the benefits of RAID-5
- 15 - 20% performance improvement for smaller arrays
- Protects data, even in the event of a two-drive failure

Orthogonal RAID-5: RAID-5 with multiple orthogonal disk adapters

- All the benefits of RAID-5
- Improved performance (due to load being spread across disk adapters)
- Improved reliability due to redundancy of disk adapters and disks

Table 31 gives you a summary of RAID performance characteristics:

Table 31. Summary of RAID performance characteristics

RAID level	Capacity	Large transfers	I/O rate	Data availability
RAID-0	Excellent	Very Good	Very Good	Poor[1]
RAID-1/1E	Moderate	Good	Good	Good
RAID-10	Moderate	Good	Good	Very Good
RAID-5	Very Good	Very Good	Good	Good
RAID-5E	Very Good	Very Good	Good to Very Good	Very Good
Orthogonal RAID-5	Very Good	Very Good	Good	Very Good
[1] Availability = MTBF of one disk divided by the number of disks in the array				

If you want to learn more about RAID, the RAID Advisory Board, of which IBM is an active member, exists to standardize terminology and provide information about RAID technology. Its Web site can be found at the following URL:

```
http://www.raid-advisory.com/
```

Appendix B. Special notices

This publication is intended to help customers, business partners and IBM employees implement SuSE Linux. The information in this publication is not intended as the specification of any programming interfaces that are provided by SuSE Linux. See the PUBLICATIONS section of the IBM Programming for more information about what publications are considered to be product documentation.

References in this publication to IBM products, programs or services do not imply that IBM intends to make these available in all countries in which IBM operates. Any reference to an IBM product, program, or service is not intended to state or imply that only IBM's product, program, or service may be used. Any functionally equivalent program that does not infringe any of IBM's intellectual property rights may be used instead of the IBM product, program or service.

Information in this book was developed in conjunction with use of the equipment specified, and is limited in application to those specific hardware and software products and levels.

IBM may have patents or pending patent applications covering subject matter in this document. The furnishing of this document does not give you any license to these patents. You can send license inquiries, in writing, to the IBM Director of Licensing, IBM Corporation, North Castle Drive, Armonk, NY 10504-1785.

Licensees of this program who wish to have information about it for the purpose of enabling: (i) the exchange of information between independently created programs and other programs (including this one) and (ii) the mutual use of the information which has been exchanged, should contact IBM Corporation, Dept. 600A, Mail Drop 1329, Somers, NY 10589 USA.

Such information may be available, subject to appropriate terms and conditions, including in some cases, payment of a fee.

The information contained in this document has not been submitted to any formal IBM test and is distributed AS IS. The use of this information or the implementation of any of these techniques is a customer responsibility and depends on the customer's ability to evaluate and integrate them into the customer's operational environment. While each item may have been reviewed by IBM for accuracy in a specific situation, there is no guarantee that the same or similar results will be obtained elsewhere. Customers

251

attempting to adapt these techniques to their own environments do so at their own risk.

Any pointers in this publication to external Web sites are provided for convenience only and do not in any manner serve as an endorsement of these Web sites.

The following terms are trademarks of the International Business Machines Corporation in the United States and/or other countries:

AIX	AS/400
DB2	Home Director
IBM	Netfinity
OS/2	RS/6000
ServeRAID	ServerProven
SP	System/390
TechConnect	WebSphere

The following terms are trademarks of other companies:

Linux is a registered trademark of Linus Torvalds.

C-bus is a trademark of Corollary, Inc. in the United States and/or other countries.

Java and all Java-based trademarks and logos are trademarks or registered trademarks of Sun Microsystems, Inc. in the United States and/or other countries.

Microsoft, Windows, Windows NT, and the Windows logo are trademarks of Microsoft Corporation in the United States and/or other countries.

PC Direct is a trademark of Ziff Communications Company in the United States and/or other countries and is used by IBM Corporation under license.

ActionMedia, LANDesk, MMX, Pentium and ProShare are trademarks of Intel Corporation in the United States and/or other countries.

UNIX is a registered trademark in the United States and/or other countries licensed exclusively through X/Open Company Limited.

SET and the SET logo are trademarks owned by SET Secure Electronic Transaction LLC.

Other company, product, and service names may be trademarks or service
marks of others.

Appendix C. Related publications

The publications listed in this section are considered particularly suitable for a more detailed discussion of the topics covered in this redbook.

C.1 International Technical Support Organization publications

For information on ordering these ITSO publications see "How to get IBM Redbooks" on page 259.

- *Linux for WebSphere and DB2 Servers*, SG24-5850
- *Netfinity and Red Hat Linux Integration Guide*, SG24-5853
- *Netfinity and Caldera OpenLinux Integration Guide*, SG24-5861
- *Netfinity and TurboLinux Integration Guide*, SG24-5862

C.2 IBM Redbooks collections

Redbooks are also available on the following CD-ROMs. Click the CD-ROMs button at `http://www.redbooks.ibm.com/` for information about all the CD-ROMs offered, updates and formats.

CD-ROM Title	Collection Kit Number
System/390 Redbooks Collection	SK2T-2177
Networking and Systems Management Redbooks Collection	SK2T-6022
Transaction Processing and Data Management Redbooks Collection	SK2T-8038
Lotus Redbooks Collection	SK2T-8039
Tivoli Redbooks Collection	SK2T-8044
AS/400 Redbooks Collection	SK2T-2849
Netfinity Hardware and Software Redbooks Collection	SK2T-8046
RS/6000 Redbooks Collection (BkMgr)	SK2T-8040
RS/6000 Redbooks Collection (PDF Format)	SK2T-8043
Application Development Redbooks Collection	SK2T-8037
IBM Enterprise Storage and Systems Management Solutions	SK3T-3694

C.3 Other publications

These publications are also relevant as further information sources:

- *Understanding and Deploying LDAP Directory Services,* by Timothy Howes, Mark Smith, and Gordon Good, ISBN: 1578700701

- *Using Samba* by Robert Eckstein, David Collier-Brown and Peter Kelly, published by O'Reilly, available online at:

  `http://www.oreilly.com/catalog/samba/chapter/book/index.html`

- *The Linux NIS(YP)/NYS/NIS+ HOWTO* by Thorsten Kakuk, found at:

  `http://metalab.unc.edu/pub/Linux/docs/HOWTO/NIS-HOWTO.`

- *Managing NFS and NIS,* by Hal Stern, ISBN 0937175757

- "Don't make me LDAP you - Lightweight Directory Access Protocol: What it is, why you want it", available from the LinuxWorld Web site at:

  `http://www.linuxworld.com/linuxworld/lw-1999-03/lw-03-uptime.html`

- LDAP how-tos are available from the Linux Documentation project Web site at:

  `http://www.linuxdoc.org/HOWTO/LDAP-HOWTO.html`

C.4 Referenced Web sites

- http://www.redbooks.ibm.com
- http://www.suse.de/en/
- http://www.linuxbase.org
- http://www.lpi.org
- http://www.li18nux.org/
- http://www.suse.com
- http://www.suse.de/en/support/download/updates/62_update.html
- ftp://ftp.suse.com/pub/suse/i386/updates/6.2/
- ftp://ftp.pc.ibm.com/pcicrse/psref
- http://www.pc.ibm.com/support/
- http://www.pc.ibm.com/us/netfinity/tech_library.html
- http://cdb.suse.de/cdb_english.html
- http://www.keylabs.com/linux/linux_results.html
- ftp://ftp.suse.com/pub/suse/i386/update/6.2/disks/servraid
- ftp://ftp.suse.com/pub/SuSE-Linux/suse_update/XFree86-3.3.5-SuSE/SuSE-6.2/xsvga.rpm
- http://www.rpm.org
- http://www.developer.ibm.com/welcome/netfinity/serveraid.html
- http://www.linuxdoc.org/HOWTO/DNS-HOWTO.html
- http://www.samba.org
- http://www.oreilly.com/catalog/samba/chapter/book/index.html
- http://www.linuxdoc.org/HOWTO/SMB-HOWTO.html
- http://www.netcraft.com/survey/
- http://www-4.ibm.com/software/webservers/httpservers/
- http://www-4.ibm.com/software/webservers/httpservers/download.html

- http://www-4.ibm.com/software/webservers/httpservers/doc/v136/readme_httpserver.htm
- http://www.apache.org/docs/misc/perf-tuning.html
- http://www.rustcorp.com/linux/ipchains
- http://www.bb-zone.com/FWHowTo/index.html
- http://www.linuxdoc.org/HOWTO/Firewall-HOWTO.html
- http://www.sendmail.org
- http://www.linuxdoc.org/HOWTO/Mail-User-HOWTO.html
- http://www.linuxdoc.org/HOWTO/Mail-Administrator-HOWTO.html
- http://www.postfix.org
- http://www.linuxdoc.org/HOWTO/NFS-HOWTO.html
- http://www.linuxdoc.org/HOWTO/NIS-HOWTO.html
- http://www.suse.de/~kukuk/
- http://www.openldap.org/incoming/roaming-073099.tar.gz
- http://www.linuxdoc.org/HOWTO/LDAP-HOWTO.html
- http://www.OpenLDAP.org
- http://www.linuxworld.com/linuxworld/lw-1999-03/lw-03-uptime.html
- http://tune.linux.com
- http://www.tunelinux.com
- http://www.linux-mandrake.com/lothar/
- http://www.textuality.com/bonnie/
- http://www.netperf.org/netperf/NetperfPage.html
- http://www.estinc.com/
- http://legends.dm.net/beowulf/index.html
- http://www.lnstar.com/literature/beowulf/beowulf.html
- http://www.povray.org
- http://www.raid-advisory.com/

How to get IBM Redbooks

This section explains how both customers and IBM employees can find out about ITSO redbooks, redpieces, and CD-ROMs. A form for ordering books and CD-ROMs by fax or e-mail is also provided.

- **Redbooks Web Site** http://www.redbooks.ibm.com/

  Search for, view, download, or order hardcopy/CD-ROM redbooks from the redbooks Web site. Also read redpieces and download additional materials (code samples or diskette/CD-ROM images) from this redbooks site.

  Redpieces are redbooks in progress; not all redbooks become redpieces and sometimes just a few chapters will be published this way. The intent is to get the information out much quicker than the formal publishing process allows.

- **E-mail Orders**

  Send orders by e-mail including information from the redbooks fax order form to:

	e-mail address
In United States	usib6fpl@ibmmail.com
Outside North America	Contact information is in the "How to Order" section at this site: http://www.elink.ibmlink.ibm.com/pbl/pbl

- **Telephone Orders**

United States (toll free)	1-800-879-2755
Canada (toll free)	1-800-IBM-4YOU
Outside North America	Country coordinator phone number is in the "How to Order" section at this site: http://www.elink.ibmlink.ibm.com/pbl/pbl

- **Fax Orders**

United States (toll free)	1-800-445-9269
Canada	1-403-267-4455
Outside North America	Fax phone number is in the "How to Order" section at this site: http://www.elink.ibmlink.ibm.com/pbl/pbl

This information was current at the time of publication, but is continually subject to change. The latest information may be found at the redbooks Web site.

IBM Intranet for Employees

IBM employees may register for information on workshops, residencies, and redbooks by accessing the IBM Intranet Web site at http://w3.itso.ibm.com/ and clicking the ITSO Mailing List button. Look in the Materials repository for workshops, presentations, papers, and Web pages developed and written by the ITSO technical professionals; click the Additional Materials button. Employees may access MyNews at http://w3.ibm.com/ for redbook, residency, and workshop announcements.

IBM Redbooks fax order form

Please send me the following:

Title	Order Number	Quantity

First name _____ Last name _____

Company _____

Address _____

City _____ Postal code _____ Country _____

Telephone number _____ Telefax number _____ VAT number _____

☐ Invoice to customer number _____

☐ Credit card number _____

Credit card expiration date _____ Card issued to _____ Signature _____

We accept American Express, Diners, Eurocard, Master Card, and Visa. Payment by credit card not available in all countries. Signature mandatory for credit card payment.

List of abbreviations

AIX	advanced interactive executive	IDE	integrated drive electronics
BIOS	Basic Input/Output System	IETF	Internet Engineering Task Force
BOOTP	boot protocol	I/O	input/output
bpp	bits per pixel	IP	Internet Protocol
BRU	Backup and Restore Utility	IPX/SPX	Internet Packet exchange/Sequenced Packet exchange
CGI	Common Gateway Interface	IRC	Internet Relay Chat
CIFS	Common Internet File System	ISA	Industry Standard Architecture
CPU	central processing unit	ISDN	integrated-services digital network
DARPA	Defense Advanced Research Projects Agency	ISO	International Organization for Standardization
DAT	digital audio tape	ITSO	International Technical Support Organization
DHCP	Dynamic Host Configuration Protocol	ITU	International Telecommunications Union
DMA	direct memory access		
DNS	Domain Name Service	KB	kilobyte
FQDN	fully qualified domain name	KDE	K Desktop Environment
FTP	file transport protocol	LAN	local area network
GB	gigabyte	LDAP	Lightweight Directory Access Protocol
GPM	Gereral Purpose Mouse	LILO	Linux Loader
GUI	graphical user interface	MB	megabyte
HTML	Hypertext Markup Language	MHz	Megahertz
		mm	milimeter
HTTP	Hypertext Transfer Protocol	MTA	Mail Transfer Agent
Hz	Hertz	NAT	Network Address Translation
IBM	International Business Machines Corporation	NFS	Network File System
		NIC	Network Interface Card

NIS	Network Information System	URL	Universal Resource Locator
PCI	Peripheral Component Interconnect	VGA	video graphics array
PCMCIA	Personal Computer Memory Card International Association	WINS	Windows Internet Name Service
		WWW	World Wide Web
PNP	Plug and Play		
POP	Post Office Protocol		
RAID	redundant array of imdependent disks		
RAM	random access memory		
RFC	Request for Comments		
RPC	Remote Procedure Call		
RPM	Red Hat Package Manager		
SCSI	small computer system interface		
SMB	Server Message Block		
SMBFS	Samba File System		
SMP	symmetric multiprocessing		
SMTP	Simple Mail Transfer Protocol		
SNMP	simple network management protocol		
SSA	serial storage architecture		
SSL	Secure Sockets Layer		
SVGA	super video graphics array		
SWAT	Samba Web Administration Tool		
TCP/IP	Transmission Control Protocol/Internet Protocol		

Index

IBM Redbooks evaluation

Netfinity and SuSE Linux Integration Guide
SG24-5863-00

Your feedback is very important to help us maintain the quality of ITSO redbooks. **Please complete this questionnaire and return it using one of the following methods:**

- Use the online evaluation form found at http://www.redbooks.ibm.com/
- Fax this form to: USA International Access Code + 1 914 432 8264
- Send your comments in an Internet note to redbook@us.ibm.com

Which of the following best describes you?
_ **Customer**   _ **Business Partner**   _ **Solution Developer**   _ **IBM employee**
_ **None of the above**

Please rate your overall satisfaction with this book using the scale:
(1 = very good, 2 = good, 3 = average, 4 = poor, 5 = very poor)

Overall Satisfaction   _____

Please answer the following questions:

Was this redbook published in time for your needs?   Yes____ No____

If no, please explain:

_____

_____

_____

_____

What other redbooks would you like to see published?

_____

_____

_____

Comments/Suggestions: **(THANK YOU FOR YOUR FEEDBACK!)**

_____

_____

_____

_____